4 -

# CIRCLES
## OF
# INFLUENCE

# CIRCLES OF INFLUENCE

## Robert C. Anderson

MOODY PRESS

CHICAGO

ISBN: 0-8024-1126-6

1 2 3 4 5 6 Printing/VP/Year 95 94 93 92 91

*Printed in the United States of America*

*To Rosella Mae Bohlen Anderson,*
*by far the most significant person in my life*

*For these many years she has been my wife, companion, and love*
*She is truly a "Proverbs 31 woman"*

# CONTENTS

## PART 3

### A Compassionate Agent of Change:
### The Leader's Defining Role

## PART 4

### Circles of Influence:
### Organizing the Church for Dynamic Impact

# FIGURES

# FOREWORD

In the early 1960s it was my privilege to meet Chaplain Robert Anderson at Ford Ord, California. Even at that time I was impressed with the organization and structure he had created in his ministry at the army base. I have followed his teaching and ministry over the past twenty-five years and was delighted to be asked to write a foreword for this thorough and insightful book.

For the veteran pastor at the helm of a large congregation to the young seminary graduate starting with thirty people, this book will be a welcome volume. In a time of church history when the variations of church programs and ministries multiply constantly, *Circles of Influence* is a basic book that will lend stability to a transitional period.

One of the continuing problems that has plagued the local church is leadership. Here is a volume that will give clarity and guidance to the ministerial staff as well as to the board members of the congregation. This is not a book to be devoured just by the ministerial staff, but rather it will be appreciated by every person on the church board. Seminaries and Bible colleges will welcome this work as a text to introduce their students to a major part of their ministry—selecting and training leaders within the church.

The author's years of serving in the local church as well as seminary teaching are evident in the thorough coverage of this book. Schools and churches will applaud its availability for their ministry.

H. Norman Wright
Adjunct Professor, Talbot School of Theology
Director, Christian Marriage Enrichment

# ACKNOWLEDGMENTS

My sincere appreciation is extended to three graduate assistants who helped me complete this book. Douglas Soleida did countless hours of research uncovering biblical words that apply to change. He dug deep into their meanings and helped form many of the insights that I have shared in my chapters on change. David Beseler and Daniel Klender, in turn, provided valuable assistance both in uncovering additional bibliographic sources for each chapter and in helping to formulate the questions and exercises at the end of those chapters.

Many thanks are due as well to Western Conservative Baptist Seminary. This fine family of Christian people lent understanding, support, and encouragement as I invested the hours necessary to produce this work.

Finally, I would like to express much gratitude to my students and to the churches with whom I am constantly working. They continue to teach me new ways of looking at things every day.

# INTRODUCTION

In warfare, planning is divided into the tactical and the strategic sectors. *Tactical* planning concerns itself with the immediate deployment of troops on the battlefield; *strategic* planning concentrates on the larger picture. It deals with such key questions as the basic principles of warfare under which an army must operate to be successful, where and when is it best for the army to deploy its efforts, and the type of units that would be best deployed in view of the terrain.

The church of Jesus Christ is involved in warfare. In order to be the offensive force against Satan that our Lord wants it to be, the church must be engaged in strategic as well as tactical decision making. Yet as I think over my more than thirty years in the ministry, I see few church leaders who understand strategy, the big picture. Most engage only in the small picture, meeting only the pressing needs of the moment.

This book is designed to challenge church leaders to look at the larger picture, to develop a comprehensive philosophy of ministry and then live by it.

I am convinced that when church leaders establish overarching principles and place those principles in an orderly system, pastors and church boards will not have constantly to be making tactical decisions as each crisis approaches. Nor will they need to engage in a "band-aid ministry," running from one program to another applying spiritual and emotional first-aid as any particular program faces an emergency.

God calls no local church to the task of perpetuating the status quo. The church of Jesus Christ must be a dynamic force in the society around it, changing that society through the regenerating power of God's Word. Though the facts of the gospel remain the same, the application of those facts must change from generation to generation. God calls church leaders to become agents of change.

This change needs to be implemented with care. Too often change has been initiated by people who did not have the slightest idea about the damage they were causing the church. God's church is a delicate organism. My prayer is that this book may teach leaders and prospective leaders how to bring about change in the church without causing harm to the body and its members.

When my book *The Effective Pastor* was published some wag approached me and asked, "The effective pastor—is that you, Anderson?" I was quick to respond, "I am writing a sequel. It is to be called *The Defective Pastor: An Autobiography.*"

Thankfully that second book was never written. Moreover, as my first book was primarily geared to pastors, so this one is aimed at all leaders of the church. Here I make few distinctions between professionals and lay leaders. All are equally needed in the church.

But back to that frivolous title *The Defective Pastor.* There is a sense in which God is always seeking to accomplish His work through the efforts of defective people. If we doubt that, all we have to do is look honestly in the mirror. I have often remarked that it would not be a great accomplishment for God to use perfect people to carry out His plans. The miracle is that He accomplishes His purposes through people who are imperfect.

So take heart! God does not expect super-giftedness or perfection. He does expect a willing heart, a humble spirit, and a determination to be obedient. Then, as we give Him what little we have, He will multiply, perfect it, and use it to His glory. I thank Him for those facts of faith as I give my own imperfect offering to Him.

# PART 1

# The Body of Christ: The Church

# 1

# THE
# NATURE
# OF THE
# CHURCH

It is Sunday afternoon, and you are watching the ball game. The doorbell rings. Half asleep, you gather your energies, open the door, and find a well dressed couple, Bible in hand, standing on your doorstep. After greeting you politely, they ask if you would like to study the Scriptures with them. At this point you are not really interested in doing anything more strenuous than reading the paper. However, studying the Bible seems harmless enough, and these people are so likable, cordial, and persistent that you make the mistake of inviting them in.

A frustrating hour begins that is unlike any Bible study you have ever experienced. At first you are puzzled, but as you begin to tune in, you find that they are using isolated Bible verses to paint a picture you know is unbiblical. As you analyze the situation even more carefully, you find that they are taking Scripture verses entirely out of context. Heresy occurs as a result.

Even the beginning Bible student knows that each verse must be considered in its context. The context of a verse includes the whole thrust of the book in which the verse is found; the historical, geographical, and cultural setting of the book; and the specific intent and meaning of the set of paragraphs within which the verse is contained. Without this information it is easy to make serious mistakes in understanding and applying a Scripture verse. If we are to be serious and accurate students of the Bible, we must study each verse in its context.

When we are serious about church leadership, we have a similar need to study the context in which legitimate ministry occurs and through which leadership guides that ministry. That context is the church, the only lasting, God ordained, biblically supported means for carrying on God's program here on earth. For that reason, I believe it is proper and necessary to begin a book on church leadership by taking a good look at the context of that leadership, the church. Such a study must begin with what the Head of the church, the Lord Jesus Christ, has to say about the church and include as well the references to the church in the book of Acts. Jesus mentions the church by name on only two occasions, Matthew 16:18, which deals with Jesus' role in building the church and with the invincibility of the church, and 18:15-17, which deals with discipline in the church. References to the church are made in numerous places in Acts and in the epistles.

## THE UNIVERSAL CHURCH INCLUDES ALL BELIEVERS

Jesus' reference to the church in Matthew 16:18 is the only place in Scripture where Jesus speaks directly to the subject of the universal church. His declaration occurs at a high point in His ministry. He has asked His disciples who He really is. In response, Simon Peter fairly blurts out his marvelous confession of faith: "Thou art the Christ, the Son of the living God" (v. 16).

Jesus replies to that declaration by saying, "Blessed are you, Simon Barjona, because flesh and blood did not reveal this to you, but My Father who is in Heaven" (v. 17). Then He adds, speaking of the institution that will become His earthly body when He returns to heaven, "I will build My church; and the gates of Hades shall not overpower it" (v. 18). When Jesus promised to build His church He had in mind the adding of the men and women who will make up the universal church and the nurturing of them to spiritual maturity. So in this passage He is not speaking of a physical building but is referring to the universal church. That church includes all believers from all of the world for all of history.

## The Church Belongs to Christ

With Jesus as the builder, a great responsibility is removed from our shoulders as leaders. He is the major contractor, and we are merely His workmen. Instead of having continual worries about the construction, all we are called to do is follow His orders. What a relief! If I had to serve as the builder, I would worry continually about whether the structure was built properly. But I have no need for such worries. He will build His church!

Jesus promises to build *His* church. Aren't you glad that it's His church and not yours? If it were your church, you would have to worry about maintaining it. Since it is His, He also becomes the maintenance supervisor. He is responsible for its success or failure. But it won't fail. He has already made that guarantee. Even though local assemblies of believers should cease to function, other assemblies will be raised up in their place. His universal church is certain to succeed.

Moreover, when Jesus asserts that it is His church, that establishes Him as head of the church. That leaves no room for church bosses, whether or not they be "bossy": pastors, elders, deacons, or presidents of women's missionary societies. He is the only boss, and He is jealous of His authority. He will not share His headship with anyone.

Just as the universal church belongs only to Jesus, individual assemblies of that church enjoy similar ownership. How terribly debilitating to a local church when it ceases to belong to Jesus and becomes the property of an individual or group.

A broken-hearted pastor once told me of a losing battle he was waging. His church was run by a woman who had succeeded in driving off every pastor who had served in that church. Her husband, who fairly jumped at her command, not only served as moderator of the church but also employed twenty-five of the wage earners in the church, including most of the board members.

When the pastor confronted this woman about her unscriptural behavior, her reply was, "Pastors come and go. This is my church, and I'm going to run it the way I want." No wonder pastor after pastor quit in discouragement and the church did nothing of value for the kingdom of God.

The church is *Christ's* church. As leaders of individual local churches, let us never forget that.

## THE CHURCH IS AN IRRESISTIBLE WEAPON

Christ's church is an irresistible weapon. That is the meaning of Christ's assertion in Matthew 16:18 that the "gates of Hades" (or "gates of hell") will not be able to prevail against the church. Some commentators have suggested that Christ was using the phrase "gates of Hades" figuratively to describe death. I do not believe that was the intent of our Lord. Instead, I am convinced that "gates of Hades" should be used in the literal sense. When we do that, it gives the verse an entirely different and much more powerful meaning.

We think of gates as just standing there. To us they are defensive guards to keep the enemy out, not offensive weapons to overpower him. Jesus sees the church as His great and powerful weapon against Satan, and the "gates of Hell" as Satan's defensive counter-weapon.

As a defensive weapon the "gates of Hades" are not strong enough to contain the church of Jesus Christ. Instead, the church is an irresistible force that will storm the very strongholds of hell. Not even the most formidable defense built by Satan will be able to contain or withstand it.

What a wonderful promise. You are a leader in a winning institution. Jesus absolutely guarantees it. None of your efforts on behalf of the church is in vain as long as they conform to scriptural guidelines and glorify God.

## THE CHURCH IS AN ASSEMBLY

To some people "church" is the white frame building in which they spent happy childhood hours. To others, church means a body of believers who worship together on a regular basis. To still others, church is a gigantic socioeconomic system that has its headquarters in Rome, Salt Lake City, or Nashville. The biblical word used to describe Jesus' spiritual body on earth today is *ekklesia.* In its root form it is the combination of two words, *ek,* which means "out," and *kaleo,* "to call." People are "called out" of their normal pursuits to carry on a specific function.

*Ekklesia* means "an assembly." Robert Saucy reports that in classical Greek usage the word meant "an assembly of citizens summoned by the crier, the legislative assembly."[1] He notes further that in Athens the word *ekklesia* "signified the constitutional assembly which

1. Robert Saucy, *The Church in God's Program* (Chicago: Moody, 1972), p. 12.

met on previously fixed dates."[2] In Acts 19, the word is used in the same context to denote first a mob in verse 32, then a lawful assembly in verse 39.

When the Lord used such a common, yet all encompassing, word to describe His strategic, long-range weapon against Satan He may have been saying that within the concept of assembly there is room for far greater diversification and variety than many Christians are willing to admit. There is no biblical prohibition, as far as I can discover, against a highly liturgical type of church group on one hand, the free and spontaneous group on the other, and all the varieties in between. All are possible within the concept of *ekklesia*. Since the Lord has created all of us differently with varying needs, why not use different expressions of the church to meet those needs?

The Lord may also have been warning against the disease of individualism that grips the church today so strongly. The very word *assembly* presupposes that parts are put together to make a usable and useful product. Although the parts are important, the assembled product is what actually accomplishes the job. The computer on which I am writing this book is made up of many component parts. The parts taken individually are incapable of doing much. Only when they are assembled in the proper structure is the mechanism sitting on my desk useful. Likewise, though each member of the Body of Christ may be important, it is only as an integral part of an assembly that he or she will realize optimal usefulness for Christ.

No person is a church in himself. Saucy, pointing to the work of J. W. Campbell, stresses identity and importance through assembling, saying, "In secular Greek, *ekklesia* refers only to the assembly or meeting and never to the people which compose that assembly. When people are not assembled, they are not considered as composing an *ekklesia*. A new *ekklesia* existed each time people assembled."[3]

The genius of the Body of Christ as described in 1 Corinthians 12 is that it depends on its assembled parts, not upon each of those parts working by itself. Christians are not complete in themselves. They need each other to make up an intelligible and functioning whole. In a technical sense the church exists when Christians are assembled. In that light, it might be proper to abandon the word *sanctuary* and use

2. Ibid.
3. Ibid.

the term *assembly hall* for the place where the church meets. If the true sanctuary is within the Christian, then Christians are a group of sanctuaries assembling together.

*Ekklesia* does not require a specific type of place in which to meet. It is wonderful when the assembly can meet in a pleasant and inviting place. Generally it facilitates the program of the church if it has a meeting place of its own to use in carrying out its functions. It can hold church meetings at times convenient to the members, and it does not have to adapt its time schedule to accommodate other users of rented facilities. Nevertheless, it does not take a special kind of building or even a building owned by a congregation to constitute an *ekklesia*. God is in the midst of His church wherever believers are gathered together to accomplish His purposes. *Ekklesia* exists whether Christians congregate in a beautiful, expansive edifice or in a rented school cafetorium.

## The Church Is a Living Organism

The Bible also describes the church as a living organism. This is a hard concept for some people to understand. How can a group of people assemble in a given place and, all of a sudden, become a living organism? For something like that to happen is nothing short of miraculous. Exactly! That is the essence and genius of the local church as the New Testament pictures it.

"But that doesn't make sense," you may say. "Why would God select an organism rather than an organization to accomplish His purpose on earth? After all, organizations are much more efficient." Humanly speaking, you have a point. Were I, in my limited wisdom, to have chosen a plan for redeeming the world, I would probably have chosen an organization. Organizations can move quickly and decisively. If people get in the way, they are removed. Organizations are likely to look at things objectively and factually. When the organization no longer serves its intended function, it can be terminated quickly and with little pain. But God did not choose an organization to save the world from sin. He chose an incarnation. This plan must have been very important to God, because it was immensely costly to Him.

First, it cost the life of His only Son. From then on, the cost has been the suffering and death of generations of His adopted sons and daughters, who, like Paul, have been able to say, "Now I rejoice in my sufferings for your sake, and in my flesh I do my share on behalf of His body (which is the church) in filling up that which is lacking in Christ's afflictions" (Colossians 1:24). And what is lacking in Christ's afflictions? Nothing, except their application to each subsequent generation. This is accomplished through the afflictions of Christians, which they, like Paul, endure cheerfully for Christ's sake.

There is an important philosophical distinction between viewing the church as an organism rather than an organization. As leaders, it is important that we grasp this distinction so that we may carry on our ministry in a biblical manner. Lawrence Richards has been one of the most important sources in helping church leaders understand the significance of this most basic concept. He writes:

> While secular management theorists have attempted to treat the organization and administration of institutions using the analogy of an organism, these attempts have failed for a simple reason. An organism is by its nature an entity with a single will. That single will is transmitted from the head to the various parts of the body so that a coordinated response to the environment may be made.[4]

It is this single will that is necessary to get the job done. When an assembly lacks this single will, or the concept of a single will breaks down, the organism begins to disintegrate. In an organization, leaders impose their will from the top down to their employees. In an organism, leaders have no will of their own. They, along with the members of the congregation who are believer-priests, are merely to seek the will of the Head, the Lord Jesus Christ. It is as they carry out His will that the organism flourishes.

Jerry Wofford and Kenneth Kilinski write:

> The church of today is failing to fulfill its purpose largely because it has ceased to be an organism. A church in which one person preaches, a few teach, and a few others work in an administrative ministry, but the vast majority simply listen, learn and follow without becoming functioning members of the body, is not an integrated organism. . . . In the face of the demands of today's society, the survival of the church is dependent upon its being "fitted and held" together by that which every joint

4. Lawrence Richards and Gib Martin, *A Theology of Personal Ministry* (Grand Rapids: Zondervan, 1981), p. 296.

supplies, according to the proper working of each individual part to fulfill its purposes in Christ.[5]

These men are alluding to 1 Corinthians 12:12-26. There Paul outlines what should be three of the most important features of the organism called the church.

UNITY

The first of these features is unity. After stating in verse 24 that God has combined the members of the body and has given even "more abundant honor to that member which lacked," Paul goes on in verse 25 to tell why. It is "so that there should be no division in the body."

The unity he is talking about is not the organizational unity sought by ecumenical movements today. Nor is it a unity that demands that every one think and act exactly alike. It is a unity built out of the respect of one part of the body for another part. It is a unity based upon the fact that in the Body of Christ, everyone is important and honored by God.

Sometimes we forget this. In our enthusiasm to carry out the leadership function to which God has called us we get caught up in a false sense of our own importance. Or we listen closely to the opinions expressed by the "beautiful" people in our congregation, those whose speech, appearance, or dress are the most impressive. We may take action more quickly in response to the demands of the movers and shakers in our congregation than to the wishes of the rank and file.

When we ignore or listen less carefully to the opinions of the poor, the aged, those who are divorced, children, and others who do not meet the corporate image we expect, we miss the point of this passage. Paul is telling us that God has given more honor to the rank and file, to the otherwise unnoticed members of our congregation, to those we see as less beautiful or important. He has done that for a specific reason—"That there should be no division in the body" (v. 25).

How important is unity to our Savior? It is of such importance that one of the major desires Christ expresses to the Father in His high priestly prayer in John 17:21 is "that they may all be one, even as Thou, Father, art in Me, and I in Thee, that they also may be in Us." In this

5. Jerry Wofford and Kenneth Kilinski, *Organization and Leadership in the Local Church* (Grand Rapids: Zondervan, 1973), p. 134.

prayer, Jesus notes the reason for this wish: "That the world may believe that Thou didst send Me."

The credibility of the Christian message in the eyes of the world depends on unity among Christians. This unity, John 17:21 says, stems from the fact that Christians are already in unity with the Father and the Son. Only when we are in the right relationship with the Lord will we be able to be in the right relationship with each other. In turn, when we are in right relationship with one another, we will become credible witnesses to the world.

What about church splits? By a church split I do not mean an instance where an assembly amiably agrees to establish a daughter church. Every church should be engaged in such church-planting ministries. It is the essence of effective activity against Satan. By church splits I refer to those occasions when there is disunity among the people in an assembly. Hard feelings build, factions develop, and a group decides to leave the church and form a new one. When such a move is made in a spirit of anger, the end product is always undesirable. God desires His church to function in a spirit of unity. When disunity occurs and His church is fractured, it always grieves His heart.

Moreover, since it is our ability to love each other and to work with each other that makes us a credible witness for Christ in the community, it follows that the inability of Christians to get along with one another destroys that credibility. Church splits always leave an unmistakable stench in the community that lasts for years. No matter that two good churches may eventually result from such splits. God is able to bring order out of chaos and success out of disaster. The Bible makes clear that God does not want to perform this service. He would rather see amicable behavior on the part of Christians and a church that functions in love and unity than have to pick up the pieces left by a fractured church.

Leader, God calls you to a ministry of unifying, not dividing, the church. Do everything in your power to respect and honor all of the members of the body and to preserve the unity our Lord longs to see.

CONCERN FOR ONE ANOTHER

The second essential ingredient called for in 1 Corinthians 12 is mutual concern. In sharp contrast to the lack of unity warned against in the first part of verse 25, the second part of the verse says, "But that the members should have the same care for one another."

We need an extended family concept to produce a caring church. Caring is more than an attitude. It means putting action to our feelings. It means meeting people's physical and emotional needs as well as their spiritual and social needs.

The Bible commands us to help those who are in need. It is bad enough to see a stranger in need, have the wherewithal to help him, and yet not do so. When the person in need is a member of one's own family, it is inexcusable not to help him. First Timothy 5:8 says, "If anyone does not provide for his own [his relatives], and especially for those of his household, he has denied the faith, and is worse than an unbeliever." The principle applies even more strongly to our spiritual families. It is wrong to know that there is a person in need within our congregation and yet neglect that need.

First Timothy 5:8 does not necessarily refer to those who are destitute because they continually make poor choices, are irresponsible, or refuse to help themselves. Later in the chapter Paul says that even the widows are to live up to certain responsibilities: "But if any widow has children or grandchildren, let them first learn to practice piety in regard to their own family and to make some return to their parents; for this is acceptable in the sight of God" (v. 4). In verse 6 he makes a strong statement against indolence, saying, "But she who gives herself to wanton pleasure is dead even while she lives."

Nor does caring for others mean the endless distribution of charity doled to people who have little intention of helping themselves. It means that we provide every care necessary for people who are industrious and conscientious but are temporarily down.

Caring for my Christian brother may not be convenient for me. It may make an appreciable difference in my lifestyle. Nevertheless, in the sight of God, I have no alternative. The loving, truly caring church is a congregation that takes action on behalf of its people. People get to know each other, care for each other, and keep track of each other. They learn one another's needs. As a result, the church functions as a true living organism: "If one member suffers, all the members suffer with it; if one member is honored, all the members rejoice with it" (1 Corinthians 12:26).

DIVERSITY

How dull a local church would be if everybody in it were exactly alike. God does not run a franchise operation. He deals in originals.

There are no clones in His kingdom, only first editions. A major problem can occur when, in our enthusiasm to meet our goals, we try to turn everyone in our congregation into a clone to accomplish the job exactly as we would.

Diversity as God's glorious, creative gift to the church is the theme of 1 Corinthians 12:17-20. In verse 19 Paul says, "And if they were all one member, where would the body be?" He has already written in verse 17, "If the whole body were an eye, where would the hearing be?"

The combined and concerted effort of all the members God has placed within the Body of Christ is necessary for the proper functioning of the body. We need each other, and we need each other's differences. Leaders need to remember that each person is unique. The functions of all the members of the body are needed as are their ideas. Different people who look at things from different perspectives can keep the church from making serious blunders.

Utilize the diverse giftedness of your people, and thank the Lord for diversity. Celebrate differences, and capitalize on them for strength. Do that even if it means throwing out the traditional agenda and opting for an entirely new approach, one that matches the abilities of the people God has sent to your church.

Rejoice in the people the Lord has sent you as members. Identify what those people are in the body. Are they hands, feet, eyes, or what? Utilize them according to their identity, and on that basis determine how your church will evangelize the lost and edify the saints. That is a vastly different philosophy from merely choosing programs and then trying to find people who can fill the slots in those programs. Subsequent chapters will deal more fully with the establishment and reaching of goals and objectives for your church.

## THE EFFECTIVE LOCAL CHURCH IS A DISCIPLINED ASSEMBLY

A good offense is necessary to a winning team, but so is a good defense. An offensive team is useful as long as it has the ball. That is how a team scores points. But without an effective defense it cannot keep the other team from scoring. In Christian terms, when the other team scores, the casualties are church members.

Jesus spoke about the local church only once, and He did so in a defensive context. Matthew 18:15-17 tells us, "And if your brother sins, go and reprove him in private; if he listens to you, you have won your brother. But if he does not listen to you, take one or two more with you, so that by the mouth of two or three witnesses every fact may be confirmed. And if he refuses to listen to them, tell it to the church; and if he refuses to listen even to the church, let him be to you as a Gentile and a tax-gatherer."

Jesus is speaking specifically to the subject of church discipline. J. Carl Laney has observed that though "church discipline applied strictly according to biblical guidelines is a rare occurrence these days," in "earlier times church discipline was a regular part of church life."[6] Could this be the defensive strategy that was so effective in the early church but eludes us today?

Why is church discipline ignored or mishandled today? Could it be that we as leaders would like to avoid engaging in church discipline? Do we regard the task as so unpleasant and distasteful that we reserve it for the most desperate situations and then exercise it only as a last resort? If so, we have developed an unbiblical concept of church discipline. I believe that there is an important connection between Jesus' remarks about the universal church in Matthew 16 and His observations about the local church in Matthew 18. I am convinced that if the universal church is to be the irresistible force Jesus promised, it will be so only as local assemblies are disciplined churches. Church discipline should be the essence of church life.

CHURCH DISCPLINE IS FOR RESTORATION

What is the formula the Bible gives for church disciple? In the Bible the end product of church discipline is restoration, not excommunication. God does not want us to get rid of our problems by kicking them out the door. He wants us to help erring Christians become obedient to His commands and productive in His church. God's design for Christians who have strayed is that they be restored to fellowship and service in that church.

Notice the process Christ decrees in Matthew 18. Discipline is to be a one-on-one procedure. If that pattern were followed faithfully and offenses dealt with expeditiously before they were allowed to grow into large scandals, most of the problems we experience with people in the church could be avoided.

6. Carl Laney, *A Guide to Church Discipline* (Minneapolis: Bethany, 1985), p. 36.

Through the years I have often been called upon to serve as consultant to churches that are experiencing trouble. In many cases, the major problem stems from the fact that the disciplinary process has broken down. When I examine the situation to find out why, it is almost always that the first step of that process, the one-on-one step, has been bypassed.

Meaningful confrontation is not easy. Our culture conditions us against it. We are reluctant to contact other people when something goes wrong, or when we have been wronged. Instead, we let a small matter become a sore. The sore festers until it develops into a serious infection and is virtually incurable. Then we contact board members, and the board initiates the second phase of the disciplinary process Jesus outlined.

But the process does not work properly when you start at the second step. When more than one person approaches a person about a problem, the confrontation is necessarily intimidating. Especially is this true when the persons making the initial approach are official board members. The end result of this application of church discipline is always less than desirable.

CHURCH DISCIPLINE MUST BE
BASED UPON GENUINE FELLOWSHIP

One reason it is so difficult to follow the procedure Christ laid out for church discipline is that we lack a genuine fellowship base in our churches. Fellowship, *koinonia* in biblical terms, is more than sipping coffee in the social hall with a person between Sunday school and worship service. It is more than talking with someone during a church potluck or Sunday school picnic. In the New Testament sense *koinonia* refers to an intimate kind of friendship.

*Koinonia* fellowship was present almost from the birth of the church: "And day by day continuing with one mind in the temple, and breaking bread from house to house, they were taking their meals together with gladness and sincerity of heart, praising God, and having favor with all the people" (Acts 2:46-47). In the context of such fellowship practices, the church thrived and disciplinary problems were kept to a minimum.

A proper disciplinary process will occur in a local church only as that process is based on a proper fellowship foundation. Why? Because people generally will not receive discipline well unless it is addressed to them in a kindly fashion by a person whom they know genuinely cares for them. In order to be able to discipline people properly, we need first to have earned the right to be heard.

We need networks of people within the local church who are responsible for one another, are in constant contact with each other, and know each other's needs. This concept is much like the extended family commonly found in agrarian societies. It is a feature the New Testament church had going for it that we are lacking today.

In an agrarian society the nuclear family, composed only of father, mother, and children, is almost unknown. Often several generations of a family live together. Young mothers and fathers have the benefit of grandparents, aunts, uncles, cousins, and siblings to call upon as resources. Those extended family members lend insight, expertise, and baby-sitting services to the young family. They provide financial assistance when needed and care for the elderly when they grow too feeble to care for themselves. In times of crisis, they are there to provide any help that is needed.

In contrast, the nuclear family in which most of us grew up is of recent origin. It did not arise until the Industrial Revolution, when economic conditions led people to leave the farm and their extended families for jobs in the city. There they discovered how difficult it was to sustain a marriage and bring up children without the resources they had back home.

Things are even rougher today because in many cases we don't have even the limited resources of the nuclear family to draw upon. With the increase of divorce, even among Christians, we see the proliferation of single parent families and the rise of the multiparent families. Confused and lacking the resources families formerly had, more and more people are giving up. They say of marriage, the family, and life in general, "I can't do it all by myself."

This is where the resources of the church should come in. Christians can care for one another by letting the local church become an adopted extended family to its people. Such a program would work the way an extended family worked. Just as in an extended family members related to one another with differing degrees of intensity, so in the church members will relate to one another with differing degrees of intensity. People will be the closest to those with whom they spend the most time. They will share their most intimate feelings with those close friends and count on them the most when they need help. Some members of the church family will be more distant, but they will still be considered family members and persons who can be counted on for help. Sometimes those more distant members can offer resources and expertise that the closest friends cannot. Sometimes it will work the other way.

In such a system, where people are constantly in touch with one another, keep track of one another, and demonstrate that they care for one another, discipline can occur naturally and in a loving and sensitive way. In turn, the disciplined assembly will function as an important part of the great, offensive, universal church that Jesus promises will be invincible and unstoppable.

If your church is not acting as an extended family and is not providing care and discipline for one another as Jesus described, that may be its greatest deficiency. Make this subject a matter of prayer between yourself and God. Then, if He directs you to take action, be the kind of leader He has called you to be.

CHURCH DISCIPLINE SHOULD NOT BE DELAYED

An acquaintance poured out his heart to me on the telephone. Problems he faced with his teenage son had reached such intensity that he had to tell the boy to move out of the house. The sad thing is that many of us had watched the situation deteriorate for years. The dad, driven by the success syndrome that is such an important part of our culture, had ignored his kids as they grew up. Like many other parents of our day, he salved his conscience by claiming he was working so hard to provide good things for his family that he did not have time to take corrective action when the kids needed it.

If the kids got any discipline at all, their mother did it. But she was busy with a full-time job and a variety of interests outside the home. Lacking consistent, loving discipline, the children grew up with few restraints, by-and-large doing their own thing. Not until the situation got entirely out of hand and the teenage boy began to do terrible things did the father wake up to what was happening and attempt to clamp down. By that time it was too late, and he was forced to evict his son.

Too often, a similar pattern of discipline is practiced by the local church. Instead of administering consistent, loving correction to one another on a regular basis, church leaders allow a person's problems to reach horrendous proportions before they take disciplinary action.

It should not be that way. We should be in constant tune with one another, helping each other in our Christian walk. We should be providing loving, corrective discipline for one another as a way of life. When we neglect to do so, we are as culpable as the father who neglected to pay consistent, proper attention to his children and, ultimately, had to evict his son.

## Additional Resources

Banks, Robert. *Paul's Idea of Community: The Early House Churches in Their Historical Setting.* Grand Rapids: Eerdmans, 1980.

Baumann, Daniel. *All Originality Makes a Dull Church.* Santa Ana, Calif.: Vision, 1976.

Cole, Alan. *The Body of Christ.* London: Hodder & Stoughton, 1964.

Crabb, Lawrence J. *Understanding People.* Grand Rapids: Zondervan, 1987.

Getz, Gene A. *Sharpening the Focus of the Church.* 1975. Reprint. Wheaton, Ill.: Victor, 1984.

Griffin, E. M. "How to Gauge the Closeness of a Group." *Leadership* 5, no. 4 (Fall 1984): 84-90.

Henry, Carl F. *The Christian Mindset in a Secular Society.* Portland, Oreg.: Multnomah, 1984.

Johnstone, Patrick. *Operation World.* Kent, England: Send the Light; Portland, Oreg.: Multnomah, 1987.

Metzger, Bruce M. "The New Testament View of the Church." *Theology Today,* October 1962.

Radmacher, Earl D. *The Nature of the Church.* Portland, Oreg.: Western Conservative Baptist Seminary, 1966.

Richards, Lawrence O. *A New Face for the Church.* Grand Rapids: Zondervan, 1970.

Robbins, Paul. "Must Men Be Friendless?" *Leadership* 5, no. 4 (Fall, 1984): 24-29.

Schaller, Lyle E. *Hey, That's Our Church.* Nashville: Abingdon, 1975.

Snyder, Howard A. *The Problem of Wine Skins.* Downers Grove, Ill.: InterVarsity, 1975.

_____. *The Community of the King.* Downers Grove, Ill.: InterVarsity, 1977.

Stott, John R. W. *One People.* Downers Grove, Ill.: InterVarsity, 1968.

## Questions for Discussion and Projects

1. Christ truly is the builder of the church. What modern misconceptions of church leadership does this concept expose? What is the responsibility of church leadership, and in what areas are church leaders to be held accountable?

2. Why do you suppose Jesus used the term *assembly* to describe His body on earth? What common modern notions does the word *assembly* tend to contradict? What place does individuality have in the assembly?

3. What are some ways in which the church is to be different from other corporate institutions? In 1 Corinthians 12:12-26 Paul speaks of the church as an organism. How should this description influence how a church should be organized? Why is it necessary for us to regard the church as an organism if it is to carry out its mission properly?

4. What are some specific ways church unity should be demonstrated? What things cause discord in the church? How can we guard against discord? How can we determine what each other's needs really are and show mutual concern for one another? How can diversity bring about an increase in unity in the church?

PROJECT: Make a list of people who are not engaged in any ministry in your church. Find out why they are not involved. Is it partially because your church demands conformity and discourages diversity? How can the programs of your church be altered in order to employ the giftedness of these unique people?

5. List some of the reasons people fail to develop close Christian fellowship with one another. What do those reasons have to do with the inability of many churches to minister to dysfunctional families? As a

church leader, how well do you know the needs of your families? How about the needs of people moving into your community?

PROJECT: Pass out an anonymous questionnaire to your congregation and find out areas of personal interest, problems, conflicts, likes and dislikes, and specific needs. Find out how often your people are in contact with each other through Bible studies, meals, and other fellowship occasions. Is there a solid fellowship base in your church? If not, why not?

Analyze how close your people actually are to one another. Develop goals and objectives for meeting the expressed needs of your people and promoting deep and lasting Christian fellowship support systems among your people. Promote "care groups" where everyone in your congregation will be looked after by someone else. Make yours the exceptional church where no one slips between the cracks.

6. Keeping in mind the principles of church discipline taught by our Lord and the epistles (for example, Galatians 6) what should your role be in the formal disciplinary process? Of what duration and how harsh should formal church discipline be? For what offenses should a person receive formal discipline? What if the person refuses to submit? How should counseling fit into the process of discipline? How will the closeness or lack of closeness in your church family affect the way church discipline is carried out?

# 2

# THE BIBLICAL FUNCTION OF THE CHURCH

What in the world should the church be doing? That question is meant to get your attention and to make a point. The church is in the world and should be ministering to that world. How well is your church fulfilling that mission? Are the activities it sponsors truly worthwhile, and do they contribute to the principal, biblical goals of the church? Is your church even aware of what those goals are?

## AUXILIARY GOALS OF THE CHURCH

A goal is "a state of being toward which one is heading; it is qualitative in nature."[1] Originally the auxiliary goals of the church were not goals at all, but were means of reaching those goals. In many churches today, however, they have become primary ends. As a result, the church has become sidetracked from performing its principal biblical mission. In *Getting the Church on Target*[2] Lloyd Perry introduces us to secondary institutional goals by referring to the work of sociologist Amitai Etzioni. In his analysis of secular organizations Etzioni says

1. Lloyd Perry, *Getting the Church on Target* (Chicago: Moody, 1977), p. 35.
2. Ibid., chap. 2.

that any established institution, no matter what its focus, has six kinds of goals: organizational, stated, order, economic, cultural, and social.[3] Each of those goals has a foothold in most local churches.

## ORGANIZATIONAL GOALS

Perry defines organizational goals as "the state of affairs which the organization is attempting to realize."[4] A church might have as a goal the planting of a church of four hundred members in Tualatin, Oregon, that will be self-supporting in one year. Does this organizational goal sound right to you? Is it a workable one? We will examine this goal later in the chapter.

## STATED GOALS

Stated goals are slogans or statements made for publicity purposes. They may or may not reflect the real goals of a church. I know of many churches that advertise themselves as "missionary minded," but when you examine their budgets, it is evident that not much of their minds are on missionaries.

Or how about those who say, "We are a friendly church"? I have attended many of them and found that they are indeed friendly—to each other, people exactly like themselves. Visitors don't always find them friendly, especially if the visitor is of another race, a different socioeconomic class, or divorced. One church advertised itself as "the friendliest church in town." After visiting there, I concluded that the rest of the churches in town must have been very unfriendly.

Think about stated goals. Are they helpful or harmful?

## ORDER GOALS

Order goals are rules and regulations that attempt to define deviant behavior. These rules let church members know what conduct is improper in the hope that they will avoid that conduct. The rules also list procedures for disciplining the offender and isolating him from the group, should he remain unrepentant. Order goals may be written or

---

3. Amitai Etzioni, *A Comparative Analysis of Complex Organizations* (New York: Free, 1971), pp. 71-73.
4. Perry, *Getting the Church on Target*, p. 36.

unwritten. Sometimes the unwritten ones are much more binding than the ones that are written.

Think about order goals. What are their benefits and their dangers?

## ECONOMIC GOALS

No matter what a church says, its economic goals indicate its priorities. Economic goals, Perry says, "usually concern producing commodities and services to outsiders."[5] Not so in the case of many churches. As you look at the budget of your own church, note the large amount of money designated for the needs of the member saints. Is that a bad thing, or is it a laudable arrangement? Think about it.

In many churches, the sole exception to the budget for edificational activities is that for foreign missions. In some churches, little emphasis is placed upon evangelism or church-planting in North America. I serve on the regional mission board for my denomination. Recently we encouraged a young man to contact churches in order to raise support for planting a church. When he did so one church told him frankly, "Do not ask us for money for any domestic project. We give only to foreign missions."

Economic goals are revealing. Is this a good time for you to stop reading this book and look at your church budget? Why not also review the expectations your church has concerning the ministry of its pastor? Are they balanced? Are they realistic?

## CULTURAL GOALS

Cultural goals sometimes arise out of ethnic origins, as for example when a congregation does its best to preserve the use of the language and culture of its forefathers. I am currently working with a Vietnamese church that is experiencing criticism from the younger generation, who want to speak only English and to participate only in American customs.

It is not only recent immigrants whose churches are shaped by ethnic origins. Some groups, such as the Evangelical Free Church, the Baptist General Conference, and the Missouri Synod Lutherans carry the culture of their ethnic origins into many subsequent generations.

5. Ibid.

Cultural mind-sets profoundly influence the way these bodies make and carry out decisions.

Still other church bodies were formed through a conflict with a parent group. That affects the way those people think and operate. Talk to any old-timer in the Conservative Baptist Association of America, for instance, and he will quickly tell you that it is of utmost concern to remember "from whence we came," so that new churches in the denomination do not fall into the errors of the parent denomination.

Cultural goals may not be apparent on the surface. But scratch beneath the surface ever so slightly and you find out how important they are. Every group has a tradition it wishes to perpetuate. If you plant a new, nontraditional church, give it a year or two and it will have a tradition of its own. Cultural goals are a real concern to most congregations. What about such goals? Do they contribute to or detract from the ministry of your church?

SOCIAL GOALS

Social goals are the last of the institutional goals Etzioni lists. Few people want to be hermits. We all need other people. The programs and events of a church are often structured to minister to the church's social needs. Often these programs involve food consumption. The unofficial slogan of one church I know is "Till we eat again."

In chapter 1, I placed a heavy emphasis upon the needs of Christians to enjoy genuine fellowship with one another. Social occasions can be used effectively to foster genuine *koinonia*. But does that mean that as many social gatherings as possible should be planned? Can there be too many social events? Are there possible dangers here?

## ASSESSING AUXILIARY GOALS

At first, when we examine the six institutional goals the worst we can say about them is that they are harmless. Some even appear to be helpful to the ministry of the church. But when we examine the goals more carefully some dangers are evident. The most noticeable danger lies in their becoming ends in themselves instead of means to an end.

ASSESSING ORGANIZATIONAL GOALS

There is nothing wrong with establishing a self-supporting church of four hundred members in Tualatin, Oregon. However, that particular goal raises questions not answered by the goal itself. Tualatin is a yuppie community. Is this church to minister solely to yuppies?

Although the goal of having a self-supporting church in Tualatin within a year may be realistic for that area, it may set a precedent that is not realistic for other areas. For example, should we ignore the inner city and responsive ethnic groups because those kind of churches cannot support themselves in a year's time?

What about the people whom we hope to attract to our Tualatin church? Are we going after the nonchurched, or do we plan to "sheep steal"? Will this church build its membership by bringing the lost to Christ or by attracting people who are dissatisfied with other churches? In other words, does the establishment of this church, which is an organizational goal, actually contribute to reaching the prime biblical goals of evangelism and edification?

ASSESSMENT OF STATED GOALS

Stated goals are sometimes helpful to interpret a church's real personality to a community. Also, they can be helpful in encouraging members to live lives that will aid the church in living up to its stated reputation.

Stated goals are helpful as long as they are considered means to an end and not ends in themselves. A church that puts undue emphasis on them may become almost entirely taken up with public image. Being "the largest church" or "the best church" or the church with the "highest quality music" becomes the consuming drive. Winning the lost and edifying the saints becomes subservient to enhancing the church's reputation.

Stated goals may prove harmful to a church if a visitor reads the goals and is then disappointed. If you advertise, be prepared to deliver the goods. Otherwise change your advertisement to reflect the true situation in your church. Don't mislead people with false promises.

ASSESSMENT OF ORDER GOALS

Every church needs order and goals, and every church must set standards. Order goals are a means of accomplishing those ends. However, when order goals are judgmental, are imposed arbitrarily, and do not follow the biblical formula, trouble follows. Throughout history witch hunts and inquisitions have arisen when order goals became ends in themselves.

### ASSESSMENT OF ECONOMIC GOALS

It may be all right that the economic goals of most churches reflect a heavy emphasis on edification. Our people need to be cared for, and we have an obligation to give our staff a living wage. There are many needs for the church to meet among the people it serves. Also, it is important that the church have a global vision and support missionaries here and overseas. Money is important to the operation of the local church, no doubt about it. But money should be thought of as a means to an end, not the end itself.

When paying the mortgage becomes more important than winning the lost, we are in trouble. After all, even that beautiful building is to serve only as a tool to win the lost and equip saints for ministry. Meeting the yearly budget is an important economic goal to most churches, but is it of supreme importance? Many times the budget we are trying to meet reflects emphases that serve only to support other auxiliary goals, not the primary goals of the church.

### ASSESSMENT OF CULTURAL GOALS

Cultural goals may help a church to concentrate its resources on a particularly needy segment of society. Any new immigrant will appreciate attending a church in which he feels culturally comfortable. But we have to keep sight of the fact that we are to preserve the culture in order to win people to Christ, not simply to perpetuate cultural customs and values.

We must never allow cultural goals to make us exclusivistic or limit the scope of our outreach to the lost. We must avoid making cultural references that make newcomers feel uncomfortable in our midst. When we do so, cultural goals become delimiting rather than beneficial to the mission of our church.

### ASSESSMENT OF SOCIAL GOALS

Social goals can make great strides in promoting genuine Christian fellowship. However, too many churches have become little more than social clubs in which the gospel is seldom preached. In those churches no one would think of saying anything that was socially unacceptable. As a result, the type of message that convicts of sin and calls for repentance is often considered in poor taste and thus never given.

ASSESSMENT OF INSTITUTIONAL GOALS

Institutional goals may be necessary in carrying out the mission of the church. But they, too, should be thought of as merely tools, means to an end. The end is the reaching of the true, biblical, organic goals of the church: evangelism and edification. When concerted effort is made to keep institutional goals subservient, they can become valuable allies. If they become dominant, the church loses its vision. It becomes mired in the philosophy of institutional maintenance, keeping the institution alive for the sake of keeping it alive. Would that a local church die before it falls into that trap.

## IDENTIFYING THE PRIMARY MISSION OF THE CHURCH

What on earth *should* the church be doing? So far we have been looking at what the church *is* doing. Should it be doing those things? Probably, as long as those are not the only things it does, or as long as those things remain in second place instead of becoming primary.

The primary purpose of the church is to glorify God. The scriptural evidence that this is so is overwhelming. What does *glorify* mean? I like to define it in this way: "To draw attention to God's glory." But what do we mean by "God's glory"? God's glory is all that He is and does, His essence. To glorify God is "to enhance His reputation."

Everything we do and say as individual Christians and as assemblies of believers should enhance God's reputation. If His esteem is not enhanced by our attitudes and conduct, both individually and corporately, then we are out of line. We are thinking and acting improperly.

How much pain could be avoided if individual Christians and local churches gauged their activities against the standard of enhancing God's reputation. We would then have answers to all kinds of questions that face us as leaders.

How does the church glorify God? It does so through evangelism and edification. To accomplish those tasks, a church constructs goals (which are, as we learned earlier, articulations of "a state of being toward which [it is] heading."[6] A goal must be built upon a purpose. Our evangelistic and edificational goals should be built upon the purpose of the church, "to glorify God.

### EVANGELISM DEFINED

Throughout this book I will be referring often to evangelism and edification. At this point, however, I would like to comment briefly on each and show how they are inextricably linked.

Broadly defined, evangelism can be described as *all efforts directed toward leading a person to commit his life to Jesus Christ as Lord and Savior and become a productive, reproducing member of a local church.* Those efforts may include witnessing, nurturing (providing a cup of cold water, food, shelter, clothing, and medical or financial help in Jesus' name), instruction, persuasion, and encouragement.

### EDIFICATION DEFINED

Edification may be described as *all efforts directed toward building mature, reproducing believers and churches.* One of the root words of the term is *oikos,* a "house." Edification is the act of building a "house not made with hands." Since it is the Lord's house we are building we must insure that both the materials and workmanship are of top quality. No second-rate materials or shoddy methods of construction will do.

Evangelism and edification are linked. Evangelism has a strong edificational element to it. How impatient I am with people who think that the job is done once a person commits his life to Christ! In reality, at that point the work is only partially completed. Some of the toughest work is ahead.

When we hear of a mother who abandons her child after birth, we say that is "child abuse," a tragic situation. Similarly, it is "child abuse" for the church to fail to nurture and instruct a baby Christian. With that thought bearing upon my conscience, I defined evangelism with the end product in mind. From the beginning, as we work to win someone to Christ, we must remember what God wants the new believer to be—a mature, productive member of a local assembly of believers.

6. Ibid., p. 35.

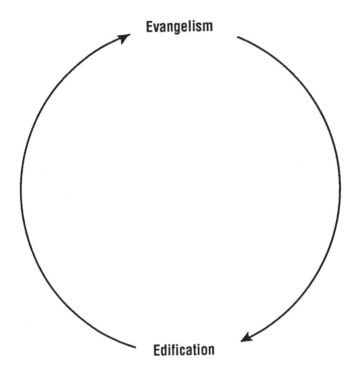

Fig. 1. The Evangelism/Edification Cycle

Look again at my definition of edification. You will notice an evangelistic dimension. One of the marks of a physically mature human is the ability to reproduce. We never know if that person has the ability, however, until a baby results. Similarly, one of the marks of a mature Christian is the ability to reproduce. However, once again, we can never tell if a person or church is able to reproduce spiritually until spiritual babies result.

Figure 1 depicts the continuing, cyclical process of evangelism and edification. When a person is saved, he must be edified. In turn, if he is edified properly so that true maturity occurs, he will share his faith, and evangelism will result.

The process is designed to continue indefinitely. The problem is that it is frequently interrupted. Therefore, it is a continual challenge to a church to watch the process carefully and get it back on track when it falters. Only as we keep the cycle going will we be able to fulfill the Great Commission of our Lord.

One more observation. We must work constantly to see that the two emphases are balanced. That's not easy because the human tendency is to swing from one extreme to the other. Sometimes that is unavoidable. There are times when pressing issues demand the majority of our attention. We must remember, however, that when a pendulum of a clock sticks in either extreme position, the clock stops.

Likewise, when the church gets stuck in either evangelism or edification, it stops. Its forward momentum is halted. A faithful leader sees to it that the pendulum gets going again, and the program of the church returns to balance. That is one of the toughest, yet most important, tasks for which God holds leaders accountable.

## A Balanced Evangelistic View

Figure 2 breaks evangelism and edification into manageable bites. On the left side of figure 2 are the three evangelistic emphases for which the church is responsible: local outreach, regional outreach, and global outreach.

### LOCAL OUTREACH

How it would please our Lord if our churches had such a steady flux of new converts that the baptistries had to be maintained full and

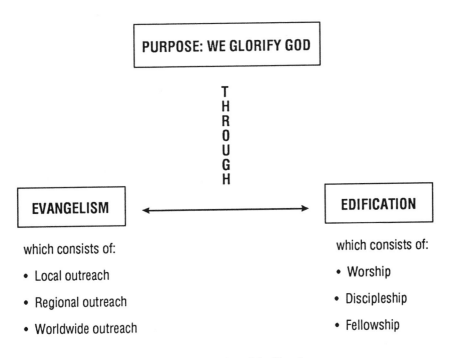

Fig. 2. The Mission of the Church

heated at all times. Instead, many churches have to clean out the cobwebs before they can turn on the faucet and fill the tank.

Here and there are a few bright lights. Many of these are new churches. Find out who they are in your community. Visit them and learn what they are doing. If they are truly evangelical in their doctrine, don't be sidetracked because they don't agree with you on every peripheral matter. Make sure that your church recaptures a biblical emphasis on local outreach and gets the pendulum swinging in that direction once again.

REGIONAL OUTREACH

Statistics are impressive. New churches are the most effective way to extend the kingdom of God. They are also more efficient in the amount of effort needed to bring a person to Christ. Church groups that plant few churches will experience little or no growth. We have to continually plant new churches just to keep up with the number of old churches that are dying each year.

New churches are a wonderful place to utilize younger, more nontraditional leaders. Here they can establish traditions of their own, for there is no need to perpetuate stereotypes of worship service formats or methods. A new church is the ideal place to attract the unchurched who are unreached because they have given up on what is to them the stodgy, established church.

GLOBAL OUTREACH

A strong emphasis on what used to be called missions is an underlying assumption in this book. That does not mean, however, that global outreach should take precedence over the local and regional outreach ministries. All three must work in concert if the evangelistic mission of the church is to be carried on effectively. The challenge for the effective leader is to maintain the balance of emphasis consistently.

## A BALANCED EDIFICATORY VIEW

WORSHIP

Nothing we do as a church is more important than worship. Public worship is and should be the essence of body life. Because we are directing our praise to Almighty God, our worship should be carried out in the most tasteful, imaginative, and professional way possible. However, our determination to do things properly should not detract from our entering into worship wholeheartedly.

For some persons, worship is important and unique enough for it to be given a separate classification of its own along with evangelism and edification. I have listed it under edification because it is impossible for a person to truly worship without his being edified.

## DISCIPLESHIP

The word *discipleship* per se does not appear in the Bible. However, we are told in the Great Commission that we are to "make disciples of all nations" (Matthew 28:19). A disciple is most commonly defined as a "follower." Once a person takes the initial step in the path of discipleship, commitment of his life to Jesus, then we are to baptize him and teach him "all things" that Jesus has commanded.

What a comprehensive job. In relation to the local church, I define discipleship as *the sum total of the church's educational efforts.*

## FELLOWSHIP

Discipleship involves fellowship. Fellowship is an important aspect of the Christian life. The trouble is that fellowship doesn't occur automatically. It must be fostered and encouraged. Most churches have a great many social activities. Few churches have an overall plan to use social activities to foster a life of genuine fellowship among members.

Fellowship has a nurturing dimension as well. When we are truly fellowshipping with people, we are aware of their needs. Those needs may be physical, psychological, emotional, or spiritual. Once we know a person's needs, we can then provide from our own assets or employ the total resources of the congregation to meet those needs. Out of the abundance God gives to each of us, we have an obligation to take care of our Christian brothers and sisters.

## LOGISTICS

In addition to the six basic tasks listed above (local, regional, and global outreach; worship, discipleship, and fellowship) there is a seventh challenge: logistics, which includes finances, supplies, and buildings. Logistics is the component that enables us to accomplish the other six objectives effectively.

The seven tasks listed above should be the focal points of the church's ministry. They are not simply nice things; they are necessary. Each of them is on the "must" list of the New Testament.

Remember the auxiliary goals with which we started this chapter? They are there to assist us in reaching the three evangelistic and three edificational goals that we have just considered. Those seven goals must be primary and they must be balanced. They are a little bit like the song about love and marriage: "You can't have one without the other" and still do the job that God has mandated for His church.

## Additional Resources

Bloom, Dorothy B. *Church Doors Open Outward: A Practical Guide to Beginning Community Ministry.* Valley Forge, Pa.: Judson, 1987.

Christensen, Winnie. *Caught with My Hands Full: Opportunity in My Community.* Wheaton, Ill.: Harold Shaw, 1970.

## Questions for Discussion and Helpful Projects

1. Define the primary mission of the church in relation to the task God has given you to do in your community.

PROJECT: List the things your church is doing. Put a check beside those things that contribute directly to the reaching of your mission. Speak with other leaders about what you have found. Discuss with them what your church should do regarding those things that either do not contribute to your church realizing its mission or actually hinder your church from realizing its mission.

2. List the reasons it is acceptable and even desirable to plant new churches in an area where there are already numbers of churches.

3. Discuss why churches that support foreign missions to the neglect of supporting home missions are really working to the detriment of foreign missions.

# PART 2

# Prepared and Gifted:
# The Leader's Qualifications

# 3

# NATURAL REQUIREMENTS

L eaders are born, not made." How many times have you heard this statement given as the sole criterion for selecting leaders?

It is true that some people seem to be unusually gifted. They are physically attractive, confident, capable, and efficient. Seemingly they have been able to charm others from the time they were delivered from the womb. "Natural born" leaders seem to have everything going for them. We are sometimes tempted to think that they should be the leaders in the church.

## ARE YOU COMMITTED AND DEDICATED?

However, let's reconsider. Just because a person is charming does not necessarily mean that he is committed to the work of the Lord. Moreover, one of God's great miracles is that He can take ordinary folks who are completely dedicated to Him and accomplish through them what would ordinarily be called impossible. Maybe that is to illustrate to the church who is to be credited with the results: not us but Him. Be assured that leaders may certainly be made as well as born.

## Do You Have Leadership Potential?

A prospective leader must have at least some leadership potential. Not everyone is destined to be a leader, and that is perfectly all right. God needs many more followers than He does leaders. But if you aspire to be a leader, you need to ask yourself, *Does anyone follow me when I lead?* If you can answer yes, you may have leadership potential.

## Do You Know How to Put Yourself in Proper Perspective?

I look at true humility as an honest self-appraisal of what one is able to accomplish. It includes knowing and admitting one's limitations, but being aware, as well, of those areas in which one is competent.

That is quite different from the definition usually heard. Many people believe that humility consists of bad-mouthing oneself. Through the years I have become impatient with people who knew that they could do something well, yet constantly disclaimed any such ability. That is far from genuine humility. It is sinful pride in a thin disguise.

The Bible plainly asserts that we are not to think more highly of ourselves than we should. But it also gives us ample reason to believe that God expects us not to think more lowly than we should of ourselves and the abilities He has given us.

Has God given you abilities that may be used effectively in the leadership of your church? Then recognize and use those abilities humbly, sensitively, and wisely to His honor and glory. Be discerning of the need for proper timing in using those skills. Then venture forth bravely, not egotistically or overbearingly but in true humility.

How does one find the balance between haughtiness and overconfidence on the one hand and a complete lack of self-confidence on the other? That is the dynamic tension in which every church leader finds himself. The answer is to be found in two sources: a person's prayer life and his relationship with the people whom he serves. Do you know how to put yourself in the proper perspective?

## Do You Know How to Practice the Doctrine of Mutual Submission?

The concept of mutual submission as a guiding posture for the Christian is expressed explicitly and implicitly in the Scriptures. Even as strong a passage as Ephesians 5, which talks about the submission of wife to husband, is preceded by the words "and be subject to one another in the fear of Christ" (Ephesians 5:21).

A colleague of mine performed a wedding recently in which he asked the bride if she would submit to her husband. She replied, "Yes," not all too enthusiastically. I sat there waiting for my friend to complete what the Scriptures seem to indicate so clearly in this passage, but somehow the pastor never got around to asking the husband if he would submit to his wife.

My colleague missed the essence of the passage. Paul's point is that we are to submit to one another. Then he spells out how that is to be accomplished. The wife is to submit herself to the leadership of her husbands. In that way, the husband is to be the head of the wife. The husband, in turn, is to love his wife as his own body. In that way, he submits himself to fulfilling the physical, emotional, and spiritual needs of his wife. Marriage must always be a partnership based upon mutual submission if it is to survive and flourish.

After making these points Paul says that he is really talking about the church and is only using the husband-wife relationship as an illustration. The principle of mutual submission Paul establishes must be applied to the church. Let's do that!

Since I am convinced that the church has only one head, Jesus Christ, and that the local assembly is the highest form of authority on earth, church leaders have no authority except that which is delegated to them by the church.

## ARE YOU WILLING TO SUBMIT TO LEADERSHIP?

From the beginning, the principle that individual members of the body must submit to leadership was given to the church as a guard against the extreme individualism that plagues the church today and often prevents it from operating effectively. Everybody wants to "do his own thing." But no institution can survive long with such a mentality.

Just as no local church is totally independent, so no person is totally autonomous. We humans need each other and must be accountable to each other. Thus the current trend toward rugged individualism that often emerges in the church is contrary to Scripture and human nature. John Snow speaks to this issue: "The concept of individual autonomy may be the craziest idea since the flat world and for the same reason. By kidding oneself one can get from day to day believing in it, but autonomy has nothing to do with reality. Human beings, simply as a part of nature, are inextricably dependent on each other as well as dependent on the physical world."[1]

## ARE YOU WILLING TO
## BE SUBMISSIVE TO THE BODY?

Just as individual members must submit to leadership, so leaders must submit to the body. Scripturally there is no other alternative.

It is unfortunate that sometimes the leadership of a church sees itself as having extraordinary knowledge far superior to that of the congregation. Often the leadership group acts as though it receives its authority directly from God instead of from the local church. It sees itself as far wiser, more mature, and better able to make important decisions on behalf of the church than is the "mere membership." The leadership considers the membership to be ill-informed and unwise.

Try not to fall into that trap. Respect the genius of the entire body acting as a unit. Learn to be submissive to the body as a whole. It is your boss rather than your being its boss. It is a tough order to practice mutual submission. We who are in leadership want to make things happen. Sometimes the body wants to move slower than we do. We may get hung up on the idea that our people are to submit to us, forgetting the other side of the coin. After all, most people find it easier to be submitted to than to submit to others. However, the essence of Christian leadership insists that submission is a two-way street. We who are in leadership must set the example for our people. To model such a principle, we must work at it, practice it, and refine it. It is a skill that must be learned on our knees and in the company of our people.

## ARE YOU FULLY DETERMINED
## TO GET ALONG WITH PEOPLE?

The ability to get along with people is the result of a conscious decision. Believe me, it can be done. However, it will not happen automatically. In order to accomplish lasting results, a leader must exercise people skills. At stake is more than a leader's ability to get a job done by

---

1. John Snow, *The Impossible Vocation* (Cambridge, Mass.: Cowley, 1988), p. 39.

using people resources, although that factor is extremely important. At stake is the fact that the actual accomplishment of the job may not be as important as the effect doing that job has upon the worker. Does doing the job strengthen the Christian worker spiritually? If not, forget about getting the job done through that person.

The ability of a worker to benefit spiritually from doing a church job may depend upon how he is treated by the leader who gives him the job. Does the leader set an appropriate example in accomplishing his tasks through people? Does he get along with people? Does he treat people as valuable in themselves, or does he use them as means to an end? How does the leader get along with his fellow leaders?

The answers to those questions often will reveal whether or not a person is truly an effective leader and a suitable Christian model to those he is called upon to lead. We are not only equipping people to accomplish church tasks; we are training them to live all of life as Christian examples to others around them.

How important is it that leaders get along with people? Jard De-Ville insists that it is of utmost importance.

> What best characterizes a successful parish leader? Why are good ones so hard to come by? The answer to the first question explains the second. No matter how well-intentioned a minister may be in his or her efforts to guide, teach, counsel, and demonstrate Christian principles to the membership, the efforts reap a limited harvest if the sower fails to realize that the key to a successful parish leadership lies with interpersonal relationships. Without a knowledge of how humans are motivated and interact with one another and the flexibility to apply "people skills" appropriately, no minister or lay-leader can be truly effective. When sound relationships are missing, people will be unenthusiastic or negative about even the most worthwhile programs.[2]

DeVille sums up his point by saying, "It is only as a parish leader draws on interpersonal strengths that desired response is reinforced and thriving congregations are built and growth sustained."[3] The greatest asset a leader has is his ability to get along with people. If you are not willing to determine to do this, you are not fit to be a leader in the church.

2. Jard DeVille, *Pastor's Handbook on Interpersonal Relationships* (Grand Rapids: Baker, 1986), pp. 14-15.
3. Ibid., p. 15.

## VALUE PEOPLE

In order to get along with people, we must value them. That involves taking a genuine interest in others. Norman Wright asks: "Who are the people you know who appear to get along well with others? What is so special about them? What qualities do they possess which make them people persons? The people I know who get along well with others are enjoyable to be with. They show genuine interest in others. When they are with you, they are really with you."[4]

## GET RID OF FEAR AND SELFISHNESS

Part of the price of getting along with others is that we rid ourselves of two stumbling blocks that cause human relationships to fail: fear and selfishness. In regard to fear Wright says, "We are fearful people, often driven more by fear than by hope. And when we live by fear, we erect barriers, act and react defensively, and fail to be open and trusting with others. Relationships ruled by fear are in danger of failing."[5]

Fear often manifests itself in our reluctance to deal with people face-to-face in a confrontational setting. Have you ever avoided dealing with a someone in person by firing off a memo or a letter in his direction? Have you ever avoided confrontation by assigning that job to someone else? I have done those things more times than I want to admit. Every time I did so the results were less than desirable.

Concerning the second reason for failed relationships, selfishness, Wright advises, "Relationships—especially binding relationships—revolve around need fulfillment. Focusing on fulfilling the needs of others is the best way to get along with them. But often selfishness butts in and we focus instead on fulfilling our own needs ahead of the needs of others."[6]

Ouch! That hurts. How much of our incentive for ministry emerges from the desire to meet our own needs, such as the need to be noticed and affirmed by people? Sometimes the position we serve raises us to a level of visibility where people give us a lot of attention. As a result, we are most eager to communicate all of the thoughts that come

4. H. Norman Wright, *How to Get Along with Almost Anyone* (Dallas: Word, 1989), p. 11.
5. Ibid.
6. Ibid.

to our fertile minds—and any other details of our lives they will be gracious enough to hear.

## LISTEN TO OTHERS

The effective leader listens to others instead of constantly speaking himself. Are you unselfish enough to concentrate your attention and energies on the other person? Are you willing to do so even when you consider that person an insufferable bore? What about people with speech defects, people who are feisty, people with a limited educational background, people you find it difficult to even like? Are you willing to concentrate your most rapt attention on those people, on their lives, their needs, and what they are saying to you? What if they persist in acting in a way that repels you? Are you unselfish enough to continue to act in an appropriate Christian manner toward them? If you are not naturally unselfish, are you willing to work at it and ask God for strength?

Dr. Wright concludes with these words of advice:

> The three most vital qualities for getting along with people are genuineness, nonpossessive love, and empathy. When these three qualities are present, therapists develop constructive relationships with their patients, making progress possible. These qualities are present in teachers who foster the greatest student achievement. Physicians and nurses facilitate a patient's return to health by expressing these qualities as they apply their medical skills. Business leaders and managers reflecting these attitudes elicit greater motivation and less resistance in their employees. Salespersons with these qualities tend to have more satisfied customers. And these qualities are essential to productive courtship, marriage, and parenting.[7]

To this impressive list of persons in whom the qualities of genuineness, nonpossessive love, and empathy appear I would like to add one other group: church leaders who are truly effective. Again, this is an area where leaders can be made as well as born. Even if we are not born with these qualities we can develop them, refine them, and use them to the glory of God. Indeed, we have no alternative. We must do so if we are to be effective leaders. Here is a formula that may help:

7. Ibid., p. 17.

1. Train yourself to exercise discipline in really listening to people. Ask your spouse or a close friend to aid you in this by nudging you when you begin to dominate the conversation.

2. Develop a set of leading questions with which to stimulate conversation in others. Learn to repeat back to people what you think you heard them say. For instance, you may ask, "You mean you and your family have actually lived in this area for thirty-five years? That must be some kind of record!"

3. Keep notes on people, especially the people with whom you are called upon to work in the church. When you learn things about these people in a social setting, first make a mental note. Then, when you get home, jot that information down on a card or log it into your computer. When you see that person the next time say, "I can't get over the fact that you and your family have lived in this area so long."

4. Develop a genuine interest in the things people find are important, and ask them about those things frequently. That doesn't mean you have to do these things yourself. For instance, I gave up golf a long time ago because I did not particularly like to play the game. However, I can be interested and enthusiastic about someone else's game.

5. Learn to listen to the point that you can truly hear when a person is hurting. Sometimes that can be detected simply from the tone of a person's voice. At other times, your clue may be what the person does not say. When you discern that a person is hurting, ask him additional questions and respond to his replies in a way that lets him know you care. It may be that you can only say, "I have never gone through those particular circumstances, and so I don't know what you are feeling. However, I can see that you are hurting. Because you are hurting so badly, I hurt for you."

Are you fully determined to get along with people? That may be the most important question you can ask yourself if you determine to be a church leader.

## Do You Have the Physical Stamina Needed to Be a Church Leader?

If you aspire to truly effective church leadership, you will pay a physical price. Just the number of hours required to do the job will exact that price from you. You will need to learn how to judge your physical strength realistically and on that basis limit the number and the intensity of the tasks you agree to perform.

Few of us are able to pace ourselves satisfactorily. Usually we tend to overestimate the numbers of tasks we can take on successfully. It is the wise leader who knows when to decline that one more vital task. To agree to undertake more than we are physically capable of doing is a disservice to our own bodies and to the ministry of the church. Inevitably our bodies rebel, and we find ourselves incapable of performing any task well. Moreover, when we spread ourselves too thin, our ministry is less than our best.

Yet we need also to remember that our physical capacities can be increased. Some people try to do this through chemical means. I have a friend who has a percolator by her bedside. A clock-radio automatically starts the coffee pot in the morning. She claims that she cannot even get out of bed without first having a cup of coffee.

Caffeine is never long-lasting, though, so she requires frequent fixes of coffee. That gets her through the day, but I wonder if she has ever considered what this artificial stimulation is doing to her system.

Other people use sugar or food to create an artificially high energy level to keep them going. Many others in our society even resort to so-called uppers to create the energy level they need.

Chemical means produce a transient, artificial energy that never approaches the natural energy the body would produce if it were cared for properly. If we are to be truly effective leaders, we can reach our ultimate energy level only as we care for our bodies properly. That means getting proper nutrition and cutting down on caffeine, sugar, refined foods, and foods with artificial additives.

It also means adopting a rest pattern appropriate to our bodies and their needs. Some people require more rest than others. Not everyone needs eight hours of sleep a night. Maybe your body demands a catnap or two during the day if you are to operate efficiently. By trial and error, you should be able to identify the rest pattern best suited to your body.

And then there's exercise. For years I fought this one. When my wife told me I needed exercise, I responded, "Exercise is against my religion. Besides, who needs it?" Just recently I have succumbed to her good advice and have joined an athletic club where I carry on a reasonable exercise program four or five days a week. My energy level has increased by almost one-half.

To repeat: limit the amount and the intensity of the leadership assignments you agree to undertake on the basis of your physical limitations. But remember—it is often possible to increase your physical capability.

## DO YOU HAVE THE EMOTIONAL STAMINA NEEDED TO BE A CHURCH LEADER?

Church leadership can be emotionally demanding. How demanding may depend upon the position the leader has, the people he must work with, the emotional climate of the church at the time, and what is going on in his life—or two or more of these in combination.

Before agreeing to a leadership position, a leader is wise to take emotional inventory of all these factors ahead of time and determine whether or not he is emotionally equipped to handle the assignment. By so doing, he recognizes that although the assignment might ordinarily be the proverbial piece of cake, there are times when he should absolutely decline the job.

Sometimes he may agree to do a job, and the circumstances are initially positive. Conditions may change, however, and he may find himself under unbearable emotional pressure. That is the time to look realistically at the job and at himself. Emotional and physical pressures often go hand in hand, so it may be that he can take steps to increase his personal physical soundness and continue in the leadership position. But there are times when the job is absolutely, unbearably taxing. Then he needs to look at the task rationally and make the objective decision to resign his position. This he should do as cheerfully as possible and without apology. He will be of little worth to the church as a leader when he is tied up in knots emotionally. Emotional strength and stability are absolute requisites for effective leadership.

## Do You Have the Moral Stamina Needed to Be a Church Leader?

Almost everyone is aware of his own weaknesses. Only you know if you are morally suitable for church leadership. It is important that you face this issue realistically. The church of Jesus Christ has been badly embarrassed by leaders who have not made this assessment. If you conclude that you do not have the moral stamina to be a church leader, exempt yourself from such positions.

There is another, more specific application of this principle. You know your own weaknesses, and you know where they are most likely to surface. Do not assume positions of church leadership that are most likely to give you an opportunity to sin. Paul speaks to this point in 1 Timothy 6. In verses 9 and 10 he lists some of the temptations to which it is easy for a church leader to succumb. In verse 11, he says, "But flee from these things, you man of God." "Fleeing from these things" involves doing all we can to avoid placing ourselves in the position to be tempted by them.

How does this application work out practically? The person who is tempted by the love of money should not place himself in a position where he is able to embezzle church finances. The person who has weaknesses toward sexual immorality should not accept a leadership role that will require him to work closely with people of the opposite sex. A person with a quick temper should not assume a high stress leadership position in which it would be difficult for him to control his temper. A person who is strongly tempted to gossip should not place himself in a position to be privy to confidential information about people.

One more caution: look at the situation realistically. Do not think you are stronger than everyone else and can therefore overcome even formidable temptations. Flee from temptation. Under no circumstances accept a position where you know that you will face temptations that are especially enticing to you.

## Do You Have the Necessary Training to Be a Church Leader?

If a person could answer all of the questions in this chapter affirmatively, yet lacked the proper training, he could fail dismally in the task of leadership. What is the proper amount of training for a church leader? It all depends. The higher the degree of responsibility, the greater the training that is required. A pastor requires a more intensive level of training than the boys' club leader. Is there a minimal amount of training necessary for all leaders? I think so. Let me share with you some of my ideas.

BIBLE TRAINING

Is it reasonable to require a person to have a thorough knowledge of the Scriptures before he is allowed to exercise church leadership? I would insist that it is. Do not read me wrong here. I am not an ivory tower professor who demands that all Christians must have mastered the biblical languages before they can teach or even lead. I would require, however, that they know where the books of the Bible are located and have a general idea of what each those books teaches.

In addition, I would urge potential leaders to become conversant with Bible history so that they know the sequence of biblical events. I would insist, as well, that they be properly trained in hermeneutics, "the study of the methodological principles of interpretation."[8] They need to have absorbed a strategic set of principles—a sound methodology—for properly interpreting the Bible.

Why do I insist on this kind of biblical training for all church leaders? I do so because the only proper decisions are biblically based decisions. Before a leader can take any significant action, he or she must be able to answer the question, Is there biblical support for this decision? If the leader is to answer that question he or she must have a general knowledge of what the Bible says, where to look for specific answers, and how to interpret the relevant passages properly. When he makes his decisions on the basis of the Scripture, he will be making aright the authoritative decisions he must make if he is to carry out his responsibilities.

Some pastors would sharply disagree with my approach. They say to their people, church leaders included, "Let me be your lifelong guru. You can't possibly interpret the Scriptures properly, so don't try. Come to me for my expert advice, and I will tell you what the Scriptures say."

8. *Webster's Ninth New Collegiate Dictionary,* s.v. "hermeneutics."

That approach is in sharp contrast to the teaching of the Scriptures. A pastor or other teacher has not properly done his job until he teaches each believer how to feed himself or herself on the Word, and church leaders are not fully qualified for their positions until they can so feed themselves.

THEOLOGICAL TRAINING

The North American church is reeling from a prolonged period of theological illiteracy. I once heard a prominent Christian speaker begin her remarks by saying, "I'm not a theologian, but . . . ," and then spend the next hour proving that statement. As a result of her doctrinal ignorance she confused her audience with all kinds of doctrinal heresy.

It is absolutely necessary that church leaders be doctrinally sound so that they are able to make doctrinally sound decisions, teach doctrinally sound ideas, and function in a doctrinally sound manner. What a person believes about the lostness of people without Christ, for instance, will have a profound effect on the ministry decisions he makes.

Not only is it necessary for a person to have theological training on the great doctrines of the church, it is also important for him to know what his own church teaches and why. Instead of floating in a sea of uncertainly when people ask him questions, how much better would it be if the leader could respond by saying, "This is what our church teaches, and here is why we believe it."

OTHER AREAS OF TRAINING

What other areas of training need to be developed? Some of those areas have already been mentioned in this book. For example, do you have the training you need to engage in realistic self-appraisal? Have you been taught how to practice mutual submissiveness? Have you learned sufficient people skills to be an effective leader?

There are other practical considerations. Have you received the proper training so that you really know your church and its background? Are you able to analyze why it does the things it does or is reluctant to do some things?

Have you received the proper training to carry out your specific job effectively? If you are a teacher, have you received teacher training along with biblical and doctrinal training? If you are involved in decision making, have you been trained to make decisions rationally and wisely?

If you are to be involved in a financial ministry, have you received sufficient training to handle finances accurately and judiciously?

God's business is the most important enterprise on earth. The principle way of carrying on His business is through the church. No business operates properly without trained leadership. Why would we think that the church would be the single exception to that rule? Never, never, never assume a position of leadership in a church without insisting on obtaining the proper training beforehand. To do so is to attach secondary importance to God's work. It is an insult to Him, to His church, and to the mission He has given the church to perform in the world.

Next to knowing God, getting to know oneself is the most important task a leader can undertake. If you do not yet know yourself, you are probably not yet ready to become a leader. Possibly you have functioned as a church leader for some time but do not yet really know yourself. It would be good for you to graciously remove yourself from leadership and devote your energies to this task. When you truly know yourself and can affirmatively answer the questions posed in this chapter, you will be a far more effective leader than you could ever have imagined. Work at it. If necessary, agonize at it. The glory of God is at stake.

## Additional Resources

Campolo, Anthony. *The Power Delusion*. Wheaton, Ill.: Victor, 1983.

Eims, Leroy. *Be the Leader You Were Meant to Be*. Wheaton, Ill.: Victor, 1975.

King, Guy H. *A Leader Led: A Devotional Study of I Timothy*. Fort Washington, Pa.: Christian Literature Crusade, 1951.

Myra, Harold. *Leaders: Learning Leadership from Some of Christianity's Best*. Waco, Tex.: Word, 1987.

Thomas, Gordon. *Leader Effectiveness Training*. New York: Wyden, 1977.

## Questions for Discussion and Helpful Projects

1. H. Norman Wright says that fear and selfishness are the two most basic reasons relationships fail. In what ways can a leader be guilty of selfishness in ministry?

PROJECT: With other leaders of your church, look objectively at the problems your church has faced over the past five years. For each of those cases, analyze which of the two factors—fear or selfishness— came into play. How might you have defused those problem situations?

2. An adequate energy level coupled with emotional strength and stability are two characteristics the Christian leader should endeavor to maintain. What measures may the leader take to enhance his physical capabilities and emotional stability? What precautions must a person take when he suspects that he may be emotionally unfit for a specific ministry?

PROJECT: List the ministries with which you are now engaged. Do any of those ministries cause you an unusual amount of stress? Or are you constantly exhausted physically when you engage in any of those ministries? Is it a good sense of exhaustion? Examine ways you can increase your physical and emotional stamina. After you have done that and a specific ministry is still overwhelming you, prayerfully consider discontinuing your activity in that area.

3. A soldier is not placed on duty until he has been properly trained. This principle should apply for Christian leaders. A biblical leader is not fit for the task of shepherding God's flock until he has received the proper training. What are some of the nonnegotiable areas of training a Christian leader must have before being given leadership responsibilities?

PROJECT: List the leadership positions in your church. Alongside each position, describe the type and extent of training a person must have in order to accomplish that task effectively. How do your present leaders measure up to your list? How can you help your church secure the necessary training for present and potential leaders?

# 4

# BIBLICAL REQUIREMENTS

The requirements given in the Bible for Christian service are stringent. Not everybody should think of applying. However, before reviewing those biblical standards, let us look at the titles the Bible uses to describe the leaders of its time. From them we may get an idea of the kind of job God has in mind for us.

## DEACON: "CALL ME SERVANT"

In the Scriptures *diakonos* is a generic term, not one that restricts the office to one gender. In Romans 16:1, for instance, Phoebe bears the title. Beyer indicates that *diakoneo* often means "provide or care for," and "in this sense . . . [was] often used of the work of women."[1]

Such talk alarms some evangelicals who are skeptical as to the kinds of offices in which women can serve. Their alarm is probably due to the fact that in our present culture the job of deacon has gone far afield from what it was in Bible days. Today deacons often serve in capacities that were reserved only for elders in New Testament times.

1. Gerhard Kittel and Gerhard Friedrich, *Theological Dictionary of the New Testament* (Grand Rapids: Eerdmans, 1964), p. 82.

There is no biblical indication that New Testament deacons sat on the ruling board of a local church, if, indeed, such a board existed. A deacon is a servant, no more, no less. If you as a deacon have any higher concept of your job, you are operating with other than a biblical view.

That does not rule out supervisory roles for deacons. The requirements set for them in 1 Timothy 3 indicate that they must have been considered important in the local church and were assigned important responsibilities. Leon Morris supports this view, saying that "the functions of these officials may well have been administrative and financial."[2]

James De Young points out that at the time the New Testament church was being formed there was already a pagan equivalent of *diakonos,* people who held a definite office and assisted in temple worship. De Young says that since pagan temple worship included acts of immorality, it is likely that pagan deacons assisted worshipers in those acts as well.

No wonder that since the early church used the term *diakonos* to describe some of its officers, Paul wanted to make sure that everyone knew the difference between a pagan deacon and a Christian deacon. That may be the reason he so strongly stressed the character requirements for Christian deacons in 1 Timothy 3.

The Scriptures give us little more than a clue as to the duties of deacons. We do know that the biblical requirements for the offices of deacon and elder are strikingly similar, with one exception. Elders are required to have the ability to teach.

What can we deduce about the servants who bore the title and occupied the position of *diakonos?* The overall job of serving in this manner (*diakoneo*) was assigned to the saints in Ephesians 4. I think it is safe to conclude that a special group of people were chosen and used by God to administer and facilitate the serving ministry of the saints. Those areas of service, Kittle says, were primarily "administration and practical service," which, he says, "may be deduced a. from the use of the term for table waiters and more generally for servants; [and] b. from what we read elsewhere in the NT concerning the gift and task of *diakonia.*"[3]

2. Leon Morris in *Baker's Dictionary of Theology,* ed. Everett F. Harrison (Grand Rapids: Baker, 1960), p. 157.
3. Kittel and Friedrich, *Theological Dictionary,* p. 90.

Moreover, this was a special kind of service. Kittel tells us that *diakoneo,* distinct from other forms of service, "has a special quality of indicating personally the service rendered to another."[4] Thus it is a special, intimate, people-oriented form of service. Kittel adds that in *diakoneo* "there is a stronger approximation of a service of love"[5] than in the other forms of service we considered in the last chapter.

Just what does all of this add up to, and how does it affect leadership? I believe that in *diakoneo* we are dealing with a special concept of ministry. This service is to be rendered in a loving and personal manner by all the saints. To ensure that this service was not carried on in a haphazard fashion, the early church appointed people they called deacons to supervise, coordinate, and facilitate the work of deaconing carried on by all the saints.

Notice that although the deacons were supervisors, they were to do their supervising in the loving, personal way indicated by the meaning of the word *diakoneo.* Never were they to be haughty, proud, or puffed up. Never were they to become overbearing or to assume illegitimate authority. There is not a single hint in the Scriptures that they were ever to consider themselves church bosses.

Nor is there indication that they sat in board meetings and made arbitrary decisions concerning the details of the church's program. They were too busy "doing the work of ministry" to get involved in such things. When they were given supervisory responsibilities, they always remembered that they were servants of no more rank than the slave who waited on his master's table. The cry of every church today should be "God give us deacons who serve humbly."

## ELDER: "CALL ME SERVANT OF ALL"

At least two Greek terms apply to those who were called upon to assume the greatest responsibility in caring for and equipping the saints. The first, *episcopos* (overseer), seems to refer to a function. The second, *presbuteros,* seems to denote a title. I believe that Titus 1 indicates that the two words often applied to the same persons. In verse 5, Paul instructs Titus to "appoint elders." Then in the next verse he specifies some of the character requirements for those people, justifying those requirements by saying in verse 7, "For the overseer must be

4. Ibid., p. 81.
5. Ibid.

above reproach." (Some commentators see the two terms as being interchangeable; others disagree. Dunham believes that though overseers always were elders, there is no certainty that elders were always overseers.)

The word *overseer* indicates that the bearer is in charge of something. Kittel[6] indicates that the word took on all kinds of new meanings when the Septuagint (an early translation of the Old Testament from Hebrew to Greek) used it to describe Hebrew biblical terms. One of the meanings of the term is "to care for something," such as a shepherd caring for his sheep, or a rancher who is "to be on guard" for the sake of his cattle. In classic Greek the term was also used in the religious sense to indicate the "gracious care of the gods for a territory under their protection."[7]

Leon Morris lends further light. He reports:

> It is likely that the Christian presbyter was patterned on the synagogue model. Any ten Jewish men could form a synagogue, and the first Christian assemblies were simply Christian synagogues, . . . complete with presbyters. The functions of oversight discharged by these men were such that they might well be designated "bishops" (*episcopoi*) in Greek. In the course of time one presbyter in each church tended to become the leader, and "bishop" was restricted to him.[8]

Kittel recounts that *episcopos* was always used in the sense of someone who is concerned about people, "with a sense of responsibility for others."[9] In 1 Peter 2:25, the term is applied to Christ Himself, the supreme Servant.

## DEFINING ELDERSHIP

If first-century Christian churches began as Christian synagogues, it is logical to conclude that the responsibilities of Christian elders much resembled the duties of their Jewish counterparts. But the term *elder* seems to have had a cross-cultural application as well. Wallace reports, "Other nations had elders (cf. Gen. 50:7, Num. 22:7), the

6. Ibid., p. 601.
7. Ibid., p. 602.
8. Leon Morris in *Baker's Dictionary of Theology*, ed. Harrison, p. 97.
9. Kittel, p. 604.

right to the title being due to age, or to the esteem in which an individual was held, or to the holding of a definite office in the community (cf. Saxon alderman, Roman senator, *gerousia*). The elder in Israel no doubt at first derived his authority and status as well as his name by reason of his age and experience."[10] Notice the term the Romans used, *gerousia.* Do you see the resemblance to the English word *geriatrics?*

Wallace goes on to say, "At Jerusalem, [elders] are associated with James in the government of the local church after the manner of the synagogue (Acts 11:30; 21:18) but in association with the apostles they also shared in the wider, or more sanhedral, government of the whole church (Acts 15:2, 6:23; 16:4)."[11]

ELDERS WERE MATURE IN YEARS

The word used in Scripture to describe elders makes it reasonable to assume that most elders were mature in years. I believe that when Paul wrote to Timothy, "Let no man despise your youth" (1 Timothy 4:12), he was referring to the fact that in Timothy's case an exception to the rule had been made. It was no doubt unusual to employ so young a man in such an important position as that which Timothy occupied in Ephesus.

Paul thus felt it necessary to encourage Timothy to defend the office of elder that he, so young a man, occupied. Undoubtedly Timothy was an unusual young man. At least he had a most extraordinary teacher. Consequently, he was a younger man of unusual maturity who had been given a heavy set of responsibilities for someone his age. Just as this was an exception to the rule in Timothy's case, I believe that the employment of a young person in such a responsible position should also be the exception to the rule today.

There is a desperate need to employ seasoned, mature people in the office of elder in our churches today. We need to recapture the true meaning of the term. In some places the word *elder* has become all but meaningless. The other day I saw two young men about eighteen years of age wearing white shirts and thin black ties and riding bicycles. Each of them wore a name tag that read, "Elder _____." I couldn't help but think, *How ludicrous!*

10. R. S. Wallace in *Evangelical Dictionary of Theology*, ed. Walter A. Elwell (Grand Rapids: Baker, 1986), p. 347.
11. Ibid.

But the Mormons are not alone in this. There are many evangelical churches in which a cult of youth has taken over. Their war cry? "We need young leadership." A quick look at their "elder board" reveals men of such tender age it is doubtful they need to shave. How is a man of that age and experience to have the wisdom and knowledge to guide the affairs of a complex congregation? How is he to deal with the problems of people of all ages in this complex society?

What a disservice we do to young men when we impose such heavy responsibilities on them. No wonder they burn out so soon. If "elder" is to be the highest office to which a person can aspire, what does he have to look forward to if he reaches it in his twenties? Worse yet, look at many so-called senior pastors. Is it even wise for Bible colleges and seminaries to train young men with the expectation that upon graduation they will be able to bear the heavy responsibilities of being the pastor of an established church? No wonder there are so many casualties in the ministry.

ELDERS BORE PASTORAL RESPONSIBILITIES

The Scriptures indicate that elders bore pastoral responsibilities. In Acts 20:28 Paul instructs the Ephesian elders, "Be on guard for yourselves and for all the flock, among which the Holy Spirit has made you overseers, to shepherd the church of God which He purchased with His own blood." Here we see two important functions, "guarding"[12] and "shepherding,"[13] outlined as the duties of elders.

Peter reinforces the need for these functions in 1 Peter 5:1-2, where he writes, "Therefore, I exhort the elders among you, as your fellow elder and witness of the sufferings of Christ, and a partaker also of the glory that is to be revealed, shepherd the flock of God among you."

Despite my concern about selecting pastors who are too young, I think we can safely conclude from these verses that the pastor, whoever he is, generally should be considered an elder. I think most churches would agree to that. However, the question of who else should be an elder is open to wide speculation and disagreement.

12. The following verses are helpful in describing the godly leader in his role of "watchman" or "guardian": Isaiah 56:10-11; Ezekiel 3:17-19; Jeremiah 6:17; Hebrews 13:17.

13. Among the many that refer to the leader as a shepherd, I have found the following to be helpful: Jeremiah 3:15; 23:1-2, 4; John 21:17; Acts 20:28-31; 1 Peter 5:2.

WOMEN DID NOT SERVE AS ELDERS

From my examination of the Scriptures, though the term *dia-konos* seems to have referred to both men and women, I can find no proof that women can or should serve in the office of elder. Nowhere do I see the female form, *presbutera,* used in Scripture to designate such an appointment. In Titus 2:3 there is reference to how the "older women" should act, but the word used there is not *presbutera,* but *presbuti-das.* In the verse immediately preceding, the male form, *presbutas,* is used, referring not to the scriptural office of elder but merely to "older men" in general. Likewise, *presbutidas* refers to "older women" in general instead of to a specific church office.

Dear ladies reading this book, there is no greater champion than I for the cause of women in ministry. However, search as I may, I cannot find a scriptural example of women occupying the office of elder. At least in Bible times, this seems to have been the job of a man.

ELDERS WERE SET ASIDE
FOR SERVICE IN A SPECIAL CEREMONY

The Scriptures indicate that elders were recognized and set aside for ministry in a special ceremony. In the King James Version of Acts 14:23 this ceremony is called "ordination." The word used is *keirotoneo,* "to elect by stretching out the hand." It seems to have been a public ceremony. Its purpose was to recognize that the people so identified had met all of the biblical qualifications and were specifically chosen by the church for that office. It is reasonable to assume that they underwent some kind of formal or informal examination prior to the ceremony.

Since the office of elder is so awesome, I am concerned that many of those selected as elders today seem to be have reached the office too quickly and too easily. I am convinced that if a church decides to appoint elders in addition to the pastor, those elders, like the pastor, should undergo ordination. Moreover, the ordination process should be as rigorous for them as for a pastor.

An examination of a candidate for elder should be given by questioning peers from other churches. They will test the prospective elder's biblical and theological knowledge and question him on his philosophy of ministry. In conjunction with the host church, the peers from other churches will help determine the person's fitness for this kind of ministry. Such an examination will make it considerably harder to become an elder than it now is in many churches. Only when the office of elder is sufficiently difficult to obtain will a person properly aspire to it, appreciate it, and guard it once he gets it.

The Scriptures seem to indicate a multiplicity of elders. There is sharp debate on this point, however. Many believe that when Paul mentioned "the elders at Philippi," he was referring to numbers of congregations in that city, each of which had one elder.

Once again, do we accept the premise that the early church adopted the leadership arrangement of the synagogue? Then we are left with multiple eldership. Note, however, that there are also biblical references to the "chief ruler of the synagogue" (e.g., Acts 18:8). In each case this rulership seems to reside in one man.

As we examine these passages, it looks as if the "ruler" established orderly processes and coordinated what happened in the synagogue. History seems to indicate that early in the history of the Christian church a similar position evolved. As a result, one of the elders emerged as the principal coordinator or leader. In our day the pastor generally occupies this position. Nevertheless, it is essential that he depend on others for help.

Does that mean it always has to be done that way? In all of Scripture, I find no prescribed form of church government. However, from experience alone, I know that church leadership is too big a job for any one person. As a pastor I always needed all the help I could get.

Sometimes, however, we have to start the job alone. Perhaps God has called us to church planting or to a church that has had little leadership training. In such cases, there may be little leadership potential upon which to draw. Even then, however, the servant of the Lord remembers that he is called upon to be an equipper. His first emphasis must be to train saints in such a way that they grow able to counsel him, advise him, and assume leadership responsibilities.

## Requirements of the Christian Leader

The basic requirements for elders and deacons are found in 1 Timothy 3. An additional set of guidelines for overseers/elders is contained in Titus 1. All of these requirements are character requirements. Many books discuss these requirements in detail. In this chapter I would like to concentrate on the basic principles these lists establish.

ABOVE REPROACH

The principal requirement of a Christian leader is rendered in the King James Version by the term "blameless." *Today's English Version* uses the expression "without fault" to describe the character requirement. If we took this combination of translations and applied it to ourselves, probably few of us would venture into church leadership of any kind.

What does "above reproach" mean? The word for "reproach" used in 1 Timothy 3:2 is *antilego*.[14] It carries with it the thought of "dispute," "refuse," "speak against," "oppose," and "contradict." It calls attention to the need to ask people in the church and in the community how they feel about a potential Christian leader. Is he controversial? Then maybe we should look elsewhere for a leader. Troublesome, quarrelsome, and balky people should avoid leadership tasks in the local church. Nobody can more fully tie a church in knots and keep it from forward progress than they.

Another word used in the text is *anegkletos,* which seems to have had a legal connotation. The term means "not arraigned," "unaccused," "irreproachable." Paul is talking about avoiding appointing people with poor records to the role of elder. Have you examined the personal lives of the people who are to become church leaders? Are there skeletons in their closets that may come out to haunt them in times of duress?

There are practical and scriptural reasons for insisting that the leader be above reproach. Foremost is that a leader needs to be credible for anyone to follow him. Who wants to follow a would-be leader who has a questionable reputation? So we need to consider the credibility of a potential leader and see if there are areas of his life that could call his credibility into question. Paul gives an imposing list in 1 Timothy 3.

THE HUSBAND OF ONE WIFE

Most scholars say that "the the husband of one wife" means "a one-woman" type of man. Traditional polygamy is not a problem in North American culture today. It is, however, in Africa, for with the industrialization and urbanization of the African nations, there has come about a resurgence of polygamy. It is a serious problem the Afri-

14. Another verse that gives description and meaning to the phrase "above reproach" is 2 Corinthians 6:3.

can church must face when selecting leaders. North Americans wrestle with "progressive polygamy," the marrying of several women in succession. Is that a factor in choosing who will be a church leader? You had better believe it!

## TEMPERATE, PRUDENT, RESPECTABLE

The qualities of temperance, prudence, and respectability indicate a lifestyle that avoids excesses and conducts itself with dignity and decorum.

## HOSPITABLE

The King James says the leader should be "given to hospitality." The Greek word is *philoxenos,* which indicates being "fond of guests," a "lover of hospitality." How concerned I am with church leaders who constantly guard their privacy. People in the congregation find their front door an impenetrable barrier. If you aspire to be a church leader, make up your mind that your home is a tool of your work. If you do not plan to be hospitable, it is probably a good idea for you to forget about being a church leader. Especially seek an office other than the pastorate.

## ABLE TO TEACH

The requirement of being "able to teach" seems to be a unique one for elders and not necessarily for deacons. Note that the meaning is not that every overseer should carry on a formal teaching function. It requires him simply to have that ability. There are many ways in which we teach. Not the least of those is by our actions.

In the early church there seems to have been a division of labor among the elders. Some of them seem to have been set aside for the more formal teaching of the Word. The Scriptures say that those individuals should be given "double compensation" for their labors (1 Timothy 5:17). However, they were also held to a higher degree of accountability than were other leaders (James 3:1).

## NOT ADDICTED TO WINE OR PUGNACIOUS

Paul says that leaders should not be "addicted to wine or pugnacious." Notice how he links the two together: "gentle" and "uncontentious." Whole books could be written as to the necessity of the church leader evidencing the fruit of the Spirit in his life. Gentleness attracts our attention especially because our "macho" society makes gentleness seem an undesirable quality for men. How the church of Jesus Christ needs leaders who are "gentle men." How wonderful the result when leaders handle people with gentleness instead of riding rough-shod over them.

## FREE FROM THE LOVE OF MONEY

When Paul says that the leader should be "free from the love of money" he does not mean that a person has to be a pauper to be a Christian leader. However, if money is the supreme, driving force in a person's life, he should not be a church leader. Do not misunderstand me. I do not think that every Christian leader is expected to live in a shack with a tin roof, although throughout the world many do. If God permits you to live in comfort, remember that extravagance and super-opulence have no place in a Christian's lifestyle. Modify your tastes and desires for the glory of God.

Even here be careful. What is extravagant and super-opulent is dictated in large part by the culture in which a person lives and works. God expects us to use the good judgment He has given to us. We are to live appropriately and modestly in the culture into which He has placed us. Neither money nor possessions is to be a driving force in our lives.[15]

## ABLE TO MANAGE HIS OWN HOUSEHOLD WELL

The "one who manages his own household well" will spend quality time there. Absentee managers don't do well. The effective manager works hard to communicate with those he manages, and he re-members that communication is a two-way street. The manager who forever dictates orders and receives no feedback soon finds himself with a rebellious work force. A person who cannot successfully manage his own household is foolish if he thinks he can effectively manage the church. The home is the first test of managerial ability.

This passage brings up an interesting question upon which Bible scholars are divided. It reads, "He must be one who manages his house-hold well, keeping his children under control with all dignity." Does "with all dignity" refer to the way the father handles the children or how the

15. A good rationale for the Christian leader to shun the love of money is given in 1 Timothy 6:9-11.

children respond to the father? The textual form seems to say it describes the father. However, both should be true. If the father is to expect the submission and respect of the children, he must treat them with commensurate dignity and respect. The father who forever flies off the handle and abuses his children either physically or verbally, or both, is not displaying qualities that would single him out as suitable church leader material. The parent who acts like a bully at home is likely to become a bully at church. I would avoid him were I looking for church leadership.

On the other hand, there is a burden on the children. Titus says that they are to be believers and "not accused of dissipation or rebellion" (Titus 1:6). Here we are looking at the end result of the father's abilities as a household manager.

If a father genuinely conducts himself with dignity with his children (not all the time—none of us is perfectly consistent) and genuinely manages his household well, is he disqualified for leadership if his child goes astray? I believe that when a child approaches adulthood, he must take over the management of his own life and make his own decisions. If he makes poor ones, I do not think his parents should be held totally accountable for those actions.

NOT A NEW CONVERT

Think of the tremendous responsibilities placed upon a church leader. Would we assign those duties to an infant child? Why then should we do so to an infant Christian? To do so may permanently stunt his Christian growth. Likewise, because he still acts in many ways like a baby, his displays of immaturity may well set back the cause of Christ in that church and community. That is why Paul charges that the leader not be a new convert.

HAVING A GOOD REPUTATION
WITH THOSE OUTSIDE THE CHURCH

Paul asserts that the leader must have "a good reputation with those outside the church." Once again, this has to do with the leader's credibility in the Christian community and in the secular world. Is he a credible witness for Jesus Christ? Do non-Christians respect him? Were I to consider a person for eldership, the first thing I would want to look into is his credit rating. The second thing I would do is talk with his neighbors.

FAITHFUL AND OBEDIENT

To those major qualities, add a whole list of other values that describe a self-controlled person of sound faith, moral lifestyle, and exemplary behavior. Two words sum up his entire deportment: "faithfulness" and "obedience."

POSSESSING THE ABILITY TO LEAD

Add to those, the ability to lead. This is basic to any consideration of leadership. But remember, there are different kinds of leaders. On one hand we need the leader who dreams great dreams and is able to get his people to accomplish great things for God. On the other hand we require the leader who sees a simple task to be done and says, "Follow me." We need both kinds of leaders and every kind in between. The trick is to employ all of them in the right spots and profitably for the kingdom of God. Regardless of how glamorous or mundane the tasks of leadership, all must be done in a sense of great humility before God.[16]

To properly comment on the character guidelines for leaders listed in 1 Timothy 3, Titus 1, and other passages would take many volumes. I do not want to convey by my brief treatment of these passages in this chapter that I believe they are unimportant. To the contrary, I believe they are of great importance. The Christian leader should read these passages at least once a month, see how he measures up to them, and make concrete plans for improvement. He should remember, too, that none of us lives up to these high standards perfectly. All of us need continually to be setting goals in many of these areas.

## CHARACTER GUIDELINES SHOULD BE APPLIED NONSELECTIVELY

We face two problems when we apply the biblical guidelines for leadership. First, "above reproach" may sometimes be hard to determine as an absolute. Many times that is because churches are arbitrary as to the criteria they select. I know of few churches that would disqualify a potential elder because he had "bratty kids," or a gossiping wife. Those problems are by and large overlooked. "After all, nobody's perfect. Right? And we need all the help we can get. Isn't that true?"

---

16. Examples of humble leaders in the Bible can be found by their reactions recorded in the following passages: Exodus 3:11; Judges 6:15; 1 Samuel 18:18; 1 Kings 3:7; Isaiah 6:5; Matthew 3:14. One of the finest records of a humble, servantlike attitude is the example of the apostle Paul as written in 1 Corinthians 2:1-16.

That is probably the reason many churches would give if you challenged them on those points.

Moreover, many churches are reluctant to enforce the guidelines against an elder's being pugnacious or loving money. Those faults they can overlook, along with the apparent inability of a man to manage his family. Yet the same churches would absolutely exclude from leadership anyone who has ever had a divorce. They would do that even if it meant placing a relatively new Christian or a person who enjoys a bad reputation with his neighbors into office. Sometimes it doesn't even matter if the divorce occurred prior to a person's conversion.

I am not suggesting that your church place a divorced person into a place of church leadership. You will have to decide for yourself whether or not he meets the biblical guidelines. I am appealing for justice and parity. If a person is excluded on the grounds of divorce, people should also be excluded for the other infractions listed in 1 Timothy 3, Titus 1, and other Scriptures. Let us use the complete list and not engage in a selective application. Moreover, before a church excludes a person on the basis of divorce alone, it should have substantial evidence that this is what the phrase "husband of one wife" means. I am a champion of the sanctity and permanence of marriage. I hate divorce as, I believe, God hates divorce. However, after a thorough study of the passage, I am not thoroughly convinced that "husband of one wife" refers specifically to people who have never been divorced.

## "Above Reproach" Is Sometimes Culturally Determined

The nature of "above reproach" is inevitably culturally defined. What is above reproach in the eyes of European Christians may be entirely inappropriate behavior for North American Christians. What is above reproach in California may be entirely unacceptable in Illinois. What may be acceptable among Southern Baptists may not fly with Free Methodists.

What practical applications should be made from this point? The first is that in order to work in a particular context, a person may have to change his style of living.[17] If he is unwilling to do that, he will have to find a context where his practices are considered acceptable.

17. For a good description of a man who could truly be "all things to all men," see 1 Corinthians 9:19-23.

Understand, I am not talking about moral practices. Those are prescribed by Scripture. I am referring to peripheral areas where Scripture is less definite. As a leader, how willing are you to become "all things to all men"? Does doing so offend your sense of Christian liberty, or can you make a concession in order to serve God effectively in a particular context?

On the other hand, conditions may exist over which you have no control. One of my seminary students believed it was God's directive will for him to marry a recent convert. She had been divorced and had conceived two children out of wedlock, all before she became a Christian. Now she was a radiant child of God. He was her spiritual father, had become her friend, and they had fallen in love.

But could she ever be a pastor's wife and could he ever be a pastor if he married her? "Not in Washington or Oregon in our evangelical circles," was the quick answer. However, my former student is now serving his second church in Northern California. In each place he has had a fine, successful ministry, and the people have accepted his wife and children without reservation.

If you have problem areas in your background, try to understand when people are not eager to place you into a church leadership position. If you believe you are being called to serve God in a geographical location and denominational context that limits your kind of service, do so humbly, graciously, and lovingly. Do whatever you can within the limitations that have been set. God did not call you to start a war in a local church because they restrict where and how you can serve. If, on the other hand, you feel unmistakably called of God to engage in forms of service that you think are more exciting and challenging than your church allows, you may well have to move to a different geographical, cultural, or denominational context.

Before you move, however, make sure that you are fit for service and are being discriminated against because of something that is "buried under the blood of Jesus." Look to make sure that you are not carrying other unwanted baggage with you. Even then, don't lash out on the people who have set the standards and have kept you from church leadership. Understand that it is their conviction, whether or not you believe they are right. Love them and leave them graciously and lovingly. Then, when you have reached your "new heights of service," don't write or telephone back to rub it in. In all, act like a Christian gentle-man or gentle-lady! Remember, you are a servant—and nothing more!

## Additional Resources

Anderson, Clifford. *Count on Me.* Wheaton, Ill.: Victor, 1980.

Campolo, Tony. *The Power Delusion.* Wheaton, Ill.: Victor, 1983.

Engstrom, Theodore W. *The Making of a Christian Leader.* Grand Rapids: Zondervan, 1976.

Jefferson, Charles. *The Ministering Shepherd.* Paris: YMCA, 1912.

Jones, Curtis. *The Naked Shepherd.* Waco, Tex.: Word, 1979.

Stott, John R. W. *The Preacher's Portrait.* Grand Rapids: Eerdmans, 1961.

Warkentin, Marjorie. *Ordination: A Biblical-Historical View.* Grand Rapids: Eerdmans, 1982.

## Questions for Discussion and Helpful Projects

1. How closely should twentieth-century churches try to model the church structure of the first century? Look at the vast differences in time, culture, geography, facilities, and resources between the first-century and twentieth-century churches. In light of those differences, what would you say are the irreducible minimum requirements in a church governance structure that all churches must accept?

2. If, indeed, the nature of the word *elder* implies maturity, discuss the means by which your church determines who is qualified to be an elder. What are some of the reasons many churches use to justify choosing less than mature men to be elders? What can be done to change this unbiblical pattern?

3. Should all pastors be considered elders? Should all elders be capable of functioning as a pastor? What church leaders should bear the title "pastor"? Should this title be granted only to paid workers?

4. Why is it that the author believes so strongly that elders should be ordained? If this is to be done, what should be the requirements for ordination? Should those requirements vary according to the task for which each elder is to be held responsible? If so, should a person be examined and ordained only to the specific office he will occupy?

5. Discuss the ways the guarding and shepherding functions are carried out in your church. In the New Testament these responsibilities are given specifically to elders. Who then is responsible to guard and shepherd the elders, assisting them to be faithful to their task and upright in their lives?

PROJECT: Construct a step-by-step plan for guarding and shepherding the principal leaders in your church. Tell in detail how the church intends to provide care for its leaders and their families.

6. Examine how spiritually fit for ministry you are. With which areas of weakness in your life do you need to deal? Explain specifically to yourself and to God how you are going to do this.

# 5

# SERVANT

The vision statement of the seminary I serve describes it as "an educational institution, nurturing for the Church godly leaders committed to and competent for Christ's redemptive purpose throughout the world." This book is exclusively designed for godly church leaders. Does that describe you? Is that the kind of leader you are or aspire to be? It is important that you consider the question carefully, because godly leaders are the only kind of leader our Lord wants for His church.

What is your concept of a godly church leader? Were you to ask a variety of people for a definition, you would likely get several different and conflicting answers. Unfortunately, many of those answers might even contradict the scriptural description of the term.

## TWO UNBIBLICAL EXTREMES

As you inquire, you might hear described the stereotypical aggressive, confident, coercive leader who expects people to jump when he barks. He sees himself as action oriented and goal motivated. He expects to be able to whip people into shape and utilize them to accomplish his goals—which he knows are necessary for the success of the church he supposedly serves. Some people are reluctant to make decisions on their own and appreciate this kind of leader telling them what to do. They feel comfortable under his leadership—for a while.

At the other extreme is the milquetoast conciliator. He never gets much done except to appease people, but when he is in charge, life is peaceful—at least on the surface. The super-conciliator may be able to please people for a long time. He may even be able to keep the lid on an explosive situation during his tenure. However, a seething volcano eventually blows. Then someone must deal with the problems of the church in a decisive manner.

Both kinds of leaders are self-serving. Look at the first type, the super-aggressive leader. Were I that kind of person, in my insecure moments I would be forced to ask myself if my goals were necessarily the best ones for the church I serve. Was my revelation directly from God? Unfortunately, some leaders would automatically say a hearty yes to both questions and try to convince us as well.

When a self-satisfied attitude prevails and a leader concludes his remarks by saying, "God has revealed to me that this is His will," that certainly ends all discussion, doesn't it? After all, who can argue with God's revelation? How unfortunate when a leader uses such a statement to browbeat his people into accepting his will. Instead of being a servant of God, he is attempting to make his people his servants and coerce them into carrying out his desires. He wants to be able to bask in the results of what he conceives to be his own efforts if and when his people succeed.

The conciliatory leader may appear on the surface to be selfless, but he, too, may actually be self-serving, even a coward. After all, it is pleasant for a leader to work in an environment where he does not have to face strife, conflict, or differences of opinion.

But is it really so pleasant for the congregation he serves? Peace at any cost often extracts a higher emotional and spiritual cost than a church can stand. Unchecked compromise eventually leads to a surrender of the essentials. If a church is to maintain its integrity, there is a time when its leaders must confidently and lovingly draw the line. Godly leadership calls for leaders who are wise enough to distinguish peripheral matters from the essentials. Where important issues are involved, regardless of the immediate cost, the godly leader has no alternative except to declare the right and decry the wrong.

Indeed, even though the milquetoast may keep the peace and perpetuate the status quo for a while, he seldom is able to lead the church forward. The resulting stagnation always leads to disharmony and dissatisfaction. Moreover, the problems seething under the lid eventually come to a boil, and trauma to the church is the inevitable result.

As a church leader, God does not call you to be a dictator or a doormat. He calls you to be His servant and a servant to the church. As we discuss service to our Lord through the church, let us remember that the ecclesiastical buzz word, "ministry," simply means service. Sounds easy. But many churches and church leaders have lost sight of that. How sophisticated and self-elevating to say, "I am involved in ministry." Doesn't that have an important ring to it? It is more ego-inflating than saying, "I serve." But saying, "I serve," puts the task in its proper biblical perspective. To adopt the role of a servant is to follow in the steps of the Savior.

## THE LEADER AS A SLAVE TO CHRIST

The New Testament uses at least four terms to describe Christian service. One of these is the word *doulos,* "slave," or "bond servant." Paul, a true apostle, one who could have become overly impressed with his own importance, often used the word to describe himself. He was a slave, a bond servant, to the Lord Jesus Christ and to the church.

In New Testament times, a slave could be bought or sold as property. His master had life and death control over him. In *I Believe in the Church* David Watson writes, "A servant is someone of no importance to himself. In humble obedience he is simply required to speak and at in his master's name. In this way his master speaks and acts through him."[1] Completely expendable. Of no self importance. That is the biblical description of Christian servanthood. Notice that in the way Paul used this term it really represented a philosophy of service rather than a form of service. That is the leadership posture our Lord expects of all of us.

## THE LEADER AS THE UNDERDOG

Another word used by the New Testament in connection with service is *huperetes.* Its early classical meaning derives from *hupo,* "un-

---

1. David Watson, *I Believe in the Church* (Grand Rapids: Eerdmans, 1978), p. 216.

der," or "subservient to," and *erresso,* "to row." Originally the word meant an "under oarsman," someone on the lower end of the totem pole on the Roman ships that sailed the then known world. Duane Dunham says that the term pictured a person who was required to respond instantaneously and without question to any order given him. The drumbeat would indicate "speed up," "slow down," or "maintain speed." He would respond, flexing his muscles and pulling for all he was worth.

Even in Bible times, the word *huperetes* still retained much of its original flavor, describing an inferior position or condition, menial labor of some kind. In Acts 20:34, Paul used the word to say, "You yourselves know that these hands ministered to my own needs and to the men who were with me." Even though he was the foremost leader of the church, Paul did not consider himself above engaging in hard, physical, menial labor with his hands to accomplish the task God had set out for him. It was all part of the job description.

Moreover, Paul's friends were not above serving him in the same way. Upon Paul's imprisonment, we see that Felix gave orders for Paul "to be kept in custody and yet have some freedom, and not to prevent any of his friends from ministering to him" (Acts 24:23). Think of the endless tasks those friends performed. Often they were perfunctory jobs, such as serving as Paul's secretary or delivering his coat to him. The jobs had no particular glamour attached to them. Nevertheless, they were essential if Paul was to serve the Lord effectively. What unglamorous tasks would you be willing to perform to help another servant of God perform his ministry more effectively?

## THE LEADER AS THE "CHIEF COOK AND BOTTLE WASHER"

The term most frequently used in the Bible to describe service is the word *diakoneo.* That is the descriptor used in Ephesians 4:12, where Paul talks about "equipping the saints for the work of service." In some ways, *diakoneo* seems to be a generic term to describe the type of service expected from every Christian. In Ephesians 4, for instance, the emphasis is on the equipping of all of the saints for the work of service.

In classical Greek *diakoneo* described a kitchen servant, one who waited on tables. It was not a pleasant task, not a desirable job. Even today, when food is considered unacceptable by the customer, the waiter generally takes the brunt of the abuse. From classical Greek literature we find evidence that this was often a task reserved for women.

Therefore, in those extremely chauvinistic days to call a man a deacon certainly was no mark of distinction.

In the early church, those engaged in deaconing might also be called upon to exercise people skills and to serve in administrative capacities, such as is indicated in Acts 6. At times the giftedness of those people stretched far beyond what might normally be expected of them. Philip and Stephen, for instance, were effective preachers, and Philip was also given the title "evangelist."

Paul uses *diakoneo* in Romans 15:25 where he states, "Now, I am going to Jerusalem serving the saints." You may find it interesting in your Bible studies to locate the many uses of this word and see how many times it involves service to or on behalf of people.

## THE LEADER AS A PUBLIC FIGURE

The final term related to Christian service I wish to discuss is the word *leitourgeo*. *Leitourgeo* denotes those who "perform a public service, serve in a (public) office."[2] In Romans 10:11 the word is used to describe the daily service carried on by the Jewish priests at the Temple. This is the more up-front, visible, platform service envisioned when many people think of the ministry.

*Leitourgeo* is used in Acts 13:2 to describe the public service carried on by the prophets and teachers. In Romans 15:27 it refers to the financial ministry carried on by the Gentile churches in behalf of the destitute Christians in Jerusalem. Public service such as this is necessary, fitting, and proper. It is here that the church acts and speaks as one.

## WHICH IS THE MOST IMPORTANT?

Having looked at these four kinds of service in behalf of our Lord, which do you suppose is the most important? The last one, *leitourgeo,* is certainly more prominent. It is the one that usually gets the most notice and public credit. It is the service that projects a picture of the church to the public, and it is the type of service that ministers to the greatest number of people at the same time. Certainly public service of this kind should be done with the greatest planning and care. There is no excuse for slipshod methods or poor performance at this level. But is it the most important kind of service?

2. William F. Arndt and F. Wilbur Gingrich, *A Greek-English Lexicon of the New Testament and Other Early Christian Literature* (Chicago: U. of Chicago, 1973), p. 471.

Which type of service is the most important? Every form of service! Notice that the apostle Paul engaged in all of the forms of service we have talked about in this chapter. Not everyone is gifted enough to do that. Some people are private people. They do not have platform skills and strenuously avoid the limelight. They are the unsung heroes and heroines who work in the background. Nevertheless, largely because of their faithful service, the church advances.

## A BIBLICAL PATTERN OF SERVICE FOR CHRISTIAN LEADERS

Is there a biblical pattern of service for Christian leaders? I believe there is. Here are some general principles to apply:

### CHRISTIAN LEADERS SHOULD SERVE IN THE SPIRIT OF *DOULOS*

All who serve in any way must do so in the spirit of *doulos*. We are not important in ourselves but are only bond servants to the Lord Jesus Christ. Therefore, we should view ourselves as personally expendable and not come unglued or become sulky when we don't receive what we think is the proper recognition for our services.

### ALL CHRISTIANS ARE TO SERVE

The command to Christian service is a universal order to all believers. The entire body of saints is to be engaged in the work of *diakoneo*, ministry. (Remember, ministry means service.)

### CHRISTIANS MAY BE ASKED TO TAKE ON MENIAL SERVICE

Any Christian may be expected to perform even the most menial type of service on behalf of our Lord at any time (*hupereteo*). I believe it is even beneficial for leaders who are always in the limelight to engage often in the more menial tasks. That will help to keep them humble, and it will show the people that their leaders actually regard themselves as human.

### MULTITALENTED LEADERS SHOULD BE ALERT TO NEEDS

Like Paul, the multitalented leader should be alert to perform the type of service that the circumstances and the occasion demands. Good use of common sense will alert the leader as to how he should serve at any particular time.

THE MORE PROMINENT THE JOB, THE
MORE A SERVANT'S HEART IS NEEDED

There is a fifth principle, one I would like to explore at some depth. It is expressed by the song line, "If you want to be great in God's Kingdom, learn to be the servant of all." This foundation stone for ministry teaches us that the more prominent the job, the more public your ministry, the more you should exhibit a servant's posture and a servant's heart.

How does such an attitude differ from what we normally encounter? If we look at the world of business and transport its attitudes to the church, as many have done, we will see a leader-service triangle that looks like this:

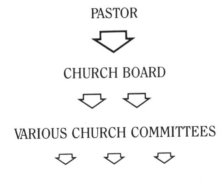

PASTOR

CHURCH BOARD

VARIOUS CHURCH COMMITTEES

THE CONGREGATION OF THE CHURCH

The operating principle in the chart is that the higher one goes on the triangle, the more important is the person who fills that position; the lower one goes, the less important the person who fills the position. The "lower" people are expected to serve the "higher" people. In addition, the "higher" people are the ones who receive all the good ideas, the great "revelations from God." The "lower" people are expected to carry out those ideas. If they are reluctant to do so, they are labeled "carnal" and chastised for their refusal to submit to the authority of their leaders.

I do not see that kind of pattern justified in the New Testament. Instead, what I see is something like this:

## THE COMMUNITY OF MINISTERING SAINTS

## FACILITATORS AND EQUIPPERS

## PRINCIPAL SERVANT
(pastor)

In this diagram the leaders are the people at the bottom. They are responsible for serving all the people above them. In both diagrams the person or persons on the top are considered the most important and, consequently, the diagrams represent radically different and conflicting views of leadership ministry.

In the first diagram the ministry is regarded as the responsibility of the pastor. He is at the top and is therefore considered the most important person. Those below him on the pyramid are there to assist him in various ways, but the real ministry is his business. How often I recall, as a pastor, urging my people to share their faith with non-Christians and hearing the response, "Pastor that's your job. That's what we hire you to do."

In the first diagram the pastor and to some extent the board pull the strings. The people take the "grungy" jobs. When the enterprise succeeds, it's because the pastor is doing his job well. When it fails, well, we had better get rid of this guy and call a new pastor.

In the second diagram the principal work of ministry falls to the saints. What, then, is the job of church leaders and of the principal leader? It is to aid the serving saints in discovering their spiritual gifts, talents, and abilities and to equip them for service in such a way that they use those gifts, talents, and abilities to maximum effect. Communication in the second diagram consistently moves in both directions rather than just from the top down.

Leaders are to become facilitators. It is not their job to lay heavy extra responsibilities upon the workers. It is not their task to hold workers to unrealistic goals. It is not their mission to keep workers in a continual state of uproar and confusion.

Instead, it is the task of the leadership to make everything as smooth as possible for the workers and to aid them in as many ways as is plausible. In that way the leadership enables the workers to function in their jobs with a minimum of distractions.

Do not misunderstand me. I am not suggesting that the leader lower his standards and settle for shoddy performance on the part of his workers. The standard of service in behalf of the Lord must always be improving. What I am crusading against is the assignment of many needless, routine, and perfunctory tasks to the worker. In no way do those tasks aid him in accomplishing his ministry. It is the duty of the leader to relieve the worker of such tasks so that the worker can experience the full joy of ministry.

Instead of being a critic, the leader is to be an encourager. Instead of asking the worker to work for him, the leader works for the worker. Always, the welfare and ministry of the worker are of prime consideration to the leader. Perpetually, the leader takes steps to relieve the worker from attending perfunctory meetings or performing redundant, meaningless, administrative tasks.

In the model with the pastor on top the workers may come to be considered means to an end. In the second model they are the end in themselves. Instead of the primary allegiance being worker to leader, it becomes leader to worker.

In the model with the pastor on the bottom the pastor (whom I consider to be the chief coordinator of most church programs) becomes the servant of all those above him in the pyramid. In that role he ministers to all and works as the equipper of all. But he has special responsibility to the people immediately above him in the pyramid. It is one of his primary jobs to provide or secure whatever is necessary to equip the leadership so that they, in turn, may equip the other saints. The pastor is thus not only a servant of the saints but a servant of the leadership. The leadership in turn becomes servants to the other saints.

In the inverted pyramid, the leader learns the true meaning of the servant-leader concept introduced by our Lord. When leaders catch this vision and begin to see their primary job as servanthood to the saints, a revival of ministry takes place. Likewise, when the pastor sees himself as servant to all, a new dynamic takes charge and wonderful things begin to happen in and through him. Most exciting of all, the saints learn what it is like to glow with the excitement and exhilaration of serving Jesus.

## Whom Is the Leader to Serve?

A quick answer to that question would be, "Why, the Lord, of course." But that's too nebulous. Through what vehicle do we serve the Lord? "Through His church," would be the quick reply. Come on, now, who makes up His church? The saints do.

Saints are VIPs in the sight of God. Paul acknowledged this fact when he began his letter to the Philippians by addressing the saints first, even before he mentioned their leaders.

## Saint: "Call Me Special!"

Why are the saints so important? There are a number of reasons. First, in purely practical terms, they represent the greatest potential source of manpower (and womanpower). One of the problems faced by the contemporary North American church is that it is plagued by a consumer mentality. The most frequently heard question is, "What does the church do for me?" Rather it should be, "What should I be doing for the church?"

How inefficient and ineffective is the church that is not able to marshal its manpower to the task our Lord sets for it. How tragic it is when the saints never move beyond being consumers to people who know the joy of actively serving the Lord. How criminal it is for the leadership of a church to perpetuate a consumer mentality instead of equipping the saints for the work of ministry.

Consider the church that sees the job of ministry as the responsibility of the pastor alone. How much can one person actually do? No wonder so little of importance is happening in the life of that church. Consider the church that sees ministry as the responsibility of the board alone. How much can several people accomplish in comparison to a whole congregation working together in a concentrated effort?

The greater the number of people involved in ministry, the greater the amount of ministry that will be accomplished. Let us tap the manpower resources of the church rather than trying to do the job by ourselves!

The second reason the saints are so important is that they represent such a wide spectrum of spiritual giftedness. The greater the number of saints, the more the chance of multiple spiritual gifts within the congregation. The more gifts that are utilized, the greater the potential for a richer and more highly successful ministry in and through that congregation.

But be careful about spiritual gifts. They can be counterfeited and abused. When they are genuine, it is important that they be used properly. To aid us in doing that, David Watson poses some questions that should be asked concerning the person wanting to serve. They are the following:

1. Is Jesus Lord of that person's life?
2. Is Jesus acknowledged as perfect man and perfect God?
3. Is the manifestation of the gift in accordance with the Scriptures?
4. Is there true holiness and godliness about that person?
5. Is there submission to church leaders?
6. Is the church edified through this gift?
7. Is love the controlling factor?[3]

How many spiritual gifts are there? The Bible gives lists in 1 Corinthians 12, Romans 12, and Ephesians 4. I believe that these lists are not delimiting but merely illustrative. Certainly a creative Holy Spirit is capable of giving a far greater array of gifts than is listed in these passages.

## How to Help Saints Discover Their Spiritual Gifts

Since it is the task of the servant-leader to help the saints discover their gifts, it would be helpful for that leader to have a set of procedures to help him do that. Below is a set of guidelines he may find useful.

### DEFINE WHAT A SPIRITUAL GIFT IS

The term *spiritual gift* is far simpler in meaning than the average Christian suspects. God in His sovereign wisdom created every Christian with a spiritual potential in mind. From the beginning He made each of us with talents and abilities. It is my sincere conviction that when a person is converted and begins the path of sanctification, the Holy Spirit takes his innate abilities, baptizes them, and begins to use them for the edification of the church.

3. Watson, *I Believe in the Church,* pp. 112-13.

David Watson's comments on the gifts of the spirit are challenging. Regarding spiritual gifts, Watson asks, "What, then, makes something a 'gift of the Spirit'? It is not some strange, inexplicable, supernatural quality. Rather, something becomes a gift of the Spirit when it fulfills two functions."[4] Those he lists as glorifying Christ and edifying the Body of Christ. He then comments on the two functions, saying,

> If any gift or ability, therefore, is used to glorify Christ and to edify his body, it becomes a gift of the Holy Spirit. Of course there must be some conscious dependence on God, together with the inspiration of the Holy Spirit, before a natural ability becomes a spiritual gift. Without this, the gift can all too easily become an occasion for self-display. Our attitude to these natural talents is important. Do I see my talent as "my gift," so that I am looking for personal fulfillment for my gift? Or do I see it as entirely a gift from God, which he could remove at any moment, and must consequently be used humbly and prayerfully to his glory and for the benefit of his people? Only then can it become a genuine spiritual gift.[5]

Watson demystifies the subject of spiritual gifts, and we might not want to go as far as he does in doing so. However, he provides stimulating commentary for us to study. The major point he makes is one with which I am in full accord. Spiritual gifts are a natural part of the person the sovereign God created. They emerge from a person's natural talents and abilities when he becomes a Christian. They spring to full fruition when they are used by the Christian to glorify God and edify the Body of Christ.

PAY ATTENTION TO WHAT A PERSON ENJOYS DOING

What do you really enjoy doing, and what have you dreamed of doing in the service of Christ? That is a question you need to ask the saints. We serve a God who wants us to delight in the joy of serving Him. Even though we will be called upon from time to time to do things we do not consider desirable, that is not the general pattern for service. Those hard, undesirable tasks are designed to build character in us, but they are the exception rather than the rule if we are paying

4. Ibid., p. 105.
5. Ibid.

attention to what God is trying to teach us. In addition to fulfilling graciously the undesirable tasks, God wants us to "dream dreams and see visions" of even greater areas of service than those in which we are now engaged. Work with the saints to help them make their dreams a reality. Help the saints to know the real meaning of spiritual gifts.

PAY ATTENTION TO THE RESULTS THAT FOLLOW FROM THE SERVICE

Observe the saints as they practice the kinds of service they like to do. Is a given saint successful in performing his task? What do other people in the church think about his abilities in that area? If he does poorly, is it because he lacks giftedness or because he lacks the necessary training?

A person may give evidence of being a gifted and vibrant teacher but may be short on content or not know how to vary his methods appropriately. Others who are professional teachers may completely fail when they teach Christian education classes in the church. Merely because a person works at a secular profession is no indication of spiritual giftedness in that area.

MAKE TRAINING AVAILABLE

Provide the saints with whatever training is necessary for them to perform their ministry effectively. Spiritual gifts are not given to us in polished form. They are given to us as do-it-yourself packages. All the necessary components are there, but we have to polish them into the effective tools for service that God has designed them to be. Inspiration without perspiration is futile. God will always do His part. In turn, He expects us to do our part. A person's willingness to receive instruction to develop a certain ability may indicate whether or not it is truly an area of spiritual giftedness for him.

BUILD IN TIME FOR THE ASSESSMENT
OF THE EXERCISE OF THE GIFT

Once the person has had the necessary training, allow him some time to apply it to his ministry. After what you consider to be suitable time, invite church leaders to observe him in action once again. Does his service glorify God? Does it edify the church? Is he (or she) effective in what he (or she) does? If so, you are probably observing a spiritual gift in operation.

## The Value of the Collective Wisdom of the Saints

We have spent some time discussing the manpower resident in the saints. However, there is still another reason the saints should be held in high regard: nothing on earth can surpass the cumulative wisdom of a group of saints working together in unity in the body.

Certainly no pastor has wisdom of this scope and dimension. Surely no church board or committee has this kind of discernment and wisdom. The leader who regards himself as superior in wisdom to his congregation and who holds the opinion of the saints in contempt or derision is unfit for leadership. Indeed, he is not "smart enough to come in out of the rain," no less lead a church. It is God who has constituted the assembly of believers you serve. He depends on the assembled parts to work together in harmony to do His will. There is no room for a Lone Ranger mentality in the service of the Lord.

The message of this chapter is so simple it cannot be missed. Yet, how elusive it is to those who greet it with deaf ears. They are the would-be builders of their own kingdoms. Only God's kingdom will survive, and, as the song says, "If you want to be great in God's kingdom, learn to be the servant of all." What a simple but profound message. All of us in leadership need to remind ourselves of it continually.

## Additional Resources

Crabb, Lawrence, and Dan B. Allender. *Encouragement: The Key to Caring.* Grand Rapids: Zondervan, 1984.

Enroth, Ronald M. "The Power Abusers." *Eternity,* October 1979.

Getz, Gene A. *The Measure of a Man.* Glendale, Calif.: Regal, 1974.

Greenleaf, Robert K. *Servant Leadership.* New York: Paulist, 1977.

Piper, John. *Desiring God.* Portland, Oreg.: Multnomah, 1986.

Sawchuck, Norman. "The Local Church: Who Works for Whom?" *Leadership* 1, no. 1 (Winter 1980).

Swindoll, Charles. *Improving Your Serve.* Waco, Tex.: Word, 1981.

## Questions for Discussion and Helpful Projects

1. How would you characterize yourself as a leader? Generally, what kind of leadership styles have you used? How successful have you been in using those styles?

2. What are some of the advantages and disadvantages of having a church leader who seeks to achieve peace at any price? Is it ever desirable for a church to have a benevolent dictator as its principal leader?

3. What does the word *servant* imply that the word *minister* does not? Which of the four Greek words that describe service is the most important, and why?

PROJECT: The biblical concept of servant-leadership implies an organizational structure that is opposite to the structure used in many churches. Sit down with a group of your church's leaders. Discuss the possibility of changing your church's structure to one more closely resembling the one proposed in this book. What would that mean to the current officers of your church? What changes would the pastoral staff, the elders and deacons, and other church leaders be called upon to make?

4. What is the greatest potential source of manpower in the church? Why are people hesitant to become involved in the church? What can leadership do to counter their reluctance?

5. Is your church laboring under the misconception that spiritual gifts are given for the benefit of the individual? What can you as a leader do to correct this error?

6. In what ways might the leaders of your church help people to know their spiritual gifts? Who can help you realize yours?

PROJECT: Survey your congregation to find out those people who desire to know their spiritual gifts. Select one or two of these individuals with whom to work. Follow the formula given in this chapter for helping people discover their spiritual gifts.

# 6

# EQUIPPER

S o far we have looked only at leaders who hold formal title as elders or deacons, yet the Scriptures suggest that a variety of other people shared the leadership tasks. Priscilla and Aquila, for instance, did not bear the title of elder or deacon but with Paul were essential members of a church-planting team. Lydia was another of these titleless leaders.

Euodia and Syntyche were so influential in the Philippian church and community that it became a local scandal when they couldn't get along with each other. These days we are quick to point an accusative finger at them and cite them as a horrible example. How easily we forget that Paul talked about their past work in glowing, thankful terms.

Add to these individuals the large number of other people who were described as co-laborers with Paul, and we have a diversified group of leaders, all who were needed in the effort.

What about today? Is it legitimate for a church to consider others besides deacons and elders as its leaders? In *Leadership in Christian Ministry* James Means not only gives an insistent yes but proclaims, "Anyone who influences the lives of other church members or the decision-making process may be thought of as a leader, whether or not

103

there is popular recognition of that fact. Informal, nonelected or non-appointed leaders are often the most powerful people in the church."[1] There is a broad spectrum of leaders with which to deal.

Recognizing that a variety of leaders is needed, in this chapter I will look at twelve tasks a leader may be called upon to perform. Some of these tasks are what I would call "function gifts" and are related by name to the title of the person exercising the gift. They are listed in Ephesians 4:11, which talks about apostles, prophets, evangelists, pastors, and teachers (or pastor/teachers). The other tasks relate less to titles than to activities: leading, administering, disciplining, protecting, praying, studying, and giving to the financial welfare of the church.

All of these leaders fulfill a principle task of a church leader, that of *"equipping* . . . the saints for the work of service"* (Ephesians 4:12; italics added). The Greek term for equipping, *katartisis,* is a wonderful word signifying "making complete." It also has a utilitarian dimension, to "fully train," to "make complete," to "put into proper condition." Equipping is the umbrella term describing the overall task of a leader. Much of what follows is a description of the methods used to do the equipping.

## PROPHET

Ephesians 2:20 tells us that the church was built upon a unique group of people called the apostles and the prophets. I believe that those special offices were foundational and that there was no further apostolic or prophetic succession. As the apostles had a unique authority that was necessary to get the church started, so the prophets had a unique message to guide the church. However, just because the prophets as a special group are gone does not necessarily mean that the prophetic function has been withdrawn from the church.

When asked to describe a prophet, the average church member would probably describe a wild-looking fanatic peering into a crystal ball and predicting the future. Most of us have forgotten that a small amount (perhaps 5 percent) of a prophet's ministry was given to predicting the future. With the closing of the canon, God had said it all. There was no more need for predicting the future. As a result, the foretelling aspect of the prophets' ministry ceased. However, I believe that their forthtelling function continues to this day.

1. James E. Means, *Leadership in Christian Ministry* (Grand Rapids: Baker, 1989), p. 30.

The prophetic task has a negative and a positive dimension. The negative dimension points to spiritual and moral discrepancies in the culture, in society, in religious life, and in the personal lives of people. The prophet warns people of their wrongdoing and calls them to repentance.

The prophet of the Old Testament told people to repent because their priorities were wrong. He warned the people about spiritual coldness because they substituted an opulent lifestyle for a life of service to God and to their fellow man. The prophet often spoke against social injustice and called people to responsible behavior toward their neighbors, especially the poor.

The prophet was not popular. Often people did not want to hear his message. They did terrible things to the prophets. They placed one prophet in a cold, dank pit in the ground; others they stoned; still another they sawed in pieces.

The negative message of a true prophet is no more welcome today in our society or even in our churches than it was in Old Testament times. That is sad, because the society and the church need that message badly. If God calls you to this kind of prophetic task, be aware that you may not be well received. If you enter this kind of ministry be sure that God has called you to it and that you are delivering His message and not airing your own gripes. We have enough complaining malcontents in the church now who are merely grinding their own axes and airing personal peeves rather than delivering scripturally substantiated truth.

The positive aspects of a prophet's ministry are much more exciting. A prophet is a visionary, a person who "dreams great dreams." He lives continually in the context of possibility. How desperately our contemporary church needs visionaries, dreamers, "possibility thinkers." How profitable to have people who "think big" about what God can accomplish through His church. The Bible says, "Where there is no vision, the people perish" (Proverbs 29:18; KJV). We might paraphrase that verse to read, "Where there is no vision, the local church dies."

How painful the slow, lingering death of thousands of congregations today primarily because there is no vision, are no plans, goals, or dreams. Vision has given way to the perpetuation of the status quo or institutional maintenance. Yet even today hundreds of exciting congregations are being born around the world mainly because there is this kind of vision. People become excited by a vision because there is a visionary, a prophet, to tell them about that vision. Moreover, that vision is usually contagious, and an epidemic often results. Wherever the church is having a vital, exciting ministry the origins of that ministry can be traced to someone who has successfully functioned in the role of prophet.

In biblical times the prophet was not only a "he" but a "she" as well. The Old Testament tells us about a prophetess named Huldah (see 2 Kings 22:14; 2 Chronicles 34:22). She was so prominent that the main south gates of the Temple at Jerusalem were named after her. Miriam, the sister of Moses, also bore that title along with Deborah, Noadiah, and an unnamed prophetess in Isaiah 8:3.

In the New Testament Anna, the prophetess, confirms that the baby Jesus is the Messiah in Luke 2. Acts 21:9 indicates that Philip's four daughters engaged in this ministry. In 1 Corinthians 14:22-24 Paul encourages the use of the prophetic function in the assembly, telling his readers that it was far more valuable than tongues. (But it, too, had to be done in the spirit of decency and order). In 1 Corinthians 11:5 Paul tells us that the appropriate way for women to prophesy in the assembly was to do so with their heads covered. Apparently that exemplified "decency and order" in the culture within which Paul wrote.

If we strip away the mystique often associated with prophecy by extremist groups, we will find a usable and helpful role for prophecy in the church. How desperately we need people who will call us to accountability and repentance and dreamers who will help us see what is possible for us to do with the help of the Lord. What a shame that this function has been pushed aside and is unused in many evangelical churches today. No wonder we have so little vision.

The prophet is the dreamer and the visionary, but he may not be able to get people to bring his vision to reality. That takes an initiator such as the apostle Paul.

## APOSTLE

I have already mentioned that the apostles and the prophets were a foundational group upon which the church was built. The apostles were a unique group of people who had known Jesus personally and had been equipped by Him. There was one exception, the apostle Paul, whom I believe was picked by God to replace Judas and who carried with him the same kind of authority as the other eleven.

The unusual authority given to the apostles was necessary in order to get the fledgling church started. I do not believe in apostolic succession, the theory that apostolic authority was passed on from person to person. Outside of the twelve, however, there were a number of other people to whom the Bible gives the title apostle. Barnabas was one (Acts 14:4). Galatians 1:9 indicates that James the brother of our Lord was also so regarded. Silvanus and Timothy appear to have borne that title (1 Thessalonians 2:6), as did Andronicus and Junias (Romans 16:7).

In order to understand this concept and give substance to my theory that the apostolic function still exists in the church, it is good to consider the original meaning of the word *apostle*. The Greek term was *apostolos,* from the word *apostollein,* "to send." An apostle was a person who was sent forth. E. F. Harrison states, *"Apostollein* emphasizes the elements of commission—authority of and responsibility to the sender. So an apostle is properly one sent on a definite mission, in which he acts in full authority on behalf of the sender and is accountable to him."[2]

I have been told that the Latin Vulgate translates *apostolos* as "missiones." The translator believed that the terms were synonymous. A cursory look at an English dictionary indicates that the terms *apostle* and *missionary* are identical in meaning as "one who is sent forth."[3]

Unlike the prophet, the apostle does not necessarily need a vision of his own. He is able to respond to someone else's dream, to do the necessary spade work, to enlist people in the effort and bring a dream to reality. He is the person who gets things going and is able to enlist people to help.

Is the apostolic function operating in the church today? How easy the answer is, but how confusing people have made it. Of course it is. Just as Barnabas was commissioned, sent out by the church at Antioch, and held accountable to that church, today's missionaries often follow the same pattern. Notice, however, that missionaries are people sent out with a mission. That mission is to evangelize the world for Jesus Christ, to "make disciples." Every New Testament example of their work that I can find involves them in church planting as a principal means of carrying out their mission. The formula seems to be consistent: Win disciples and establish churches for them.

2  E. F. Harrison in *Evangelical Dictionary of Theology,* ed. Walter A. Elwell (Grand Rapids: Baker, 1986), p. 71.

3. *Webster's New World Dictionary of the American Language,* s.v. "evangelism."

Today the term *missionary* is greatly misunderstood because of the number of ways we currently apply it. Vehicle mechanics, computer programmers, teachers, medical personnel, bookkeepers, hydrologists, and those serving in a host of other support vocations all bear the title "missionary." Mission boards justify this practice by saying that all of the support vocations are needed because they aid the church planter in his tasks. Perhaps the term is so widely used because it is sometimes easier to raise funds to support missionaries than it is to monetarily support other kinds of outreach activity.

I would in no way demean those who serve in an auxiliary fashion on the mission field. I have done so myself. However, just as I would not call myself a missionary, I think it would be a good idea to invent another term for support personnel.

Through confusion, we have lost sight of the apostolic function of the church. Let us redefine it and rename it. Then let us pursue the apostolic function with the same fervor with which it was pursued in the first century. The mission fields of the world are exciting places of harvest. Better yet, today it is not even necessary to go overseas to reap a harvest. The world is coming to us. There is no better way of meeting the needs of that world than winning people to Christ and planting churches in which the new converts, in turn, may be "equipped for the work of ministry." The need to which God is calling you may be right in your home town. Look around you. Is there a field in your town that is "ripe unto harvest"?

## EVANGELIST

Evangelism may be defined as "the proclamation of the good news of salvation in Jesus Christ with a view to bringing about the reconciliation of the sinner to God the Father through the regenerating power of the Holy Spirit." The word *evangelism* derives from the Greek noun *euangelion,* "good news," and the verb *euangelizomai,* "to announce, or proclaim, or bring good news."[4] The evangelist carries on a reconciling ministry and equips the saints to do this same work of evangelism (Ephesians 4).

Who is the evangelist in the sense of Ephesians 4? We have many stereotyped images of him. As I write this, the term is not held in high regard because of the faults and foibles of certain televangelists.

---

4. T. P. Weber, *Evangelical Dictionary of Theology,* p. 382.

Unfortunately the term *evangelist* has been misused to describe many religious TV personalities who really do little or no evangelism.

The term has also been used to denote itinerant evangelists who go from city to city conducting crusades. It was my privilege to meet in assembly with some five thousand traveling evangelists in Amsterdam in 1983. Evangelist Billy Graham hosted the gathering.

Because of the visibility of Billy Graham, Luis Palau, and others, many people have come to associate evangelism with that kind of ministry exclusively. That is unfortunate, because evangelism can take many forms. The Campus Crusade worker who labors at a nearby university is certainly an evangelist. He or she not only wins people to Christ but equips new believers to reproduce themselves. Likewise, the chaplain who faithfully labors at winning the lost to Christ, either in a military or institutional setting, is "doing the work of an evangelist." This is true, as well, of the pastor who takes seriously the challenge of 2 Timothy 4:5, that he "do the work of an evangelist."

The evangelist facilitates the process of bringing new life into the local church through the addition of new Christians. He may be in a paid or nonpaid position, and he may work full or part-time. His is the most exciting, most promising task in the entire church. His work can make the difference between a stodgy, sedentary church and a vital, productive body. There is nothing like new blood to keep an organism alive and functioning. For most churches today, the most crying need is a blood transfusion brought about by a sustained, rigorous, evangelistic effort.

Evangelism should be an area of prime concern when the church decides where its financial resources are to be concentrated. Were I to become a pastor again, an evangelist is the first person I would hire after securing a good church secretary. If a church hires an evangelist it must free him from mundane administrative responsibilities so that he (or she) can carry on this more vital ministry. The evangelist should have no other responsibility than to win the lost to Christ, get them established in the faith, and equip them for the work of evangelism. When the church fully learns this lesson, we will see many more people come to Christ than we currently do.

## SHEPHERD

The term *pastor* denotes a "shepherd." I view him as the chief elder and the person with the primary shepherding responsibilities. In many cases, he may find himself the only biblically qualified elder. A few years ago, I wrote an entire book about the pastor, his qualifications and responsibilities.[5] It is not necessary nor is it possible for me to repeat all of that information here.

THE PASTOR AS HEAD SHEPHERD

Over the years I have become even more convinced of two things. First, I think that it is unfortunate that we apply the term *pastor* to almost anyone on the paid church staff. Church bulletins often list such personnel as an associate pastor or an assistant pastor. This practice confuses church members and weakens the unique position of pastor with its special responsibilities and commensurate authority. I contend that the terms *coordinator, director,* or *minister* more appropriately describe a staff member's ministry position. The pastoral office is unique and should be treated as such.

Nevertheless, that does not negate the fact that staff members, lay elders, and, indeed, all church leaders, need to be involved in the task of shepherding. Means states: "The shepherding role applies to all church leaders who are involved in ministry. Shepherding is not the exclusive prerogative of clergy, but of all spiritual leaders. All spiritual leaders, especially those who preach and teach, are undershepherds."[6]

Means believes four important elements are inherent to the shepherding role. They are as follows:

1. "First, shepherds must genuinely care for the people under their oversight."[7] Means insists that "many people in today's churches feel used rather than cared for by their leaders. People resent being pawns on the leader's chessboard or building blocks for the leader's personal kingdom. Genuine care for the spiritual and physical welfare of the church as a whole and for members in particular is indispensable to spiritual leadership."[8]

---

5. Robert Anderson, *The Effective Pastor* (Chicago: Moody, 1985).
6. Means, *Leadership in Christian Ministry,* p. 51.
7. Ibid.
8. Ibid., p. 52.

2. "The shepherding role carries the responsibility of nurture."[9] (Means goes on to describe the need to provide both wholesome spiritual food and protection for the church body).

3. "The indispensable correlate to good preaching and teaching is study."[10] "The chief (but not the only) evidence of a fragmented and secularized church," Means insists, "is dryness in the pulpit and classroom and boredom among church members."[11] Means believes that much of this can be cured through systematic and correct study practices.

4. "The shepherding role requires guidance."[12] Means defines guidance as "enlightenment, tutoring, motivation and persuasion." "Guidance is supervised assistance," he says.[13]

## THE PASTOR AS AN EQUIPPER OF SHEPHERDS

Although I see the pastor as the primary undershepherd of the flock, nevertheless under the explanation given in Ephesians 4, he has another job in addition to shepherding his people. He is to be an equipper of the saints for the ministry of shepherding. He does this through preaching and teaching and through modeling.

The truism "actions speak louder than words" is especially applicable to equipping the saints for the work of shepherding. The platform contact of the pastor with his congregation is but a brief time each week. If during the week they can see him personally modeling what he has been preaching, he will be a much more tangible and believable resource. Modeling breathes life into the abstract concepts taught from the pulpit. Teaching becomes action. As a church member, I am not convinced that I can do something just because someone tells me I can do it. Instead, it becomes much more plausible for me to try something if I see that someone else can do it fairly easily. Leader, take people along when you are carrying out shepherding duties. As they see you minister, they will learn that there is no particular mystique about it and will be willing to try it themselves.

9. Ibid.
10. Ibid.
11. Ibid.
12. Ibid.
13. Ibid., p. 53.

Shepherding ministries can be carried on by all members of the church. Although the pastor bears principal responsibility for shepherding ministries, he has a mandate to equip the rest of his leadership and his people to do this task also. How wonderful it would be to be part of a church where every member was shepherding someone else.

## TEACHER

There is speculation concerning whether teaching is listed as a separate function or listed only in connection with pastoring. Some people believe that we are dealing with a hyphenated word: "pastor-teacher." The Greek construction suggests that this may be true.

Let me insert two items of concern, however. First, even if the word should be regarded as hyphenated, note that the Bible lists the pastoring task first. That indicates that pastoring responsibilities are important. Even when the pastor-teacher is teaching, he should be doing so with a pastor's heart. The needs of the flock should always be preeminent.

My second concern arises from churches who write into the job description of their elder the title "teaching pastor." Taken to its extreme, this kind of title may encourage a pastor to spend the majority of time in his study and little time with his people. He may get the impression that this job description excuses him from the need to carry on other pastoring functions.

A genuine shepherd knows his sheep and cares for them according to their needs. If he does not know them, there is no way he can care for them properly. In order to know them he has to spend adequate time with them. That means that he must get out of the study and walk among his people on a regular basis.

Along with equipping the saints for the work of shepherding, the pastor-teacher should be regarded as the "chief teacher." In this role he is not only obligated to equip the saints for the work of ministry through his teaching, he is also obligated to equip them to do the work of teaching. The church has many and varied teaching needs. Not all of them can be accomplished by the pastor. We have already considered the biblical imperative that all elders should be able to teach. It would seem, then, that a major part of the pastor's equipping responsibility is to teach prospective elders and other saints how to teach so that they may fulfill this important requirement for eldership.

So far we have looked at the tasks of leaders in relation to descriptions given in Ephesians 4. In paragraphs to follow I will explore other tasks indicated in the Scriptures.

## PREACHER

What is the difference between teaching and preaching? There are all kinds of debates and speculations concerning this matter. Last year one of my students thought he had solved the riddle. In his Bible study, he said, he found that every time the most frequently used word for "preach" was used, it was used in connection with preaching the gospel.

My student concluded that preaching was to be addressed only to sinners. Thus, preaching, he said, is a method to be used only by an evangelist. Now, since the student saw himself as a "pastor-teacher" and not an evangelist, he decided that he would not have to know how to preach. As a result, he approached the seminary and asked to be excused from taking homiletics classes. It didn't work.

He had forgotten some important things. One was the directive given to Pastor Timothy by Paul to "preach the word" (2 Timothy 4:2) and "do the work of an evangelist" (2 Timothy 4:5), thus fulfilling his ministry. It did not matter whether or not Timothy was actually called as an evangelist. Even if he was the pastor of the Ephesian church, he was still directed to perform the tasks of preaching and evangelism.

Years ago I came to the conclusion that preaching includes elements of persuasion, encouragement, and admonishment not necessarily present in pure teaching. Second Timothy 4:2 also indicates that preaching should reprove, rebuke, and exhort. Consequently, preaching can be considered as a method of teaching. It gives teaching excitement and stimulation, and it helps hold the interest of our listeners. It appeals to them "where they live." I would hope that a Sunday sermon would be more challenging and practical than a typical seminary lecture. The lecture is there primarily to impart information. Those who hear it are not necessarily encouraged to make some kind of decision as a result of what they have heard.

Preaching is different. It is designed to lead a person to make some kind of commitment. If a sermon does not call a person to do something, it is not preaching. I believe that every sermon must be followed by an invitation of some kind. That may be an invitation to salvation or to further discipleship.

In recent years there has been a remarkable revival of evangelistic preaching. Evangelistic pastors not only are preaching messages that speak to the needs of the unsaved, they are becoming successful in drawing the unsaved to Christ. Remarkable things are happening as churches are turning the Sunday morning service into an evangelistic service. The evening service, or midweek service, becomes the primary worship service of the church. The morning service is for the non-Christian or the nominally committed, and the evening service is for those who really want to get down to business with and for the Lord. Not a bad format.

## LEADER

Lately, we have heard a great deal as to how, when a church grows large, the leaders need to become ranchers instead of shepherds. I have an urgent plea to make: If we must have a ranch, let's make it a sheep ranch and not a cattle ranch. Almost every time the Bible speaks about God's people in a concerned way, it refers to them as sheep, not cattle. Only in the most insulting and derogatory ways does Scripture use bovine terms to describe the people of God.

There is a striking difference in philosophy of ministry. Sheep, unlike cattle, are not driven. They are led. The shepherd goes in front of the sheep, looking for the danger ahead, and says to them, "Follow me." He is concerned about them, loves them, and looks out for their welfare. The cattle driver gets behind his herd and uses whatever he needs, including whips, prods, and guns, to keep them all moving together. He says impatiently, "Come on. Get going."

There are numbers of contemporary leaders who think that they can accomplish their high profile ministries more successfully by getting behind the sheep and continually whipping them into line. Sooner or later the sheep rebel, and then the leaders accuse them of lacking submissiveness. The truth is that sheep don't like being treated as cattle, and the so-called leader is using a technique of leadership that is the opposite of the one the Bible encourages him to use. No wonder the end product is often disaster.

God calls us as leaders to feed and lead His sheep. He does not call us to drive His cattle. There is a great difference in these two approaches. The leader who wants to serve effectively needs to get that fact firmly planted in his mind and then continually apply it.

## ADMINISTRATOR

Administration is one of the principal tasks of the deacon. That position may be true, but it does not excuse other leaders from the task. By definition, all leaders are administrators. They are required to be so if they are to accomplish their ministry with any semblance of order.

Good administration is the necessary companion to good leadership. But there is great danger here. People may become so enamored with administration that it becomes an end in itself. Good administration is a valid goal only when it serves as a means to an end, not an end in itself. (More about administration will appear in chap. 7, "Administrator.")

## DISCIPLINARIAN

Elsewhere I have looked at church discipline in some detail. Here I want to emphasize that the primary responsibility for establishing and maintaining a biblical system of church discipline is in the hands of church leaders. Moreover, leaders must be absolutely consistent in insisting that the order of discipline established in Matthew 18 be followed exactly.

In addition, discipline should always be executed on the lowest level possible. If someone is not doing his job properly, it is the responsibility of his immediate supervisor to do the disciplining. It is not proper for the supervisor to look to a higher echelon of leadership to carry out the disciplining responsibilities that he, himself, is reluctant to do.

## PROTECTOR

An elder is a "watchman," or "guardian," but *all* the church's leaders must be involved in this important function. What are we to protect people against? Hebrew 13:17 says that leaders "keep watch over your souls, as those who will give an account." Two things can be injurious to our souls, false doctrine and improper behavior. As leaders we must constantly ascertain where our people are. We know that many of them are immature. Are they being led astray "by every wind of doctrine" (Ephesians 4:14)? It is our task to see that they progress from theological illiteracy to a biblically and theologically mature mindset. That way they won't be an easy prey for cults and create doctrinal divisiveness within the body.

Are they lured by the "trickery of men, by craftiness in deceitful scheming" (Ephesians 4:14)? I know of churches that are in constant turmoil and pain because there is a divisive spirit resident in one or more of their members. These members recruit gullible people who become pawns in the hands of these unscrupulous schemers. We must warn our people against such dividers and do our best to dissuade our sheep from following the bad example set by them.

There are other things against which we should protect our people. The temptation of materialism is one of them. Becoming members of a popularity cult is another. Here the sheep come to worship at the feet of the "beautiful people," doing all they can to become one of them so that they may feel "accepted."

We must guard our people against exhaustion, helping them to prioritize their activities and refraining from giving them unreasonable amounts of "Christian duty." Limiting the number of jobs a person is allowed to do in a church is one way we can do that.

We are to help our people protect their marriages and their family life by fostering activities that involve the whole family in meaningful, fun times that also are spiritually productive. After all, who says that church has to be boring?

In the same way that a responsible parent gives his child enough latitude to grow up and yet guards him against harm and evil, we who are leaders are to guard and protect our people. This is an important responsibility of leadership.

## PRAYER

The need of a leader to be a person of prayer is so basic that I even hesitate to mention it. It is no secret that the answer to spiritual power is a powerful prayer life. I know of no easy way to become a person of prayer except to discipline oneself to pray, and then do it. To maintain a consistent and powerful prayer life is one of the greatest challenges to today's leadership. We often view ourselves as being so talented that we can do the task in our own strength. Unfortunately the efforts of too many churches reflect leaders who operate with that attitude.

Prayer must be in behalf of ourselves: that God will give us discernment, wisdom, and judgment; that He will keep us sensitive and responsive to the needs of our people. Prayer must be in behalf of our own families and our relationships to them, for here is the real test of effective leadership. Prayer must be in behalf of our churches, that God will put a protective hedge around them in a period when Satan's power is intense. Prayer must be in behalf of fellow leaders, that God will do the same for them as we have requested for ourselves and that He will help all of us get along—to His glory. One of the most profound and needed advice the Bible gives us is the order to "pray without ceasing." How much trouble we would spare ourselves if we followed that order.

## STUDENT

It is permissible for baby Christians to want to be fed all the time. We expect that of babies. By the time a person is a leader, however, such thoughts are inexcusable. Certainly a leader is mature enough to feed himself. Surely he is smart enough to know that he must eat regularly, or his spiritual health will be in danger. One of the supreme tasks of a church leader is to see that he feeds himself regularly on the Word of God.

The grownup requires a different diet than a baby. Likewise, the leader needs to feed on the meat of the Word if he is to have the stamina and brain power to do his job effectively. Select a balanced diet of the Word, obtain the tools with which you will know how to dissect the Word, and feed daily. As you do, ask God for concentration so that you can absorb and apply all that you are reading.

Ask Him to supply the "plus power" of His Holy Spirit so that the deeper things in the Word will be understandable to you. More than anything else, before making any major decision, ask God to show you His will and then search the Word for the proper answer. A careful study of the Word provides God's right answers to most problems faced by leadership.

## GIVER

The effective leader must regard stewardship as a way of life. That will involve careful stewardship of his time and his talents. It will also involve the diligent stewardship of the financial resources God has given him.

We have already talked about the folly of a leader who expects his people to do as he says but not necessarily as he does. Nowhere has this point become more dramatic than in the area of financial stewardship. A leader can speak ad nauseum about the need for Christians to engage in proportionate and responsible giving, but unless he himself sets the example, his words will fall on deaf ears.

This principle is so important I want to state it dogmatically. If you aspire to be a leader in the church of Jesus Christ, plan that the least you will give to your church is a tithe of your salary. If possible, do even more than that. If you are the pastor or a paid staff member, do not think that you are exempt from this responsibility. You more than any of the other leaders need to set the example. If you do not set the example how do you expect people to follow you? Either plan to be a responsible and exemplary steward of the resources God has given to you, or don't plan to be a leader. Here, more than in many other places, you need to be a proper example.

## Additional Resources

Armerding, Hudson T. *Leadership*. Wheaton, Ill.: Tyndale, 1978.

Berkley, James D. "Burning Out, Rusting Out or Holding Out?" *Leadership* 4, no. 1 (Winter 1983).

Gardner, John W. *The Task of Leadership*. Washington, D.C.: Independent Sector, 1986.

Pittenger, Norman W. *The Ministry of All Churches: A Theology of Lay Ministry*. Wilton, Conn.: Morehouse, 1983.

Smith, Donald. *Clergy in the Crossfire*. Philadelphia: Westminster, 1978.

Stogdill, Ralph M. *Handbook of Leadership*. New York: Free, 1974.

## Questions for Discussion and Helpful Projects

1. Note the list of church leaders given in Ephesians 4:11. How complete is this list in light of the many needs of today's churches? Could all of the church's leadership needs be met by the positions described in this list? According to Ephesians 4:11-12, what is the primary function of church leaders occupying these leadership positions?

PROJECT: Analyze the five (or perhaps four) leadership roles described in Ephesians 4:11. Which of those functions is most needed in your church? How could each of these functions—apostle, prophet, evangelist, pastor, and teacher—be best utilized to the benefit of today's church? Together with other church leaders, look over your membership list. Who is best suited to carry out each of these functions? Would others be suited if they received the proper training? What training should the church provide in order to properly employ these people in the service of the Lord?

2. Why is the author so concerned about the title "teaching pastor"? What dangers may lurk in that title? Why is it necessary for the person who preaches to stay in close contact with the people who hear him preach?

3. What are the key elements preaching must possess in order to be preaching? What do you think of one person's opinion that preaching is to be aimed primarily at the unsaved? Do unsaved people attend your services? Why or why not? If they do attend, how could they be made more comfortable, and how could the gospel message be made more appealing to them?

4. In what ways is leading sheep different from driving cattle? What does each of these methods say about a congregation and its leadership? Which of these is most representative of your church?

# 7

# ADMINISTRATOR

I just want to be a leader of this congregation. Don't bother me with administration," I heard one deacon say. Poor man! Do I have news for him, and it isn't good news. My friend, if you buy into becoming a church leader, God expects you to purchase the whole package, and administration is an important part of it.

"Administration," to me, is "the process by which an institution reaches its goals in timely fashion through organized and orderly means." It includes initiating, motivating, planning, organizing, managing, delegating, coordinating, and recruiting. Every leader will be called upon to exercise all of these eight administrative tasks in some way.

However, don't be discouraged. You will seldom need to exercise all of them at the same time. Moreover, if you firmly believe that God has constituted your church as a body and chosen its leaders, then He will provide help for you. Just as you function better in some areas and less effectively in others, your fellow leaders are constituted in the same way. Depend on them to complement you where you are weak. In turn, complement them where you are strong and they are weak.

Note that I have placed an institutional emphasis on this definition. Administration can only be understood properly when it is considered in light of the institution it serves. A leader is part of a team working toward mutually constructed and agreed upon goals. Good administration is not the process of merely reaching your own goals. Can you imagine a football game where each of the players was playing his own game? It is only as the team works together to reach team goals that it wins. The same thing applies with a church leadership team.

But there is an additional consideration. A church leadership team also cannot be playing its own game. It is part of a larger group, the body. Necessarily, the goals and objectives of the leadership team must be built upon the goals of the body if the team is to function effectively.

Notice, as well, in my definition of administration, I placed an emphasis on timeliness. How grateful I am that I started my ministry as a chaplain. In the army, everything reaching me which required action had a suspense date attached to it. Required action not only had to be accomplished by that date, written communication stating the action taken had to reach the proper source by the suspense date. Throughout the years, I have found the suspense date a valuable tool in my arsenal of weapons for getting things done in timely fashion.

The need for timeliness also requires that I keep careful tabs on my own time and my commitments. A "daytimer" or other appointment book is a necessity. This not only helps keep track of business and church appointments but social engagements as well. A "daytimer" book is a good place to record suspense dates. This helps you to know how heavily you are already committed, and decide whether "just one more appointment" is feasible.

I also write "family times" into my schedule book. Consequently, when someone inquires if I am available on a certain date, I can look quickly at my appointment book and can honestly say, "I'm sorry, I already have an important commitment."

Notice that my definition of administration insists that goals be accomplished not in haphazard fashion but through organized and orderly means. God expects Christians to be orderly people and for His body to operate in an orderly fashion. However, even this can be overdone. Orderliness can become a fetish that will keep us from being sensitive to the needs of people. Doing things sensibly with moderation is a norm the Bible paints for us. How much easier if we could all live up to that norm!

Church administration is more challenging than any other kind because of the unique situation in which the church leader finds himself. Briefly, let me list some of the problems faced:

1. Most other institutions pay their workers and, therefore, have built in clout, "Do what I say, or you will be out of a job and will have no source of income." The church can't say that because it staffs most of its positions with volunteers.

Church leaders sometimes forget that and try to coerce their workers. Some workers rebel at once. Others are more passive and put up with it for a while. If the workers get upset enough, they will either try to oust that leader, resign their positions, or maybe a combination of both. The attempted coercion of church workers is not a viable leadership technique. Inevitably it results in great trauma. Consequently, the only viable means of improving performance that a church leader has at his disposal are various methods of encouragement and persuasion.

2. The second great challenge of the church leader results from the unique character of the church as an organism. In other institutions, it is enough that the workers are contributing in performance to meet the institution's goals. The church, however, must concern itself not only in reaching its principal edificational and evangelistic goals. It must also concern itself with edifying the worker. Consequently, it must facilitate rather than interfere with the utilization of an individual's giftedness and creativity. But it also must be cognizant of where individual creativity leaves off and sinful individuality takes over. Trying to determine that fine line, of course, is the precarious position in which every effective church leader finds himself.

3. A third great challenge to administration revolves around the fact that it must be performed in what I call the "nomothetic" (legislative) dimension that is peculiar and unique to each church. Despite the claim of "franchisement" in denominations, each church in itself is a uniquely different organism. Affecting its unique personality are such factors as geographic location, denomination loyalty or lack thereof, background and general attitudes of parishioners, socio-ethnic mix, history, size, internal organizational structure, chief sources of support, real (as well as stated) goals and objectives, and traditional ways of carrying out policies. All of these things contribute to how a church thinks and acts. A leader must be fully cognizant of the unique personality of his church and the things that make up that personality if he is

to lead effectively. Without this knowledge, he has no real inkling as to how far and in what direction he can provide administrative leadership.

Having, then, looked briefly at the overall picture called "administration," I would like to look briefly at each of the component parts I listed above in light of the overall philosophy of ministry that this book proposes.

## INITIATING

Although all leaders will be called upon to initiate, there's no question that some are better than others at this task. The initiator takes over where the prophet leaves off. It is he who translates a prophet's vision into tangible tasks, sells it to people, and gets them moving toward accomplishing that vision.

Initiators are not always easy to live with. They seem to have that unquenchable conviction that anything is possible and will do their best to convince other people of this. In addition, they often appear to feel that they are always (or almost always) right despite what may be clear evidence to the contrary. As a result, they will often initiate to accomplish those things that they believe to be important. Because of their persuasive spirit, sometimes things that are truly more important to the church get sidetracked in favor of the initiator's pet projects.

Nevertheless, initiating is important because it helps keep an institution from becoming stagnant and ineffective. It is the initiator who gets the creative juices flowing. And, indeed, they must continue to flow if the institution is to remain on the cutting edge. Lawrence Miller insists: "A loss of creative energy is the most obvious characteristic of decline. And it is creativity—innovation in both products and ways of gaining productivity and quality—that determines competitive success. As we will see, history teaches that leadership must be creative if the organization is to be creative."[1]

Miller uses an interesting term to describe the person who is primarily an initiator, calling him a "barbarian." He is, says Miller, "the person who embraces the Prophet's values and vision, then leads his company on its conquering march."[2] A primary leader, says Miller,

1. Lawrence M. Miller, *Barbarians to Bureaucrats* (New York: Clarkson N. Potter, 1989), p. 7.
2. Ibid., p. 34.

"will make two appearances in the life cycle of a company—immediately after the birth of the business and again during times of renewal when the excess baggage of bureaucracy must be shaken loose and swept away. His forte is discipline and quick action."[3]

The true barbarian is action-oriented and has little patience with planning and other routine administrative tasks.[4] There are times in the life of a church when this kind of primary leader is needed. However, troubles arise when he stays longer than he is needed and refuses to change his leadership style.

Without routine administrative tasks that include careful planning,the fondest dreams of a prophet may reach temporary fruition in the barbarian. However, usually these accomplishments are short-lived.

What, then, may we conclude regarding initiating as an administrative skill? I think that the following are true:

- Initiating needs to be a way of life. Church leaders must always be initiating so that the church does not become stagnant and ineffective.

- Every leader needs to exercise the art of initiating and keep developing this art. Especially is this true if he doesn't "come by" the art naturally.

- If a person is not a natural initiator, he should seek the help of those who do it naturally and well.

- There are times when initiating should be the primary administrative thrust. Those times are when a church is just getting started or when it needs renewal desperately. During those periods, the principal leader of the church needs to be a person who is primarily a "barbarian" initiator.

Be appraised, however, that few "barbarian" initiators can easily adapt and change their style of leadership when the church no longer needs such dramatic, initiatory action. If you are such a person, you need to pray for wisdom so that you know when it is time to move on. Likewise, others of you who are leaders need to be brave enough to

3. Ibid., p. 36.
4. Ibid., p. 40.

tell this leader when it may be time for him to leave. Since he is generally a "charismatic" personality, if he doesn't leave quietly and graciously, severe trauma may result in the church. As a result, much of the good that he has accomplished may be undone.

Constant, steady initiation rather than drastic, flamboyant initiation will be the posture of most effective church leaders. If you are supremely gifted in initiating, it may be that you will need to discipline yourself so that your enthusiasm does not get out of hand. On the other hand, if you are not naturally gifted, this is a skill which may be developed in concert with others who do this well. Keep initiating so that the church remains flexible and healthy!

## MOTIVATING

Working hand in hand with initiating is the challenge of motivating. This is the essence of leadership. It is the ability of a leader to convince someone that he should follow that leader. Unfortunately, it is difficult to motivate a person to do something unless the leader has set the example. It is impossible to follow someone unless he has gone ahead of you. Imagine the leader, for instance, who can't control his own children but tries to motivate others to adopt biblical family values. The ability to motivate is inextricably tied to the credibility of the person who is trying to do the motivating.

Motivation is done best by people who are pleasant and agreeable, kind and considerate. In our church, the chairperson of the discipleship committee is such a person. We find ourselves saying, "How can I say no to Lucille? She is such a devoted and giving person!"

So far I have focused on the motivator. Now let's consider the "motivatee." Robert Dale points to a study 1973 conducted by Case Western University as to what motivates workers. The study found seven motivational factors: interesting work, good pay, seeing the results of their work, a chance to use their minds, a chance to develop skills and abilities, participation in work-related decisions, and recognition for a job well done.[5]

What motivates people? In business, there are external factors such as gaining rewards and avoiding punishments. Some church leaders attempt to use those upon would-be "motivatees." Seldom do they work, nor are they appropriate. Dale states:

5. Robert D. Dale, *Pastoral Leadership* (Nashville: Abingdon, 1986), p. 143.

By and large Christian leaders do not rely on external motivation methods. Volunteers simply cease to volunteer when they are enticed by artificial rewards or threatened by manipulative punishments. In most churches, manipulation doesn't work in practice and is also questionable on theological grounds. Pushing followers constantly soon discourages them or wears them out. The "swift kick in the pants" school of motivation is usually as ineffective over the long haul as the "froth and frenzy" approach.[6]

Dale has cited two motivational methods, both of which employ external stimuli. Both may work for a while in certain kinds of situations. However, in the long run, volunteers will discover what is happening and will eventually discontinue playing this kind of game.

Note the seven motivational factors listed above. With one exception, pay, people are motivated by stimuli which bring them personal fulfillment. How exciting that six out of seven of those motivational factors are available for use with workers in a church. These are the factors that leaders need to use not only in recruiting workers but in retaining them as well.

## PLANNING

As I think of planning, two "chestnuts" come to mind that are so overused that they have almost become trite. The problem is that they contain so much truth that I can't bypass them. The first speaks to the fact that the "best laid plans of mice and men" often go awry. Consequently, even after we have done the best to plan for every exigency, it is entirely possible for the unexpected to happen, necessitating a change in plans.

However, the possibility that plans may need to be changed does not in itself offer a proper excuse for not planning. Here's where the second slogan comes in. It states, "Failing to plan is the same as planning to fail." Robert Dale points to a poster he saw recently. It read, "Plan ahead, it wasn't raining when Noah built the ark."[7] Planning is not just a "nice thing to do." It is often necessary for survival.

Planning, says Olan Hendrix, "consists of decisions made in advance of action."[8] It is the ability to look ahead, project needs, and

6. Ibid., p. 150.
7. Ibid., p. 104.
8. Olan Hendrix, *Management for Christian Leaders* (Grand Rapids: Baker, 1981), p. 45.

devise ways and means of meeting those needs. Hendrix, citing the work of Louis Allen in *The Management Profession,* lists an all-encompassing view of planning. It includes:

1. Forecasting: Estimate the future.
2. Establishing Objectives: Determine the end results to be accomplished with the people involved.
3. Programming: Establish the sequence and priority of the action steps to be followed in reaching objectives.
4. Scheduling: Establish a time sequence for program steps.
5. Budgeting: Allocate resources necessary to accomplish objectives.
6. Procedure: Develop and apply standardized methods of performing specific work.
7. Policies: Develop and interpret standing decisions that apply to recurrent questions and problems of significance to the enterprise as a whole.[9]

For whom should we plan? First of all, we must plan for ourselves. We should ask ourselves, "What does God want me to be doing this afternoon, tomorrow, next month, next year, five years from now? What hopes and dreams do I have for my life? Into what great efforts do I want to invest my life?"

Having answered those questions, we need to inquire further, "How am I going to get there? What resources will it take? What help do I need and from whom? How will I reach my goals while still carrying on the necessary responsibilities of life: my obligations to my family, my church?"

In addition to making such plans for myself, I need to make plans for my family and for my church ministry. However, I cannot make these plans alone. I must involve the people whose lives these plans will affect. Since planning involves the future behavior of people, Hendrix writes, "If you expect someone to cooperate with you later in doing something, involve them in the decision to do it."[10] This makes

9. Ibid., p. 44.
10. Ibid., p. 47.

them an important part of the planning team. It also expands the knowledge base upon which to build plans. Two heads certainly are better than one, and many heads are the repository for much wisdom.

As leaders, we also need to agree to a set of church plans. These range from operational plans telling us how the day by day ministry of the church is to be carried out, to long-range plans whereby we project and plan to meet the needs of the future. Once again, it is good to involve many people in the planning process. Dale says the benefits of such planning are fourfold:

- Goal ownership. Group goals build public commitment for implementation.
- Ministry continuity. Programs and projects are synchronized by the long-range and short-term goals of the group.
- Flexible options. Even the best of plans can go awry. However, the planning process generates other possibilities that provide a Plan B to fall back on.
- Precise direction. Plans select specific targets. The purpose of the congregation is kept clearly defined and publicly understood. The congregation's decisions are openly made.[11]

Engaging regularly in planning can build singular unity into a group of leaders and into the congregation itself. It's fun to be part of an institution that not only knows where it's going but has a good idea how it's going to get there.

Once again, this is an area where some people shine and others struggle. For some people, exercising the discipline of drawing up concise plans is like eating their favorite brand of ice cream. For others, this is the most tedious and exhausting work in which they engage. The latter group is most often action oriented. They are too busy doing to worry about planning.

However, it may be difficult to move the planner into any kind of action. He loves to project but doesn't necessarily want to be involved with carrying out those plans. He finds the future to be far more satisfying and challenging than the present.

11. Dale, *Pastoral Leadership*, pp. 107-8.

We need a balance of these two types in the leadership of a local church. Moreover, these two types need to draw upon each other to add further dimension to their own ministries. They need to help each other enjoy both the excitement of living in the present as well as the delicious possibilities of flying in the future. In order to be truly effective, every leader must learn how to participate wholeheartedly in the planning process. In addition, the "natural-born" planner must learn that his primary duties consist of bringing future plans to fruition through faithful day by day service to the Lord through His church.

## ORGANIZING

I once worked in a clothing store where everything was in a major state of disarray. The most frequent slogan of the manager was, "One of these days, we've got to get organized." After graduating from college and leaving that town, I returned ten years later to find that organizing still had not occurred.

Organizing, says Hendrix, is "the work of grouping work and people so that the work can best be performed by human beings."[12] Since Hendrix is high on the managerial school of leadership, he sees organizing primarily in terms of charts, the blocks and lines "representing people and titles: director, superintendent, chairman, supervisor and so on."[13]

Hendrix has a point. It is good to have everything down on paper. In that way a leader can tell at a glance who is responsible for doing what. However, when we are dealing solely in charts, blocks, and lines, we sometimes forget that these represent human beings with feelings and needs. Moreover, the people who are higher on the chart may come to believe that they are, in some way, superior to people below them on the chart. Thus, instead of exercising leadership, they may establish a "pecking order." If there is no other point you get from this book, please remember the servant image. The higher a person is placed on most charts, the greater his degree of servanthood and the greater his degree of responsibility to all those he serves.

I am not totally opposed to charts. It is important that the church organize its human assets. It is also important that it be able to "visualize" this in some kind of chart. In this way, it will know where

12. Hendrix, *Management for Christian Leaders*, p. 29.
13. Ibid.

its human assets are employed and how effectively they are employed. It can also help the church avoid overworking some people and underworking others. It can determine if the people assets of a church are most profitably employed to accomplish the church's primary goals. It may give the leadership some idea as to who are the employable human assets that are currently not serving in their church.

Organizing applies not only to people, it also applies to other assets such as time, material, buildings, money, heritage, and spiritual resources. It is important for every church to "catalog" these so that they can see what they have to work with. Once they have been cataloged, then church leaders need to devise a system whereby they can effectively employ these assets to best accomplish the primary goals of the church. If there are not sufficient assets to adequately cover a major thrust the church wants to make, then leaders will know which assets need to be procured. They can then set up a procurement schedule, noting which desired assets have the greatest priority.

One of the problems that plagues the church today is leaders who operate their lives and leadership in a disorderly and disorganized fashion. Many times you can check any area of their lives and find it in disarray. As a result, few things that they accomplish are done well. Leader, discipline your life. Become personally organized, and then organize the tasks you are called upon to do. When you operate in an organized fashion, you will find yourself accomplishing much more than you ever dreamed you could do.

Once you have organized your own life, then, and only then, it is time for you to help your workers organize themselves and the programs in which they serve. If you, as a leader, are not personally organized, you will not be a credible example for those to whom you are preaching, "Get organized!"

## COORDINATING

This skill goes hand in hand with organizing. It is the process of making sure programs, buildings, materials, and the ministries of people are all utilized so that the maximum possible effectiveness is reached.

How do we keep two important church events from occurring at the same time? Coordination. How do two programs complement instead of compete with each other? The leaders coordinate their efforts and programs. How do we insure that two or more groups do not expect to use the same room at the same time? Someone coordinates the use of church rooms. How do we know that our people are getting a balanced spiritual diet? Someone coordinates the teaching program. How can we prevent the church calendar from becoming so full that everyone is exhausted with all the activities? Someone "rides herd" on the calendar.

Coordination is the essence of sanity. Without it, life in general and church life particularly becomes a "zoo." Coordination should be on the top of the agenda for every board and committee in the church. It should be one of the prime purposes for each group to meet.

## MANAGING

The whole subject of church management has been held in disrepute by many contemporary Christian writers. The most prominent spokesman among these, Lawrence Richards, sees great dangers at this point. He writes: "Even with the use of good management techniques, they come to think of the saints in relation to whether they help or frustrate the leaders' plans and hopes. The exercise of managerial skills begins to dominate more and more of their attention and demand more of their time."[14]

The dangers about which Richards warns are certainly real. It is easy to get caught up in buildings, programs, and finances and forget the needs of the organism and the people comprising that organism. Nevertheless, when these needs are kept foremost, managerial skills may be used to enhance service to Jesus Christ and His people. We must keep foremost in our minds that the budgeting, staffing, buildings, committees, and councils Richards decries are the tools that can be used to help serve the church the best. The trick is to use these tools properly. Foremost in our minds is that these tools always remain the means to an end, not ends in themselves.

The proper use of these tools does not happen automatically. Someone has to be in charge of using them in an appropriate and effective manner. That's where management comes in. Management has many definitions, some of them inappropriate to church application.

---

14. Lawrence O. Richards and Clyde Hoeldtke, *A Theology of Church Leadership* (Grand Rapids: Zondervan), 1980, p. 75.

The one I like the best, however, is this. To manage is "to have charge of; to direct; . . . to handle or use carefully."[15]

Imagine a church where no one is in charge of anything and where everything "just happens." What chaos. That in no way represents the "decency and order" the Bible commands us to observe. Can you envision, for instance, a Sunday school class or an AWANA program where no one is in charge and where there is no planning or forethought? Deliver me from such a church!

Someone has to be in charge. Someone has to work with budgets, committees, buildings, and equipment to see that the job is done and that the services of people are being used effectively and in concert.

Managing means that a servant-leader has the responsibility to get the job done using people and the other assets I have listed. He does so in a way as to draw upon the full giftedness and creativity of the person. He does so in a manner in which the person as well as the church is spiritually edified.

If you are assigned a responsibility, take charge confidently and organize your people to get the job done. Do so with humility and in a spirit of servanthood. Do not attempt to let things "just happen." Make them happen right. Remember that managing is a skill that is essential to the healthy, ongoing ministry of a church and is part of your job as a leader.

## DELEGATING

Delegating is the act of assigning a task for which you are responsible to someone else to accomplish. The average leader has far more responsibilities than he can successfully handle. There are three ways in which he can handle that problem. He can reduce the number of his responsibilities, which is sometimes hard to do. He can improve and enlarge his capacity to handle responsibilities. And he can delegate. In many cases, a combination of all three may be in order. However, here I want to consider only the subject of delegating. As I do, I want to give credit to my colleague Grant Howard, who has helped me to think through this subject more clearly.

When do we delegate? We do so when there are routine procedures that others can and should handle. As I observe church leaders, I see many of them bogged down in a morass of details, many of which

---

15. *Webster's New World Dictionary of the English Language*, 2d ed., s.v. "manage."

should be accomplished by someone else. Consequently, they are often wasting needless time and energy caring for the smallest details. Sadly, they seldom accomplish anything substantial and often miss seeing the "big picture."

In addition to delegating routine procedures, the leader should delegate responsibilities that are appropriate for another leader, such as a committee chairperson. He should also delegate tasks that individuals or couples would find great satisfaction in doing. How do we delegate? Dr. Howard gives us a procedure that I believe is helpful:

1. Pinpoint the task. Carefully define the what, when, how, where, who, and so on.

2. Select the person or committee. If time is short, select someone you know is capable. If there is latitude in time and performance, use someone who will benefit from the experience. Rotate delegation to broaden your base of trained people.

3. Make the assignment. If verbal, follow it up in writing. Remember to require only reasonable expectations from people to whom you delegate. Explain why this person was selected, why this job is important and the results which are expected. Through feedback, make sure that the person completely understands what is expected of him. Make sure he understands the time frame in which this is to be accomplished. If necessary, establish suspense dates.

4. Supply the support which is needed. This may vary according to the capabilities of the person you have selected. Some will require fairly detailed, ongoing support from you.

5. Periodically check on progress. Do it in a friendly, non-threatening manner. Often a casual, "How's it going?" will suffice. With more formal or detailed tasks, you may require more detailed progress reports.

6. Evaluate results. This has three purposes. It determines how well the task has been accomplished. It also is an opportunity to reward the person for his service. In addition, it gives a person a chance to understand what he has learned through the process.[16]

16. J. Grant Howard, class notes, Western Conservative Baptist Seminary.

By learning to delegate properly, a leader can greatly extend the amount of work he can effectively accomplish. But, in addition, he is fulfilling his mission of "equipping the saints for the work of ministry." Don't try to do everything yourself. Delegate widely and wisely!

## RECRUITING

Recruiting is the task of finding and enlisting appropriate workers to minister in the areas for which you, as a leader, are responsible. All of the administrative tasks we have discussed so far have been of great importance to the ministry of the church. However, none of them is more important than this one. Not only are you looking for godly workers, you must have quality workers. Moreover, these workers must possess unique qualities that are necessary for success in each particular office.

How do you recruit quality workers? Not by putting a notice in the Sunday bulletin or by asking for volunteers to respond to an announcement made in the worship service. Effective leaders have already surveyed their congregation and know who the potential workers are. This is accomplished by both formal, written surveys given periodically for the congregation to fill out and by simple, careful observations of people. These two means should give us enough information so that we can, then, approach a person directly as to whether or not he or she will serve. If the person is willing, then we must be prepared to provide the proper training so that he will be successful in that ministry.

Whatever the office, don't be in a hurry to place anybody into it permanently. After a person has received his training, he begins his "tryout" period. During that period his performance should be observed and evaluated. Only when he or she shows confidence and competence in the job should that person be given a "permanent" position. I placed the word "permanent" in quotation marks because I believe "permanent" should always be relative. After each year, a person should be evaluated as to whether he or she should continue in that ministry.

Recruiting is an important job because to a great extent it will determine whether or not the ministry of the church is going to succeed. Care exercised to see that the right person is employed in the most appropriate position does not guarantee success. But it sure helps!

Of the skills you as a leader need to develop, please place great emphasis on this one. But make it a continuous ongoing process. Don't recruit only for your immediate needs. That can get pretty frightening.

Instead, be recruiting all the time and especially for future needs. This gives you a pool of available workers from which to choose. As a result, you often can make a better choice.

This chapter is entitled "Administrator." To some extent, I have indicated how to build administrative skills even though I have spent most of the chapter describing the skills themselves. I have chosen to end the chapter by outlining a step-by-step process by which a leader can build administrative skills. As a leader or potential leader, then, you should evaluate the following:

1. In what areas of administration are you the strongest? Major in those areas, and help others who are not as skillful. Provide aid with a sense of helpfulness and humility. Don't act like a know-it-all. However, even though you perceive yourself as being strong in this area, don't rest on your laurels. Determine to improve that skill, and work hard at that task.

2. If you lack certain administrative skills, do everything you can to correct that deficiency. Read everything you can on the subject of building a particular skill, but realize that authors may differ widely. Glean from your research ideas that you believe are likely to work best for you.

   Various seminars and workshops often are offered in many of these subject areas. Inquire of other leaders and other churches as to the quality of a particular seminar, and then attend it, taking careful notes. Perhaps your church budget will even pay the workshop fee. Discuss the suggestions of the workshop leader with fellow church leaders who have strengths in administration. Begin following the suggestions given by the workshop leader, and see how well they work for you.

3. Observe others who are good at a particular skill. Notice how they do these things, and ask them their reasons for doing what they do. Ask them to provide help for you on an ongoing basis. Especially call upon them for advice when you face a serious problem in that administrative area.

4. Practice exercising the skill while others competent in that skill are asked to look on. On the basis of their observations, fine-tune the skill until you are good at it.

5. Maintain the attitude of an amateur. Always be humble. Always ask others to help you become better at your skills. Always seek ways of improving everything that you do.

## Additional Resources

Anderson, Ray S. *Minding God's Business.* Grand Rapids: Eerdmans, 1986.

Fiedler, Fred, and Martin M. Chemers. *Leadership and Effective Management.* Glenview, Ill.: Scott, Foresman, 1974.

McGregor, Douglas. *Leadership and Motivation.* Cambridge, Mass.: Massachusetts Institute of Technology, 1966.

Richardson, Marilyn. "How Our Church Benefited from Long-Range Planning." *Church Administration,* May 1990, p. 12.

## Questions for Discussion and Helpful Projects

1. You are a member of a leadership team in which the other members are obviously less gifted and creative than you. Moreover, your church has not set any formal goals in years. Despite your giftedness, list the reasons it is important for you to play as a team member, responsive both to other team members and to the congregation.

2. Make a list of all the possible things that could help you carry on the administrative task. These include "daytimers" and suspense dates. Which of those helps are you currently using well? Where may major improvements be made?

3. You begin the process of planning with your workers and one of them, a "tribal leader," insists, "Jesus may come tomorrow. Why bother to plan. After all, who can predict the needs of the future anyway?" How will you respond to him in light of the principles given in this book?

4. List both the possible dangers as well as the benefits of delegating. Why is delegating an inevitable necessity for you as a leader? How can you avoid the dangers?

# 8

# AUTHORITY

On the basis of Scripture, who has authority in the church and what kind of authority does he (or she) possess?

Before answering that question, it would be good to define authority. The definition listed first in most dictionaries is one that authoritarians love because it describes authority as "the power or right to give commands, enforce obedience."[1] Implied in this definition is the right to control, command, or determine. But who has this right, to what extent, and over whom?

Many people claim this "right," whether legally or illegally. Moreover, the multiplication of authoritarian cults and the ascent of Muslim radicalism in our day indicates that some people are searching for a religious authority. The willingness of people to submit tempts cultic leaders to abuse authority. As a result we often see leaders attempting to impose their will on the most minute details of people's lives.

Though this kind of abuse of authority is common in cults, it is rare in most evangelical circles. Yet in the name of discipleship training, evangelicals sometimes try to impose other, more subtle pressures

1. *Webster's New World Dictionary*, s.v. "authority."

upon individual Christians. Sometimes this is done to make Christians conform not to Scripture but to the will of a leader or group of leaders.

What do the Scriptures say in regard to the type of authority church leaders are entitled to wield? The principal biblical term to describe authority is the word *exousia.* In Matthew 9:6, when Jesus is criticized for healing a paralytic, He gives the reason, "But in order that you may know that the Son of Man has authority on earth to forgive sins." Paul uses the word in Romans 13:1, where he writes, "Let every person be in subjection to the governing authorities. For there is no authority except from God." The authority referred to here is that which is exercised by rulers or others in high positions by the virtue of their office.[2]

Sometimes that is the type of authority church leaders believe should accrue to them. However, I could not find a single reference in Scripture where that is indicated for church leaders. As close as I came was Hebrews 13:17, which is translated handily in the King James, "Obey them that have rule over you." My, how some church leaders love that translation of the verse. How many times have you heard an overbearing church leader try to use it as a club to get his own way?

The word used to describe a ruler in Hebrews 13:17 is *hegeomai.* Its prime meaning is "one who leads or guides"—quite a different concept from the one we have for "ruler" today. In turn, the term translated "obey" is the word *peitho,* which has as its root meaning the idea of persuasion. In view of the words used, it would seem that the verse is telling us that we should be open and amiable to the persuasive influence of our leaders, but we are not obligated to follow them blindly.

The words used in the passage suggest that leaders are not to be commanding generals barking out orders at their troops, insisting that their way is God's way. Instead, they are to be gentle persuaders of the people whom they are called to lead, not to drive. The term *lead* would indicate that instead of pushing people from behind, leaders are to be out in front serving as models. Thus they can say "Do as I do" as well as "Do as I say."

So far we have used the most common definition of authority, "the power or right to give commands, enforce obedience." Yet I can-

2. William F. Arndt and F. Wilbur Gingrich, *A Greek-English Lexicon of the New Testament* (Chicago, U. of Chicago, 1957), p. 278.

not find a single scriptural instance of that type of authority being vested by God in church leadership. So we must ask, What and where is authority as it applies to the church, and who has it?

Perhaps an examination of Matthew 28:18 will help. In this, the Great Commission, Jesus said, "All authority has been given to Me in heaven and on earth." Then He commands His followers to carry out certain actions: to make disciples, baptize them, and teach them. Though Jesus commands His followers to carry out these activities, He reserves "all authority" to Himself. He delegates to His followers only what is needed for them to accomplish the mission.

If all authority was given to Jesus and the church is His physical body on earth, then Jesus' authority is vested in the church today. But notice, I said "the church" and am talking about the church as a whole. Jesus' authority is not necessarily restricted only to the officers of the church. Jesus delegated certain responsibilities to His followers and gave them commensurate authority to carry out the mission of the kingdom. The mission Jesus gave the church is as valid today as it was when He gave it. Just as Jesus delegated authority to His followers, thus designating them leaders, it is reasonable to conclude that the church has the authority to choose leaders and delegate specific types of authority to them. If we expect leaders to exert the authority the church has delegated to them, we need to understand the kinds of authority those leaders will be using.

### AUTHORITY DERIVED FROM THE JOB

This type of authority is given to an individual when he is selected for or elected to a particular position of leadership. However, a person relying only on authority of position will have difficulty exercising it. A primary example of this is the recent seminary graduate who is chosen to become "senior" pastor of a local church. He has just gone through an intensive period of study where he has wrestled with a great deal of theory. However, he may have had little practical experience when he is suddenly thrust into this august position. The kind of authority he exercises and how he applies that authority may well spell life or death for his ministry. Even though he has authority by virtue of his position, that will not be enough in itself to command respect from his people.

Let's look at another example, a member of the congregation who finds himself elected to the post of elder or deacon. Does the fact that he occupies an office automatically flood him with such knowledge and wisdom that he is competent to become a tyrannical church boss? If we look to biblical models, it will be difficult to justify such behavior. He will find difficulty imposing his authority even though he has been elected to office.

## AUTHORITY DERIVED FROM THE PERSON

This type of authority arises out of the personal strength of the individual himself rather than the office he holds. Such a person is likely to exert a great deal of influence whether he is in a specific office or not. William Oncken, Jr., has outlined three categories pertaining to this kind of authority.[3]

### COMPETENCE

A young or untried leader may find life troubling when people grant authority primarily on the basis of competence. He has no track record so no one knows whether or not he is really competent. People will listen to him and may like his ideas, but they have no real inkling as to whether his ideas will work. Therefore, they are reluctant to grant him any significant degree of authority. Without authority to carry out his ideas, his programs will likely prove to be the failures everyone feared.

In sharp contrast to the untried leader is the experienced, veteran Sunday school superintendent. Everyone knows that he has run a tight ship for years. The Sunday school is orderly, well staffed, and growing. Nothing dramatic or exciting has occurred for years, and his ideas may be far inferior to those of the young leader. However, because the superintendent has proved himself competent, he will likely be able to exert great authority over many kinds of church ministry. He is predictable. "We know what to expect so we will follow him." Woe to the unproved new leader that crosses this battle-scarred veteran, even though the new leader may hold the exalted position of deacon or elder, or even pastor.

### PERSONALITY

Some people are so pleasant to deal with and have such a personal sparkle they could lead a congregation over a cliff. Often this type

---

3. William Oncken, Jr., "Examining Authority, " *Colorado Institute of Technology Journal,* July 1970, p. 273.

of person is not only a charmer, but is so thoughtful and gracious in his actions and so generous in helping others that people feel eternally indebted to him. As a result any action that could be construed as opposing him is almost considered a betrayal. It is never difficult for such a person to raise a large following, and as a result have a great deal of authority at his disposal.

Authority based on personality alone may be the most dangerous type of all. A person may have charm without having strong moral convictions. He or she may be externally attractive without being inwardly beautiful. This is the of type person who can easily cause factions and fragmentation in a local church. Would that we could always find the perfect combination: personal charm combined with true selflessness and godliness.

CHARACTER

The person who has the reputation of being godly often will carry a great deal of clout in a local assembly, especially if he occupies a position of respectability in the community as well. Therefore the person who has brought up his children well, is known as a tither, and has a history of honesty and respectability often will gain the reputation for spirituality, especially if he can pray eloquently.

Inwardly this person may well be unspiritual and self-serving. But people would never know that unless they crossed that person. Even then, the weapons he would direct toward such an antagonist would be "spiritual" ones. They would be so subtle and appear so pure and innocent that no one could easily pin him down to undue use of influence or abuse of power.

## When Both Kinds of Authority Do Not Reside in the Same Person

So far we have looked at two basic types of authority: authority derived from the office and authority derived from the person. Under ideal conditions no conflict should exist between the the two. Ideally we should be able to elect people to office within the church who combine competence, amiable personality, and impeccable character. This combination of official position and personal attributes should produce a credible leader people will follow.

The problem arises when the person in leadership possesses only one of those sources of authority. The church may not have people with the personal and character traits that it would desire in the persons it elects to responsible leadership positions. But the situation is not entirely bleak, it reasons. There are always people willing to serve. They may not meet the spiritual qualifications or possess the desired personal attributes, but they are *available*. The constitution specifies that the church will fill a given number of offices, and here these willing people are. "What else can we do?" the leadership muses. "How can we turn them down when there is no one else available to serve?"

As a result the church sometimes feels it must do the best it can with the people at hand. Sadly, people are sometimes elected to official positions who have neither the required qualities for that position nor credibility with the constituency. Once in that office they carry out their functions as well as can be expected but not to a standard of excellence.

There was a day when people would follow a leader just because he had been elected to an office. That no longer is true. Today authority of all kinds (including that of seminary professors) is being questioned. Some leaders cannot handle that. Perhaps they know down deep inside that they do not qualify for church leadership. As a result, when their authority is questioned they become defensive and stand on the dignity of their office. They try to exert even more authority than before they were challenged, and the struggle goes on with increasing intensity.

Sometimes the opposite dilemma occurs. A church has numbers of people possessing the necessary personal qualities for leadership, but those people are not willing to occupy an official position. Maybe a person declines nomination because he has gotten wind that the power structure is afraid of his influence. Or perhaps he has grown weary working with those he believes to be a "bunch of incompetents." Maybe he is just too committed in other areas of service and chooses not to serve in an official capacity. Yet, like it or not, he is a leader and has a following.

Unfortunately that following often may be made up of persons who are dissatisfied with those in official positions. Thus even the spiritually qualified leader with charisma and charm unwittingly may find himself a divisive force within a church when he exerts his leadership authority outside of the church's established governmental system.

What do we do with this dilemma? First, we must review with the people the fact that though the church is an organism, that does not mean it does not need a degree of organization in order to survive. God has given leaders to the church to cure the disease of individualism, which is not only strong today but has existed since the birth of the church. The church is to use these leaders in an orderly pattern, delegating to them sufficient authority to carry out their responsibilities.

Many churches could be far more creative in selecting leadership teams than they have been. Many churches need also to work hard to see that gifted leaders are not saddled with perfunctory duties but challenged to exercise their gifts of leadership in creative ways. Sometimes, however, the church has no alternative but to do the best it can with what it has available. As a result, it must pick leaders from a manpower pool that may not include the most exciting leaders within the congregation. Once the church has picked these leaders, however, it is the obligation of the people individually to submit to leadership in the areas in which the church has given those leaders authority. Gifted people especially, who could be leaders but have declined to serve, must submit to the elected leadership of the church. If they do not, they are inviting chaos.

A church must never compromise its scriptural position, though. It may not want to call all of its leaders "elder" or "deacon." But if it does establish those offices it must be careful that the candidates it chooses meet the biblical qualifications for the offices to which they are to be elected. If people being considered for these offices do not meet the proper criteria, the church should not choose them. That office should remain unfilled rather than being staffed by an unqualified person. Meanwhile, some of the work ordinarily expected by people in office may be farmed out to people without official titles.

There is an additional consideration. People who qualify for a particular office may choose not to serve in office for good personal reasons. That does not mean that their opinions should be ignored. Elected officials are wise to seek the counsel of those wise and godly people who by the vestige of their character and personality command a following. Likewise, these "natural leaders" must submit themselves to those who have been elected to official positions by the church.

Up to this point we still haven't answered the basic question, "What real authority do church leaders possess?" At this point it might be good to look at another definition of authority. According to the dictionary, authority involves "the power to take action or make final decisions."[4] Authority, might be defined as "sufficient power to get the assigned job done."

What authority do church leaders have? Certainly they have the authority they need to work together in accomplishing the twofold mission of the church, evangelism and edification. They also have the authority they need to supervise the functions that assist the church in accomplishing its mission. In short, they have sufficient authority to carry out the tasks of leadership that we considered in the last chapter as they are assigned and entrusted with these tasks by the church.

What authority does the church leader have over people? In the sense of authority as "control of one person over the personal life of another," the church leader has no such authority. When he tries to exert such authority, he is meddling into territory where he has no scriptural foundation.

As church leaders we do have the authority to work in partnership with the Holy Spirit to bring about change in individual lives and in the church. That authority must manifest itself not in dictatorship but in persuasiveness built out of our sensitivity to people and our skills in dealing with them. The ability to exercise that authority could well depend upon personal credibility built up by our own training and the example of our lives.

Anyone who would aspire to leadership in the church would do well to remember the injunction of 1 Peter 5:1-3: "Therefore, I exhort the elders among you, exercising oversight as your fellow elder and witness of the sufferings of Christ, and a partaker also of the glory that is to be revealed, shepherd the flock of God among you, exercising oversight not under compulsion, but voluntarily, according to the will of God; and not for sordid gain, but with eagerness; nor yet as lording it over those allotted to your charge, but proving to be examples to the flock."

We have asked many questions in this chapter, but we should ask a final one, Can we even speak authoritatively? The answer is that we can do so only when we speak from the authority of the Word of God itself, not from our own ideas. Where the Word of God is specific in pronouncements we can speak authoritatively on the basis "Thus saith

---

4. *Webster's New World Dictionary,* s.v. "authority."

the Lord." Where the Word of God does not speak authoritatively, all we can safely say is, "On the basis of the best evidence that I have, this is what I think is right and this is what I think we should do."

When we have learned to speak in this manner, we will have learned as well to avoid backing ourselves against the wall to defend any questionable methodology. Moreover, we will have learned to avoid seeking an obscure biblical rationale to try to force our people to adopt that methodology. When we cease putting our job and reputation on the line to support questionable methodology, it will be possible for us to be modest and patient in what we demand of others. As a result, God will transform both individuals and the church, maybe not on our time schedule, but He will transform them nonetheless.

## Additional Resources

Barrs, Jeram. *Shepherds and Sheep: A Biblical View of Leading and Following.* Downers Grove, Ill., InterVarsity, 1983.

Bertolini, Dewey. "Authority in the Church." M.Div. thesis, Talbot Seminary, 1977.

Cheney, Tom, Jr. "How to Cope When a Deacon Wants to Be Boss," *Church Administration,* February 1990, pp. 20-21.

Duane, Garrett, and Rich R. Melick, Jr. *Authority and Interpretation: A Baptist Perspective.* Grand Rapids: Baker, 1987.

Felix, Montgomery. "Authority in Ministry: Meaning and Sources." *Church Administration,* June 1990, pp. 21-23.

## Questions for Discussion and Helpful Projects

1. Many traditional definitions of authority denote images of tyrannical dominance on the part of church leaders and blind submission on the part of parishioners.

PROJECT: Make a thorough search of the New Testament to see what kind of authority Jesus and the New Testament writers advocate. How does their brand of authority differ from that so often subscribed to by our society?

2. In what ways has authority been abused by leaders of churches of your acquaintance? Cite specific examples of such abuse. What could have been done in each of those situations to prevent abuse from occurring?

3. What precautions should be taken when attempting to derive principles of church leadership from Matthew 28:18? How does the transference of Christ's authority in this text differ from the authority vested in an elder or deacon?

4. Describe how the authority vested in church leaders adequately permits them to fulfill their divinely appointed mandate.

5. What advice would you give a church that has more volunteers for leadership positions than qualified people? What considerations should be made in the election of church officers?

# PART 3

# A Compassionate Agent of Change: The Leader's Defining Role

# 9

# PREPARING YOURSELF FOR CHANGE

It is not news to any of us that we are living in a period of rapid, unprecedented change. Technology, moral values, political alliances, economic conditions, and medical treatment are just a few areas where those changes have been mind-boggling in just the past decade alone.

When Alvin Toffler wrote *Future Shock*[1] in the late sixties it burst onto the literary market as an overnight best-seller. One of the reasons for its popularity was the way in which it described what was already happening in the lives of its readers: unprecedented, overwhelming change. Today the rate of change we experience is even greater than it was when *Future Shock* was written.

Toffler defined change in terms of the way the future invades our lives. He reminded us that mankind has always lived in a state of change but that today change is occurring so rapidly people are overwhelmed by it and cannot possibly adapt to it. As a result, a new disease has come into being, the disease Toffler called "future shock." This malady, Toffler said, manifests itself in psychosomatically induced

---

1. Alvin Toffler, *Future Shock* (New York: Random, 1970).

symptoms from which an increasing number of people in our society suffer.

In the midst of a society already overburdened by massive change you may be surprised at what I tell you. If you are really called to be a church leader you can expect to be an agent of change. That's the essence of leadership. A leader guides the way by going in advance. He is an initiator. He is on the forefront of new activity, encouraging his people on to newer and better things.

The Bible never instructs leaders to preserve the spiritual status quo of their people. It calls them to examine the Scriptures constantly, discover the better things God has for His people, and lead them to greater spiritual maturity and service. That is what God has called you to do.

The leader is expected to lead people in a forward direction. I can find only one place in the Bible where God expected His servant to lead people around in circles, and in that case there was a definite reason. The Israelites had been so corrupted by the world that Moses had to lead them through the desert until an entire generation died off and a people fit to conquer and inhabit the Promised Land was left.

## THREE ABSOLUTES

If you have already been an agent of change, you have discovered that some people balk at doing things in a new way. Their conversations sound something like this: "Is there no escape from change even in the church? Are there no constants, no sturdy foundation stones upon which we can build the lives of our churches? Are there not certainties that cannot and will not change? Is change always desirable?"

Are there indeed any changeless areas left in this world? Of course there are. The Bible is rich in describing them for us. Is there any hope for the change-fractured person? There certainly is. The first and foremost job of the change agent is to ground his people in those changeless areas. When he has done that, his people will feel more secure and be better prepared to tackle the changes that need to be made.

### GOD'S NATURE IS CHANGELESS

We can state on firm scriptural grounds that the nature and character of God are changeless. Testifying personally to this fact, God the Father states in Malachi 3:6, "For I, the Lord, do not change." If that were not reassuring enough, the New Testament adds its confirmation. Speaking about God the Son, Hebrews 13:8 reminds us, "Jesus Christ is the same yesterday and today, yes and forever."

How comforting to the Christian to find out that the Bible contradicts the dominant philosophy of our society, which insists that nothing is constant and everything is changing. Such a philosophy is a lie originated by Satan.

Current secularism insists further that everything in life is relative and nothing absolute. That simply is not true. We do have changeless absolutes upon which we can build our lives. One of those is an absolutely dependable God whose nature and character are changeless and upon whom we can always depend without reservation. Hallelujah!

From that assertion we can move to other things that are changeless: God is love and will always be love. God is always just. He is forever good. He is constantly all-knowing, all-powerful, and everywhere present. He who is in us is always far greater than he who is in the world. How comforting to the Christian to know that he has a heavenly Father who is absolutely dependable. How reassuring to know that he has a Savior in whom he can trust completely, forever.

However, even that assurance is dulled to some extent for the person who is trying to avoid change. After all, although God deals with His children on the basis of His changeless character and attributes, He does not always use the same methods in His mission of maturing us. Indeed, every child of God knows that He is versatile and creative in His dealings with us. His methods differ according to the particular purpose He wants to accomplish in our lives. When He sees that we are ripe for a period of growth but unresponsive, He may use any number of dramatic means to get our attention. Some of those methods make us joyful; others cause us pain.

Sometimes we willingly step out of line. As a result, we miss God's best for our lives. When we do, He will often use discipline to bring us back into line, sometimes to our chagrin. The kind and amount of discipline may differ drastically, depending on the circumstances and our individual need. Therefore, although the nature of God is changeless, the application of that nature to our lives is changing constantly.

Conversely, it would be good for us to remind ourselves that although God is constant in His love for us, we seldom remain constant in our relationship to Him. All of us are well aware that our relationship with God has its ups and downs. But think for a moment. Would you want your relationship with God to never change? Surely there is something better than that which we are now experiencing. Surely I can live a more victorious Christian life than I am now living. Surely God is not through molding me into the person He wants me to be. Surely there is improvement ahead—but improvement inevitably presupposes change.

GOD'S WORD IS CHANGELESS IN NATURE

On the basis of God's unchanging nature, we may also insist that His Word is changeless. Many years ago that question was settled for me. Assailed by a variety of problems confronting me because of textual criticism, I made a simple but far-reaching decision. I became totally convinced that God was the author of the Bible. Since I had also put my complete trust in the Author, I reasoned that I could put my complete trust in His Word. I have never wavered from that decision. I cannot begin to tell you how many problems that has spared me.

Even when we affirm the changeless nature of the Word, we must recognize the changeable character of the medium through which the Word is conveyed: human language. Like many of my generation, I grew up on the King James Version. Portions of that translation still are my favorite. Yet though the KJV remains substantially the same as when it was written 480 years ago, our language has changed. Many of the language forms are different and many of the actual words have changed their meaning through common usage. As a result, numerous words convey meanings different from the ones they were meant to express. Consequently, though the character of God's Word remains the same, committed Christian scholars of each new age must translate God's Word into a form that will convey the original meaning to the new generation.

Here we face an additional problem. The application of God's changeless Word to the life of an individual believer must be a constantly changing pattern. What the Holy Spirit conveys to an individual depends upon how mature the intended receiver is at any particular time. Thus not only does the application of God's Word differ from person to person, it differs with the same person depending on how mature he is spiritually when the message reaches him.

This point can be demonstrated vividly in the lives of most believers. Before we were saved, we were probably attracted most to passages of Scripture dealing with salvation. When we read other passages, they didn't make sense to us. After we were saved, however, through the interpreting power of the Holy Spirit entire passages come to life that were unintelligible to us before. The more we grew in Christ, the more Scripture opened up to us. Who has not had the experience of rereading a particular passage after a period of time and saying, "Isn't this wonderful? I have never seen this truth before."

GOD'S CHURCH IS CHANGELESS IN NATURE

The church is also changeless in nature. Its purpose and its goals never change. That does not mean that the church is designed to be changeless in methodology, though.

This is the point where contemporary church members may experience their greatest difficulties. A large number of saints would like to add methodology to the list of things that should remain changeless. As a result, a major eruption occurs in some churches when even a minor change is made in format or methods. The change-minded leader in such a church will face his greatest challenge when he attempts to bring maturity and dynamic outreach to that church.

The changeless nature of God, the Bible, and the church are the foundation of our faith. They will never change. We can absolutely depend upon that. All other areas are candidates for change. It is to those areas that we must give our attention.

## EARNING THE RIGHT TO BE HEARD

Identifying which things that should be in a church is a personal and subjective decision. The exact choice will vary from congregation to congregation and from person to person in each of those congregations.

The answer to the question, What should be changed? is obvious to the teenaged boy forced by his parents to sit through a long and laborious worship service. He would opt for a shorter sermon preached in terms that are easier for him to understand and on topics he considers more relevant to his needs.

Change item number two would likely be the type of music. "Surely, the church could use some better stuff than the oldies I have to listen to every Sunday! Why do I have to put up with Grandma's music all the time?" is his complaint.

The middle-aged dowager, who has lived through a life that has seen every possible kind of change, may view this same "outdated" service with different eyes. The lengthy sermon and "good old songs" are a comforting security blanket, proof that there is something left in the world she can consider stable. That anyone would even consider changing the position of the doxology in the order of worship is a serious affront to her. The thought of including contemporary music in "her" worship service sends chills down her back. The change she would call for is in the deportment of those "irreverent" teenagers.

The seminary graduate whose diploma stills bears the hint of wet ink thinks that almost everything in the church needs changing. He is terribly disturbed that the church does not resemble the ideal church he had in mind during his theological training. He sees the major problem facing the church as its being too resistant to change. *Any* change would be an improvement, he thinks. As a result, he may opt for change for change's sake, not realizing that that may be more detrimental to the church than no change at all.

Realizing the subjective nature of what needs to be changed in a particular local congregation, please allow me to bypass the more visible candidates for change and suggest some more foundational but subtle areas that can be changed. My suggestions will be posed in the form of questions.

DO YOU REALLY LISTEN TO YOUR PEOPLE?

Have you convinced your people that you really are interested in what concerns them? There are any number of reasons people may not be inclined to follow their leaders. One of the most prominent is that they are not certain that their leaders really want to listen to them. Perhaps this seeming unwillingness on the part of leaders has built within the people a feeling of helplessness or despair, a feeling that they, the people, are not truly important.

Maybe attending services has become a tiring, obligatory exercise. Perhaps the church's program is wearing them out by sheer activity. Maybe the governmental structure has become so overbearing in its authority that church members look to business meetings as potential hassles. All that and you still refuse to listen to them or take their complaints seriously! It could be that your people have come to feel used, no longer important. Do you consider your people important in themselves, or do you see them merely as means to accomplish the objectives set by leadership?

Perhaps the facilities have become so worn and unsightly that the church building is no longer a pleasant place to be. As a result, people are ashamed to invite their friends to church and find church attendance less desirable themselves.

What I have been describing is a church whose leaders have caught the disease of institutional maintenance. Their more important energies are directed toward keeping the institution alive. Leadership no longer sees its primary mission as serving of people and their needs. It ignores the needs people express.

Does that describe your church? Then trying to change the minds and hearts of your people may be premature. After all, why should they change? What hope is there that changes they make will result in the church's beginning to respond to their needs?

In some cases the people are aware of changes needed in their own lives but will not change until they first see change taking place in the thinking and the attitudes of their church leaders.

It is my prayer that church leaders who read this chapter will use the ideas in it as a springboard for soul-searching. Before championing your ideas to your people and becoming defensive when they don't respond enthusiastically, ask yourself how you are responding to them.

ARE YOU THE ONE WHO IS DELAYING CONSTRUCTIVE CHANGE?

Is there already a consensus among the people of your church that certain changes need to be made? Are you at odds with your people because you have a change agenda of your own that is quite different? If so, despite the fact that the leadership does not agree with the congregation, it is wise for them to listen to the congregation. It may be that the leadership of the church—not the congregation—is the barrier to constructive change.

DO YOU HAVE YOUR PRIORITIES STRAIGHT?

What strategic areas and conditions need to be changed in a local church? Everything that does not help it to reach the primary purpose of the church, to glorify God. How do we glorify God? We do so through evangelism and edification. Those tasks are not just theological ones, but are people-oriented. Evangelism cannot be defined properly unless we identify it with the people who will come to know the Savior. Likewise, we are not discussing edification adequately unless we zero in on individuals to be edified.

Do you have your priorities straight? Are the major efforts of your leadership directed toward the people-oriented goals of evangelism and edification? Is your program sufficiently balanced so that equal attention is given to both? If not, that is where major change is needed.

DO YOU THINK OF THE PEOPLE YOU SERVE
AS MORE THAN "MERE LAYMEN"?

Probably the most unfortunate and detrimental term used in the church today is the term "mere layman." Why? Because it may prejudice a leader's thinking and create in his mind an improper image of the people he has been called to serve. When leaders think that "mere laypeople" are not important, they may ignore the many good ideas the lay members of the body can contribute to the whole. Moreover, those leaders are likely to conclude that the problems the people raise are unimportant and consequently may fail to take action on problems that truly have serious implications for the church.

Leader, respect and listen to your people. They are important. Don't fall into the trap of considering yourself smarter and more important than they are. Don't try to pull rank in support of your own threatened authority. Remember that only as the entire body pulls together as a unit will it reach its potential for Christ. Don't dismiss the expressed concerns of members. Unsolved, persistent problems that are ignored by leadership are the single greatest factor that immobilizes the church.

There is no such a thing as a "mere layman" in God's eyes. God describes all of His sons and daughters as saints, priests, and ministers. The fact that a few of those sons and daughters are specially trained and set apart as equipping and leading ministers does not detract from the high esteem in which God holds each of the other saints.

DO YOU THINK AND ACT ETHICALLY AS A LEADER?

Christians should be the most ethical people on earth. Unfortunately, often they are not. Perhaps one of the reasons is that sometimes their leaders fail to provide an appropriate ethical model for them to follow.

I do not believe that this is a universal problem. Most Christian leaders do well in this area. Others fail miserably. Unhappily it is often the offenders who stand out so dramatically that they overshadow the efforts of those who do well. Nor do I think it is the intention of Christian leaders to act unethically. When they do so there is often a plausible explanation for their behavior.

Instruction in leadership ethics is seldom offered by schools that train future Christian leaders. Even pastors are often ill-equipped in this area. Sometimes a leader fails ethically because he is operating on a survival mentality. That fosters unethical behavior toward other churches. Sometimes a leader is so caught up in the task of keeping his ship afloat that he rationalizes the legitimacy of almost any action so long as it contributes to the cause. *That other church is so large and successful, and here we are struggling for survival. Surely they won't miss a few people!* he says to himself. The rationalized legitimacy of his behavior is doubled when the sheep that are stolen from another congregation are tithing sheep!

The sin of individualism is one of the strongest sins plaguing the church today. This sin breeds serious problems within individual congregations and produces problems between congregations. As a local church we are not alone in the task of redeeming the world, nor are we alone in the challenge of redeeming our city. There is a sense in which the local church is made up not only of our group of believers but of all groups of believers in the community. Just as we need each other within the local church, we as a local church also need other local churches of similar evangelical persuasion.

Similarly, just as we are obligated to act ethically within our own congregation, we have an equal obligation to act ethically toward other evangelical groups within our community. When we gossip or act unethically toward another evangelical church, the entire church in that community suffers. When we steal sheep from another evangelical congregation in our community the sum total of additions to the kingdom of God is zero. We cause untold pain to the larger local church of which we, as an individual congregation, are a member.

Ethical breaches can arise from a church's being being caught up in the success philosophy of the world. The rationale reads something like this: Since success is the ultimate triumph, the end truly does justify the means. Thus any tactic short of glaring immorality is acceptable so long as its ultimate result is numerical success.

Yet when one congregation gains numerical or financial "success" at the expense of another evangelical congregation, pain always results. Pain is experienced immediately by the congregation that has been wronged and experienced eventually by the church practicing un-ethical behavior. Chickens come home to roost. The church that savors so-called success and pursues it through ethical breeches is making a serious mistake. Bad consequences always result.

What about ethical breaches within your local congregation? One ethical breach that can come back to haunt a leader is the practice of misrepresenting the facts. The tactic often presents itself as an air of overconfidence or an exaggeration. Or it may voice itself in such claims as "The large proportion of people in this congregation are in favor of this issue." Surely everyone should get on the bandwagon and support such a popular program! I am such an upbeat, enthusiastic person that I have had to watch this area the closest. The leader who pursues this tactic may think it is useful when he is trying to get the congregation to see a pet program of his in a more favorable light, but eventually the tactic will backfire. His credibility will be undermined when the con-gregation learns that his description of support for the program was exaggerated and unrealistic.

Sometimes ethical breaches take the form of little white lies produced to try to convince someone that an error made by a leader should be blamed on someone else. In practice it sounds something like this: "It's Charley's fault that this awful thing has happened. I've warned him dozens of times, but he just won't listen." Other times, the lie emerges in the context of a love offering where only a part of what is designated by the people for that purpose reaches its intended recipi-ent.

Unethical tactics are unworthy for Christians to pursue. A church leader must flee from anything that tempts him to engage in such actions. He must be above reproach in all his dealings and be a model for those he is equipping. Of the areas of the church needing change today, few are more critical or important as this one. The church as the Body of Christ must follow biblical, ethical principles in all its dealings.

If you and your church have not addressed the question of ethics, make doing so a priority. Do not wait. Work on this change immediately for the sake of Christ and the reputation of His kingdom. Put to work in your own life and in the life of your congregation the set of principles you develop.

## ARE YOU STRIVING FOR A "CLASSY" MINISTRY?

Were the casual outsider to analyze the quality of the facilities, maintenance, and program of many churches he would describe them in a single word: tacky. Yet congregations do not deliberately intend for things to be substandard. Usually the slippage occurs because the church is trying to do more than it can do well with the resources it has available. If I were able to give only one piece of advice in this area it would be, scale down.

Scale down to the number of programs your church can do well. If your church is small, acknowledge that not everybody who visits you is going to find his needs met. Then see to it that the programs you do offer are well run and effective. In that way those people who stay with your church will find that they are served exceedingly well.

Instead of strapping your congregation with a large debt, scale down your building dreams to those that will serve your needs and can be maintained properly. Engage an architect who can combine beauty with economy. Plan your facilities so that they can be expanded later to meet the needs of a growing church. Make your facilities attractive and inviting so that the moment a person walks in, the building says "Welcome." Take special concern for the appearance of the worship facility. Do not let its appearance detract from that which is supposed to take place there.

Make sure that the nursery and the rest rooms are well designed and properly maintained. Careless maintenance of those rooms can repel people who would have become productive members.

Give careful attention to the grounds. Trash around the building, weeds in the flower beds, and untrimmed lawns are deterrents to attendance and a poor testimony to the neighborhood.

Strive for class in your music program, realizing that you may have to settle for a less active program than the big church down the street. Perhaps you will need to reduce the number of selections offered by the choir or the number of soloists performing special music. Use the best you have judiciously. Encourage those who are less gifted to perform at functions other than the worship service—and, by all means, initiate this latter process gradually, diplomatically, and graciously.

Plan worship functions carefully, coordinate them extensively with those who participate, and see to it that the service is the best thing your church does. Worship is designed to be direct interaction of the congregation with almighty God. Offer Him only your best.

Strive for quality in church education. Obtain the necessary training for your teachers so that they can do their job properly. Combine their talents in teacher teams. Alter learning activities to fit the needs of the individual learner. Choose teachers carefully. The essence of quality in Christian education is a classy program where well-trained, amiable, competent teachers engage the learner in a meaningful learning experience. Nice facilities help. Attractive curriculum materials are an asset. But the real key to quality church education is well-trained, energetic, personable teachers who really care for the learners to whom God has sent them to minister.

Other people-oriented areas could be considered in detail. Handle people politely and courteously. Both privately and publicly thank people for their ministry. How sad it is when people suffer the disappointment of seeing their acts of service go unnoticed. Make church social functions classy. Make the extra effort to present refreshments attractively. Doing so will send the message "We really do things right around here."

Tastefully decorate and comfortably furnish church meeting rooms. The person who invented the stark, unpadded steel folding chairs used in most church classrooms must have been a sadist. After fifteen minutes of sitting on them, all learning become an impossibility. The appearance of many church classrooms is equally stark. How much more inviting they would be with a little paint, a few pictures, tables, lamps, and carpeting. All of that will take effort and some money, but the results will make it worthwhile.

One more target on our "classless" list is the way many churches treat visitors. There is no more awkward feeling than finding oneself alone in a strange environment with no one to talk to. Church members should be stationed strategically throughout the church to greet visitors in a friendly and polite manner and to ascertain that their social needs are met. Visitors should be introduced to other people and escorted to their places of activity. Their children should be made to feel comfortable and secure.

Assign parking spaces near the building for visitors, and place attractive and accurate information signs inside and outside the building. The ones on the outside should tell visitors what goes on inside and how to get in; the ones on the inside should direct people to the activity rooms and tell them how to find those rooms. More could be written about having an adequate public address system, a ramp for those confined to wheelchairs, a tuned piano, a tidy, readable church bulletin, and a well-printed church newspaper.

To this list, other bothersome things can be added. Remember to ban the phrase, "Wouldn't it be wonderful if somebody would do something about that!" You *are* somebody! Perhaps the fact that God has allowed you to identify a particular area as needing change is a sign that you should do something about that area yourself. It may be as simple as buying a gallon of paint and going to work.

Insist on class. Eventually the attitude will become contagious, and the resulting enthusiastic response of other people in the congregation will result in a new, more exciting atmosphere in your church. It will become a delightful place for the congregation and for visitors.

ARE YOU USING THE SCRIPTURES HONESTLY?

I hesitate to add this last section to the chapter because I would like to think that a majority of evangelical churches are above reproach in the way they handle the Bible. Despite my wishful thinking, however, reality is more grim. Misuse of the Bible has been going on for a long time.

Through the centuries, no book has been as abused in its application as the Bible. Misinterpretation and misapplication have been used to justify the worst type of atrocities, from the mass slaughter of Jews in Nazi Germany to the segregation of black people. The latter has been based erroneously on a misinterpretation of the curse on Canaan as recorded in Genesis.

But of course those are problems of the past—we don't use the Bible in that way today. We are more civilized and humane than those who engaged in abuses before. What they did couldn't happen to us! Or could it? We need to remember that the nation that spawned the Holocaust was the most technologically advanced nation in the world. Moreover, justification for the atrocities they committed was given in the name of being humane and even biblical. After all, the reasoning went, wasn't it the Jews who crucified Jesus Christ? Don't the Jews deserve all they receive?

We can use the Bible to rationalize almost anything we want to do so that our consciences can be placated. The veneer of civilization is thin in many places, and the savage easily rises to the surface when "number one" is threatened. In the church, when ideas, programs, or egos are threatened, those who are biblically astute may be tempted to use the Bible to destroy their adversaries. People who have just a little knowledge of the biblical languages may be effective in using such tactics. After all, who knows enough to refute them?

A companion to this tactic is the ability to take a Scripture passage out of context and use it to justify almost anything. All of us can point to the use of this tactic by sects and cults. Usually a thinking person can see through such a ploy, and it falls short of being convincing. A much more insidious method wreaks havoc in a church, the practice of what I call scriptural chaining. A series of events is analyzed in relation to a group of Scripture passages that have no logical relationship to one another in the scriptural narrative itself but that can be made to seem connected by skillful and adept maneuver. Thus a position that ordinarily would be indefensible is successfully defended. This use of the Scripture is entirely unjustified.

It would be interesting to know to what extent the pragmatic philosophy "the end justifies the means" is the unwritten policy behind the actions of many church leaders. Such a philosophy is untrue, unscriptural, and invalid. Dishonest use of the Scriptures will not go unnoticed by God. The Holy Spirit, who is the author of the Scriptures, will not allow such methods to be undetected forever. When the deception is discovered, the result on the congregation will be so devastating that further attempts by the offending leader to bring positive change to the church will be stifled.

As potential agents of change let us not fall into the trap of wanting change so badly that we will practice deception, even biblical deception, to gain it. Instead, as interpreters of God's Word, let us hold on to our integrity and practice a biblical hermeneutic. As wielders of God's Word let us become artisans who use it skillfully and honestly. So used, the Bible will bring about results that are designed by God rather than contrived by man.

A credible leader is one who honestly and objectively inventories the foundational areas that have been mentioned in this chapter. When he discerns a difference between what he does and what the Scriptures insist should be, he corrects that discrepancy in his own life and attempts to do so in the life of the church. By his own example and his own willingness to change, he establishes a climate in which his people are willing to institute change. May you be such a leader.

## Additional Resources

Berkley, James D. "Turning Points: Eight Ethical Choices." *Leadership* 9, no. 2 (Spring 1988).

Bustanoby, Andre. *You Can Change Your Personality.* Grand Rapids: Zondervan, 1976.

Engel, James. *How Can I Get Them to Listen?* Grand Rapids: Baker, 1987.

Hauck Kenneth, and William McKay. "Dealing Creatively with Parish Antagonists." *The Circuit Rider,* July-August 1980.

Kirkpatrick, Donald L. *How to Manage Change Effectively.* London: Jossy, 1985.

Leigh, Ronald W. "Change in the Local Church: Philosophy and Practice." *Journal of Christian Education* 1, no. 2 (Spring 1981).

Richards, Lawrence O. *A New Face for the Church.* Grand Rapids: Zondervan, 1970.

Schaller, Lyle E. *The Change Agent: The Strategy of Innovative Leadership.* Nashville: Abingdon, 1972.

———. *It's a Different World.* Nashville: Abingdon, 1987.

Swindoll, Charles. *Hand Me Another Brick.* Nashville: Nelson, 1978.

"Vital Signs: An Interview with George Gallup." *Leadership* 8, no. 4 (Fall 1987), 12.

Walrath, Douglas A. *Leading Churches Through Change.* Nashville: Abingdon, 1979.

White, Jerry. *Honesty, Morality and Conscience.* Colorado Springs: Navpress, 1978.

## Questions for Discussion and Helpful Projects

1. What is future shock, and how is it produced? What are some of the negative side effects of accelerated change that you have experienced in your church and among its people? How well has the church met the challenges of those negative side effects?

2. If you agree that a church must constantly change to meet the challenges of its culture, then answer these questions:

   a. What specifically are those things you would call the irreducible minimums, those things that should never change?
   b. Give examples of how methods should change in order to accomplish the mission of the church more effectively. How can changes in method help your church meet primary goals that are being either neglected or addressed poorly at present?

3. Reflect on your own attitude toward the people you serve. Do you occasionally put them down rather than edify them? What other terms similar to "mere laymen" have you used or heard used that might exemplify an improper attitude of service?

4. Think through your concept of the local church. Does the local church refer only to the assembly to which you belong?

PROJECT: Evaluate your church's relationships with other evangelical churches in the neighborhood. Consider ways in which relationships with other area churches might be improved and a deeper sense of fellowship and mutual support encouraged.

5. Address the ethical issues raised in this chapter. What can be done to discourage the kind of unethical behavior referred to by the author?

PROJECT: Have the principal leaders of your church construct a list of ethical principles that apply to each of the areas in which they serve and to their own personal conduct as leaders. Study those lists as a church board and draw up a set of biblical, ethical standards by which your church will operate. State clearly what the consequences will be if a church leader is found to be acting unethically.

# 10

# HUMAN NATURE AND CHANGE

$A$t this point, you may be itching to read about the possibilities that change in your church can promise. You may have even tried to initiate significant changes within your church but have fallen flat on your face. Why? It may be because you are more detrimental to the progress of your church than a leader who is change-resistant. Your enthusiasm for change may not be matched by your knowledge of how to bring about change without fracturing the church.

Or you may be failing because you are so enamored with change you worship change for its own sake. People who think like that often want change to be continual. If change is not constant, they think the church has stagnated. They try to change things that do not need any changing just so that change is constant. They keep the local assembly in a continual state of turmoil. If you are like that, slow down and give your followers a chance to catch up with you.

Are you a change agent who moves wisely and surely to change those things that really need changing? That's good. You are on the right track because change that is handled rightly can bring about positive growth and vitality in a local body of believers. That's important to remember. All around us are harbingers of doom who point to our society and the present condition of today's church and see nothing but deterioration. When they are asked to identify the cause of this so-called deterioration, inevitably change is their victim. That's when we need to assert categorically and in as loud a volume we can that many changes taking place in society and in the church today are beneficial. In many ways we've never had it so good.

Speaking to the potential offered by change, Lyle Schaller asserts in *It's a Different World* that "in many respects today is not only a different world than the 1950's, it also in many respects is a better world. The increased complexity that often accompanies change frequently is the price of a better world."[1]

## Why Do People Resist Change?

It is this better, albeit more complex, world that we long for in the church. But how do we bring it about? How do we break down the natural resistance to change that is ingrained in many congregations? How do leaders initiate change that is beneficial to the church at large and to the individual members? To answer those questions, we need first to consider why people resist change. Without attempting to be exhaustive I would like to list some of the reasons.

### CHANGE IS UNCOMFORTABLE FOR THEM

We have a tendency to be most comfortable with that with which we are most familiar. After all, what we've got might not be so great, but at least we understand it and know how to cope with it. Moreover, in this constantly changing world, there are few comfortable, familiar areas left. In most areas of our lives we have no control over whether or not change takes place. Change is forced upon us. We have to accept it or resign from the system.

The church is a sterling exception to this pattern. Individuals can and do have influence over what the church does. So people decide to exercise clout in that institution. Since keeping something change-less is the goal these people have, and since they cannot keep anything else in life changeless, they try their best to keep the church from changing. If they are successful, they find themselves in an inner sanctum, a safe place where everything is predictable. There they are isolated from the change going on everywhere else. How thankful they are

1. Lyle E. Schaller, *It's a Different World* (Nashville: Abingdon, 1987), p. 19.

for that one area of comfort and security. The church becomes change-less in form and methodology while the rest of the world is in a state of constant change. The church meets the needs of the select few but becomes unintelligible and irrelevant to the world outside of it.

## THEY ARE NOT CONVINCED THAT CHANGE IS NECESSARY

Picture the average person embroiled in a culture that imposes all kinds of changes on him. Who asks him whether or not those changes should be imposed? No one! He has an attitude of utter helplessness regarding most of those changes. After all, isn't he an insignificant little nobody? What could he possibly do to prevent change from happening?

He faces changes with an air of resignation. He may not like them, but what can he do about them? He is but one voice in a huge system. He bites the bullet and puts up with change until the sheer volume overpowers him. If he's strong enough, he might make it until he retires. If not, he may just check out of the system through mental illness, psychosomatically induced physical illness, or some form of drug abuse.

Then he hears that someone is trying to change the church. Now here's an area where he does have some say in things. Understand, he's not entirely opposed to all change in the church. But he had better be convinced that it is necessary. Moreover, in order for him to support that change he must be absolutely convinced that what the church is changing to is far better than what it already is. Frazzled by change on every hand, he will be sure that no one changes the church just for the sake of change alone.

What a dreadful mistake some church leaders make. They are perfectly sincere in their goals. They are pushing for changes that would be beneficial to the church. But they fail to communicate their dreams properly and positively to their people. As a result, the people do not see the proposed changes as necessary and beneficial. They oppose these changes, vocally and actively or quietly and passively. Consequently, few changes actually take place, forward minded leaders feel frustrated, and the church is the loser.

## THEY LACK CONFIDENCE IN THEIR LEADERS

To bring about change effectively, a leader must have earned the confidence of his people. Such confidence is usually gained only after a leader has established a successful track record. People follow those whom they have learned to trust. If a leader is young or has not yet proved himself he should move slowly and cautiously in instituting change. An older or more established leader who has already succeeded in his ministry will find it much easier to initiate change.

No matter how much success a leader has experienced or how old a leader is, if he has recently goofed rather badly, his credibility rating will drop. Following such a disaster he is wise to lay low for a while before trying to initiate further change. Then, when he has proved himself in routine matters over a period of time, people will begin to trust him once more and agree to the more major changes he proposes.

THEY HAVE NOT HAD ENOUGH TIME
TO THINK ABOUT THE PROPOSED CHANGE

When people resist change it may be because the leadership is attempting to bring about change too abruptly. They have not given them time enough to consider that specific change. In *The Change Agent* Lee Grossman observes that change that is too rapid has a negative effect on a business organization.[2] Applied to the church, the principle is even more important, for the church is an organism rather than an organization, and thus even more susceptible to damage from rapid change. Unless the entire body of the church has had enough time to consider a drastic change thoughtfully, the members of the body will resist it steadfastly.

THEY DO NOT SEE CHANGE BEING APPLIED SELECTIVELY

The byword used by impatient, indiscriminate change agents is the expression "This is good for everyone." Consequently the leadership may subject everyone in a local church to a particular change even though that change may only be necessary for a small group within the church. For instance, a forward-minded church leader may believe that the music of Bach is meaningless to young people and so opts for loud, contemporary Christian music. He may even decide to use this newer music in all the worship services of the church.

It is true that contemporary Christian music is an effective evangelism tool among unchurched teens. It may be a valuable com-

2. Lee Grossman, *The Change Agent* (New York: AMACOM, 1974).

munication tool among Christian young people, but it is a mistake to subject all members to it. Many members of the older generation may not consider such music to be sinful. They merely find it uncomfortable and offensive to their ears. They do not find it conducive to worship. Were such music to be used in its proper setting probably only a few would object. But when it is the only music used for the entire congregation it is not acceptable. Change has been applied to everyone indiscriminately instead of selectively to the group most apt to benefit from it.

THEY DO NOT OWN THE PROPOSED CHANGE

Recently a friend of mine shared with me an important lesson learned by the elders of his church. The church was overcrowding its rented facilities. In their enthusiasm for growth, the elders purchased property, hired an architect, and began to plan a building program. Only one factor was missing—money. Numerous appeals to the congregation fell on deaf ears.

Finally the elders put their plans on hold and investigated what had happened. It turned out that the people had not been consulted as to whether land should be bought and a building erected, or what kind of a building it should be. The building program was the baby of the elders. Since the people had not been consulted, they had were not the ones who had made the decision to build. Consequently, they did not consider it their responsibility to give. Moreover, since initiating the building program was a decision of the elders, the people decided to let the elders worry about how to bring it about. The people had not been involved in process; they did not own the decision.

Unless the people are involved in the major goal-setting and decision-making processes of a church they will not own the decisions that are made and consequently will be unlikely to support those decisions. Especially is that true where major change is proposed.

THEY HAVE DECIDED THAT OTHER
CHANGES DEMAND A HIGHER PRIORITY

A church at which I spoke recently was staggering under enormous indebtedness. It had grown rapidly. To meet the needs caused by this growth it had erected costly buildings and hired a large staff. One of its more exciting attractions was its youth music program. Initially that program had drawn many people to the church. Then the minister of music decided that he needed an outreach dimension. Somehow he convinced the church to purchase a road-ready bus to transport young singers to concert engagements in other churches.

But when it came time to purchase the second and third buses, the people were resistant. Not only would the home church fail to benefit from the traveling ministry, other more urgent needs of the church would not be met. The church voted against the new ministry. There were higher priorities.

In a situation where there are financial limitations and many changes to be made, people will support what they consider to be high priority items and resist those items they consider to be low priority ones.

THEY HAVE CONCLUDED THAT THE TIMING
IS NOT RIGHT FOR THE PROPOSED CHANGE

Even when a specific change is a high priority item, people may not be convinced that the timing is right for the change. For instance, even when the church is packed in multiple church services, it may not be the right time to build.

Perhaps the church has grown rapidly. Possibly many of its new members also are new converts without "baptized pocketbooks." Maybe interest rates are so high that the church would be saddled with a crippling building payment each month. The expense would keep the church from hiring additional staff members to meet the needs of the growing congregation.

A time of rapid growth may have occurred simultaneously with a time of economic recession in the community. Is it the right timing to erect a building when many people are out of work and the budget of the church is already suffering? Even though the leadership of the church may be enthusiastic because of rapid growth and is certain that God will provide, cooler heads may conclude that the timing is not proper.

THEY ARE UNCERTAIN WHERE THE PROPOSED CHANGE WILL LEAD

Will a certain change open up a Pandora's box of troubles for a church? For example, how will the purchase of an expensive bus affect missions contributions, the building fund, the senior citizen ministry, the Sunday school, and future staff expansion? Will it keep the young people on the road all the time and away from their own church? Will it mean an increase in the amount of Christian rock music that senior citizens will be forced to endure? Will the young people become egotistical about their own performing abilities and make a bad impression for the church on the churches they visit?

Sometimes the people of a church can see the repercussions of a particular change better than can the leadership. When the people are not sure that a change will take the church in a wholesome direction, they will be resistant to it. The wisdom of the people may be greater than that of their leaders. Before making major changes in any church, the leadership should launch an "environmental impact" investigation and study how the change will affect the other areas and programs of the church.

## THEY SEE THE PROPOSED CHANGE AS THREATENING TO CREATE A DIVISION IN THE BODY

Does the particular proposed change have within it the seeds of disunity or disharmony? Sometimes a congregation will not support certain changes because the people are convinced that the changes will not unify or edify the body. The addition of the wrong staff person, for example, may divide a congregation into two groups each having its own loyalties. The addition of a strongly worded statement in a church covenant may speak to what some people view as an obvious evil, but it may also brand a group within the church as spiritual lepers, thus ostracizing them from the rest of the congregation.

The unity of the church is a high priority in the mind of the Lord. As a result, most evangelicals would probably defend what they believe to be the essentials of the faith. However, they would also be reluctant to support change that causes disunity on a peripheral doctrine or lifestyle practice.

## THEY HAVE NOT BEEN CONSULTED ABOUT THE PROPOSED CHANGE

Sometimes the leadership of a church operates under the mistaken premise that they are in charge. Be aware that the workers are the people who really run the show. Sometimes teachers, youth sponsors, committee members, or other workers simply do not want to do things as the leadership proposes. Perhaps the proposed change requires skills for which the workers are not trained. Perhaps the leadership has taken the workers for granted, not asking their opinion before instituting change that affects them. Perhaps the workers find the demands of their leaders too difficult or too time-consuming to accomplish.

Perhaps the workers are in the midst of a period when change has taken place too fast and too furiously. They have not had time to catch their breath. They are burned out and confused by constant change over which they have had no control. Perhaps they are standing on their authority as volunteer workers to resist changes proposed by their leaders because they believe the leadership does not want to understand their position. In that situation a tremendous communication gap may have developed between the workers and their leaders. Since the workers are volunteers and are absolutely necessary to the operation, they know that they are really in charge. Sometimes they will object to change simply to demonstrate that fact.

THEY ARE TIRED OF CONTINUOUS CHANGE

In his book *The Dynamics of Planned Change*,[3] Donald Lippitt states that whether we like it or not, continuous change is not a possibility. The most common possible pattern involves spurts of change separated by longer periods of apparent nonchange. That is not all bad because it allows for a period of preparation between periods of change. The change agent who is driven to keep the momentum of change going may be defeating his own purpose.

Lippitt suggests that even the appearance of resistance to change is not always bad. The fact that people resist, he says, suggests that important parts of the present unsatisfactory system are weakening. As a result, people are forced to work harder to defend it. Lippitt names four additional reasons for resistance to change, reasons that are discussed in the paragraphs below.[4]

THEY ARE RELUCTANT TO CALL A CURRENT PROJECT A FAILURE

Why is there such a proliferation of programs in the local church? I believe it is because we are reluctant to call programs unsuc-

3. Donald Lippitt, *The Dynamics of Planned Change* (New York: Harcourt Brace, 1958), p. 180.
4. Ibid., pp. 180-81.

cessful. Perhaps a program is a special pet of someone with considerable influence. Who wants to cross him? Maybe sentiment and tradition would be violated if the program were discontinued and a new one introduced. Perhaps it would be a blow to the ego of a church to discontinue a program into which it has invested much money and effort. As a result, many leaders try to add new programs without examining others to see if they should be abandoned.

By not abandoning the old programs, the church stretches its resources thin. It may be impossible for it to institute the new programs that would breathe new life into the congregation. Excessive multiplication of programs thus taxes the limited pool of workers to the extent that they are unable to do anything with skill and expertise.

Many times people do not want to engage in changes that will initiate new programs because they realize that the church is already over-programmed and the workers overtaxed. In churches that try continually to start new programs without retiring old programs it is no wonder that people resist change.

THEY FEAR FAILURE

Sometimes people resist change because they fear failure. This fear of failure may be extended to fear of anything new. A church with which I am acquainted had a poor self-image. That image had been reinforced by a succession of senior pastors who saw their ministry in that church as unsuccessful. In turn, these pastors conveyed their feelings of unsuccessful ministry to the people and even intimated that the people were the ones to blame. As a result, the people of that church were reluctant to try anything new for fear they would fail. The standard slogan of the church became, "Oh, we could never do anything like that. We're too small. We don't have enough trained workers."

If a church has not had a record of success, the people will be reluctant to try new initiatives. In this situation as in others, the attitudes and actions of the church leaders will be the key to the congregation's venturing out into something exciting and different for God. If the leaders convince the people that they are a group of losers with only limited potential, fear of failure will doom the church to a life of failure. Nothing ventured, nothing feared!

### THEY HAVE LEARNED TO EXPECT FAILURE

A contrast to the church above, which never attempted to do anything of significance, is the church that tries but does not succeed. This type of church is self-burned. It poured significant efforts into a succession of programs that fell flat. Perhaps several years ago it had tremendous expectations that arose out of an evangelistic effort that eventually failed. It may not occur to such a church that the failure occurred because of improper planning and strategy. All it knows is that it tried and failed. Out of that experience has grown a fatalistic expectation of failure in anything that it might initiate. The members of such a church solemnly ask each other, "What would happen if we tried that and failed again?"

### THEY ARE AFRAID OF LOSING SOMETHING

Sometimes people resist change because they will lose something precious, some current satisfaction, if the change occurs. If the evening service were discontinued, for example, when would people get to sing the old sentimental gospel songs that have emotional overtones for so many? When would people be able to enjoy the fellowship that follows the evening service, either in the church vestibule or at a nearby restaurant over a cup of coffee?

The idea of retaining an evening service may have nothing to do with whether or not people actually receive benefits from the service itself. Retention of the service may be predicated upon an entirely different set of emotional, sentimental, or social values. It may not be readily apparent to the leader why the people are holding on to a tradition so tightly. A little study will show, however, that they are guarding that tradition or program because discontinuing it or putting something new in its place will cause them to lose what they now enjoy and believe is valuable.

The person fearing the loss may not even admit to the leader the real reason he believes it is so vital for the church to retain a function or practice. He spiritualizes the issue and gives the leader some kind of theological argument. It takes an astute leader to cut through this kind of smoke screen and find out what is really at stake with the person who is so reluctant to experience change.

Let's make it more personal. What if the church opted for a new governance pattern and I lost my position? What would happen to the power I as a leader now enjoy? What would happen to the dependency people now have on me? Could it be that I would lose my sense of importance entirely and be lost in the crowd? Undoubtedly thinking along these lines is the real reason many church leaders resist change in a governance pattern.

People whose special emotional needs are met through current church practices and structures will be reluctant to approve changes that threaten those practices and structures. Similarly, people will resist changes that threaten to reduce their status or importance within the influence structure of the church they serve.

## WHY DO PEOPLE AGREE TO CHANGE?

However, there is also good news! There are conditions under which people will agree to change. In fact there are conditions under which people will come to regard change as an opportunity rather than a threat. In the next few paragraphs I will attempt to describe those conditions.

### THEY SEE THE CLIMATE AS CONDUCIVE TO CHANGE

In *The Change Agent*,[5] Lyle Schaller suggests that a church leader desiring to see change should deliberately encourage an increase in the level of discontent with the status quo. I would add that the leader should develop this discontent not by complaining about what exists but by continually painting pictures of what could be. It is even better when he can illustrate those pictures by pointing to successful working models. When people realize that their leader's dream has already become a reality in another congregation they will be more apt to look at it as a possibility for themselves. Painting a picture of what can be is one step in creating a climate receptive to change.

What the church needs is visionary leaders who will do their homework, discover what has been done elsewhere, find out ways to replicate that success, and optimistically convey the possibilities to their people.

5. Lyle Schaller, *The Change Agent: The Strategy of Innovative Leadership* (Nashville: Abingdon, 1972), p. 64.

THEY ARE CONVINCED THAT CHANGE IS LEGITIMATE

Some areas are legitimate candidates for change, and others are not. If a congregation is theologically sound and is given time to adequately think through areas of potential change, the changes that are truly legitimate will make themselves evident. Unless people sense that legitimacy, they will be reluctant to agree to change.

Sometimes change is resisted because people lack information. When they have had an adequate chance to examine a specific change biblically and have had the opportunity to discuss the issue among themselves, even some of the diehards will agree to change. Surprisingly, many times people who have been the strongest opponents of a change become champions of that change when they are convinced it is a biblical, rational, and legitimate approach for their church.

THEY SEE THE OLD SYSTEM AS NO LONGER MEETING THEIR NEEDS

When people get sufficiently unhappy with what they have, they will often be more agreeable toward change. Unhappiness in a church may arise for many reasons: poor preaching, tight finances, meaningless programs, lack of shepherding, worker fatigue, failure to have one's needs met, inability to serve meaningfully, inadequate facilities, frustration with the leadership, interpersonal difficulties, and others.

If the dissatisfaction level rises high enough, people may become more and more willing to agree not only to change but to initiate it. Then the trick is to be sure that change moves in the right direction. The nice thing about changes such as this is that most church members will not only heartily agree to such changes but will call the leader blessed who initiates that change. When the sources of widespread annoyance are removed, then it is likely that there will be ample opportunity to change other things and set the church on its way to health once again.

When assessing the climate for this kind of change, it is important that there is ample assurance of overall, mass discontentment with the status quo rather than mistakenly identifying the complaints of a few malcontents as being the overall sentiments of the congregation. If there is not widespread discontent by a consensus of people within the church, the most dangerous thing a leader can do is to try to bring about precipitous, radical changes in areas only a few noisy people are complaining about. Look carefully and thoroughly before you leap!

## THEY KNOW THAT THEY NO LONGER HAVE THE ANSWERS

In a subsequent chapter we will discuss cognitive disequilibrium, the sensation summed up in the quip, "Just when I thought I had all the answers, they changed all the questions." The potential change agent must be aware when people experience periods of intense crisis. During those times people are ripe to realize dramatic, positive changes in their thought processes and in their lives. When a person goes through such a crisis period, the godly change agent walks with him, offering comfort, understanding, and information. In so doing he helps his friend to realize dramatic positive rather than negative changes in his mind-set.

Churches, too, go through such periods of crisis. During those periods the wise leader gently and persuasively leads his people into new paths of adventure and service in behalf of Jesus Christ.

## THEIR ATTITUDES HAVE BEEN CHANGED

What entices people to buy a product? They change their attitude toward it, becoming convinced that they can hardly do without it. As we increase the attractiveness of a goal, the proposed changes brought about by realizing that goal become acceptable and desirable.

The ingenious change agent educates people in such a way that they come to desire goals and the accompanying changes brought about by realizing those goals. He does that by bringing about a drastic change in the attitudes of his people. A chapter later in this book describes how church leaders in partnership with the Holy Spirit can bring about changed attitudes in people.

Perhaps you have tried to bring about change in the past and failed. That's why you are reluctant now. May I challenge you to try again. Having gained a better understanding of why people resist change and how people can be made open to change, you are bound to do a better job next time. Remember, God has not called you as a leader to perpetuate the status quo!

## Additional Resources

Allen, Blaine. *When God Says No.* Nashville: Nelson, 1981.
Dittes, Ames E. *When People Say No.* San Francisco: Harper & Row, 1979.
McDonough, Reginald M. *Keys to Effective Motivation.* Nashville: Broadman, 1976.
Perry, Lloyd. *Getting the Church on Target.* Chicago: Moody, 1977.
————. *The Decision Makers.* Nashville: Abingdon, 1974.

## Questions for Discussion

1. Examine your heart. How open are you to changes that are not your pet changes? What steps can you take to develop a better approach to change? Discuss the role of the Holy Spirit and prayer in bringing about change in the church.

2. What steps can leaders take to prove the necessity of change? How can they make change more acceptable and comfortable to those who resist it? If it is true that people resist change because they don't trust their leaders, what does that say about where change is needed most?

3. Discuss how people should be told of proposed changes and how much time they should be given to think about those changes. To what degree should the congregation be involved in determining what should be changed, making important decisions, setting goals, and evaluating programs?

4. What criteria should be used to determine which are high and which are low priority items? Discuss the dangers in trying to sell everything as a high priority item.

5. What are the indicators that the timing for a certain change is best and that the change will be successful? What obstacles might indicate to you that a certain change will not meet with success? How can you overcome those obstacles?

# 11

# MORAL STAGES AND CHANGE

Webster's dictionary defines the word *oxymoron* as "a combination of contradictory or incongruous words."[1] The elements of an oxymoron contradict themselves, leaving the expression meaningless. The expression "detached leader" is a classic oxymoron, for the words *detached* and *leader* do not go together. The essence of leadership demands involvement with people—loving people, understanding people, and being patient with people. None of that is easy. But all leaders need to be willing to try.

## LAWRENCE KOHLBERG'S THEORY OF HUMAN BEHAVIOR

To deal effectively with people we need to know what makes a person tick. We must get to know our people as individuals. That means spending time with them, especially those for whom we have direct supervisory responsibilities. But since we are also called upon to serve numbers of individuals, we need to go beyond individualized contacts and select methods that meet the needs of numbers of people at once. We need to operate from an orderly pattern of human behavior

1. *Webster's Ninth New Collegiate Dictionary,* s.v. "oxymoron. "

that applies to just about everybody. We need to know if there are groups of people who fit into the same pattern. Then we can employ methods that minister to individuals and groups in our church more effectively.

Does such a pattern exist? I believe it does. The pattern is one developed by Lawrence Kohlberg, a proponent of the developmental, or stage-theory, school of educational theory who built his work on the theories of the Swiss philosopher Jean Piaget. In this chapter I will outline and then apply to the leadership task what Kohlberg had to say about human behavior. I will be using as a base for my remarks a book on Piaget and Kohlberg written by Ronald Duska and Mariellen Whelen, *Moral Development: A Guide to Piaget and Kohlberg.*[2]

Kohlberg began his work in the early sixties. Initially, he interviewed young men who ranged in age from ten to twenty-eight. He interviewed those subjects once every three years for eighteen years. In his interviews, Kohlberg posed a moral problem or ethical dilemma and asked his subjects to propose solutions. Once a solution was given, Kohlberg asked the person his reason for solving the problem the way he did. Through analyzing the participant's reason for his decision, Kohlberg determined the stage of moral reasoning to which that person belonged. From the observations gained from the interviews, Kohlberg identified at least six stages of thinking his subjects went through in their social development. Those stages he defined as stages of "moral reasoning."

There were some variations. Though Kohlberg's subjects went through the same basic pattern and sequence of stages, they did not do so at the same rate of speed. Also, some reached a certain stage and progressed no further. Others who progressed fairly far did not reach what Kohlberg called the highest stages of development.

The stages Kohlberg postulated indicated a person's primary cognitive orientation, his dominant frame of mind. They were not descriptions of a person's actual behavior. After all, a person may act in a certain way for any number of reasons, not all of them necessarily a product of his rational reasoning.

In the years following that initial study, Kohlberg and his associates interviewed selected groups of people from other cultures. The

2. Ronald Duska and Mariellen Whelen, *Moral Development: A Guide to Piaget and Kohlberg* (New York: Paulist), 1975.

results were similar to those they obtained from subjects in the United States. Stage development was apparently a cross-cultural phenomenon that applied to people in general, irrespective of their background.

Other observations and assertions concerning Kohlberg's system:[3]

1. "Stage development is invariant." Everyone progresses through the stages in the same order without skipping any stages. To reach stage four a person must go through stages one, two, and three in that order.

2. A person "can be attracted to reasoning one stage higher than his predominant stage." Thus a stage one person is attracted to stage two thinking.

3. People "cannot comprehend moral reasoning at a stage more than one stage ahead beyond their own." A stage one person can understand stage two thinking but nothing beyond that.

4. People can understand and identify with thinking in any stage through which they have already come. Residuals of this thinking still influence them. Thoughts from previous stages, however, do not represent their dominant thought pattern.

5. A person may remain, or become fixated, at any stage for an indefinite period of time and fail to progress.

6. "In stage development movement through the stages is effected when cognitive disequilibrium is created, that is when a person's cognitive outlook is not adequate to cope with a given moral development."

Cognitive dissonance is what you feel when you say, "Just when I thought I had all the answers, they changed the questions." The dictionary gives a less tongue-in-check definition: "psychological conflict resulting from incongruous beliefs and attitudes held simultaneously."[4] Cognitive disequilibrium occurs when new information or experiences do not make sense within old ways of thinking.

3. Ibid., pp. 47-49, 102-3.
4. *Webster's Ninth New Collegiate Dictionary*, s.v. "cognitive dissonance."

## KOHLBERG'S SIX STAGES OF MORAL DEVELOPMENT

Kohlberg identified three distinct levels of thinking, each of which included two stages. The three distinct levels Kohlberg called *pre-conventional, conventional,* and *post-conventional.*[5]

### PRE-CONVENTIONAL LEVEL

In this phase, people are basically egocentrically motivated. Decisions as to what is right and wrong are made according to the physical consequences. The person reasons that if an action will result in punishment, it is wrong; but if it should bring him a reward or favor, it is right. Morality is practiced in terms of avoiding painful experiences and seeking rewarding ones. The pre-conventional level is divided into two stages:

*Stage one: The Punishment and Obedience Orientation.* Here "the physical consequences of action determines its goodness or badness regardless of the human meaning of those consequences." A person obeys rules to avoid punishment. He defers to authority because he believes that if he doesn't he might get into trouble. "Avoidance of punishment and unquestioning deference to power are valued in their own right, not in terms of respect for an underlying moral order."

*Stage two: The Instrumental Relational Orientation.* "Right action consists of that which . . . satisfies one's own needs and occasionally the needs of others." Satisfying the needs of others is seen only in terms of the benefits of reciprocation. "If you scratch my back . . . I'll scratch yours."

### CONVENTIONAL LEVEL

This is the "groupie" level, where people identify personal satisfaction in terms of service to the group to which they belong. Important to a person at this level are the expectations of "the individual's family, group, or nation." The "attitude is not only one of conformity to personal expectations and social order but of loyalty to it." He not only maintains, supports, and justifies the order, he also identifies with "the persons or groups involved in it." His identity is bound up in "belongingness."

---

5. Descriptions that follow are taken from Duska and Whelen, *Moral Development,* pp. 45-47.

*Stage three: The Interpersonal Concordance Orientation.* "Good behavior is what pleases or helps others and is approved by them." In this stage "one earns approval by 'being nice,'" conforming to the expectations of the group to which he belongs, whether that group is represented by the First Presbyterian Church or the Cosa Nostra.

*Stage four: The Law and Order Orientation.* In this stage, a person still identifies himself in relation to a group and that group's expectations. Yet an added dimension is introduced. Because he believes that a system of rules and regulations is necessary to keep his group alive, he will defend that set of rules almost with his life. Right behavior then becomes doing one's duty, respecting authority, and "maintaining the given social order for its own sake," regardless of any personal satisfaction he gets out of behaving in this manner.

POST-CONVENTIONAL, AUTONOMOUS, OR PRINCIPLED LEVEL

"At this level there is a clear effort to define moral values and principles which have validity and application apart from the authority of the groups or persons holding these principles and apart from the individual's own identification with these groups."

*Stage five: The Social Contract Legalistic Orientation.* Stage five people recognize that there are standards of conduct that "have been critically examined and agreed upon by the whole society." However, where standards are not defined, "right is a matter of personal values and opinion." Although a stage five person emphasizes what is legal, he does not consider the law sacrosanct in itself. If the law no longer serves society, individuals can use legal processes to change it. This is in sharp distinction from stage four, where the emphasis is on rigidly maintaining the law whether or not people feel it is desirable.

*Stage six: The Universal Ethical Principle Orientation.* Here, "right is defined by the decision of conscience in accord with self-chosen, ethical principles appealing to logical comprehensiveness, universality, and consistency." These are "abstract and ethical" principles rather than "concrete moral rules like the ten commandments." They espouse justice for all, "the reciprocity and equality of human rights, and . . . respect for the dignity of human beings as individual persons.

## General Observations Concerning Kohlberg's Work

The term "stages of moral development" is confusing to a great many people. Many people today identify "morality" in terms of a person's conduct in regard to specific moral issues. Yet Kohlberg is identifying an underlying structure dependent not only on a person's cognitive development but also his degree of interaction with his social environment. In addition, the six stages in Kohlberg's system progress on a social continuum rather than a moral one. The early stages are primarily egocentric, whereas the latter stages indicate an increasing degree of social interaction and responsibility. The stages are probably better described as stages of "social awareness" or "social sensitivity."

The stages might be renamed on another account. The reasons the subjects gave for their "moral decisions" were not in themselves truly moral reasons. In *Educating for Responsible Actions,* Nicholas Woltersdorff states: "The reasons characteristic of these first four stages are not correct ones. The ultimate reason for thinking it is right to act in a certain way is not that one will bring pleasure to oneself or earn oneself social approval, but that by doing so we will fulfill the demands of love, so none of these first four stages is ultimately acceptable as a cognitive structure for morality."[6]

Though the first four stages are fairly well defined and reasonably easy to understand, the last two are somewhat nebulous and abstract. Woltersdorff intimates that Kohlberg may even be speculating on the latter two stages rather than appealing to scientific evidence. He writes: "What does seem to be true is that stages one through four are conceptually quite clear, and have some empirical confirmation, whereas by contrast the empirical confirmation for the presence and the order of stages five and six is almost nonexistent."[7]

As a result of these observations, Woltersdorff, who in many respects is quite critical of Kohlberg, nevertheless admits: "We should probably assume that people do in fact go through something like Kohlberg's first four stages. And I think we should assume that the reasons characteristic of these stages are internalized by people in the stages."[8]

6. Nicholas Woltersdorff, *Educating for Responsible Action* (Grand Rapids: Eerdmans, 1980), p. 93.
7. Ibid., p. 91.
8. Ibid., p. 93.

In a nutshell, what Woltersdorff is trying to tell us is that stage four, the Law and Order stage, is the highest stage to which an individual may aspire in what Kohlberg calls "moral development" and what I have termed "social sensitivity." I am uncomfortable with Woltersdorff's position. Perhaps the problem lies with Kohlberg's inability to accurately define the last two stages. Certainly observation alone would give plenty of evidence of Christians who have progressed from the harshness and judgmental attitudes of stage four thinking to something that resembles stage five. Our Lord gives evidence of stage six thinking. The apostle Paul, among others, though never giving clear evidence that he had reached anything resembling stage six, seemed to comprehend and aspire to such thinking.

Though not agreeing to stages five and six, nevertheless Woltersdorff lends his voice to the testimonies of an increasing number of educators and social scientists who believe that Piaget and Kohlberg are correct in their basic premises. If we can find biblical examples to correspond with some of the work of these developmentalists, it will lead us to a system that can help us determine where people are in their thinking. Then we will be able to understand them better and know better how we should lead them.

## APPLYING KOHLBERG'S SIX STAGES TO CHRISTIAN LEADERSHIP

To clarify our thinking, let's look once again at the stages.

### APPLYING STAGE ONE:
### THE PUNISHMENT AND OBEDIENCE ORIENTATION

Initially Kohlberg included children of ages ten to thirteen in this stage along with certain adults who are fixated at this level. Probably this was the stage our original ancestors were in after they ate the fruit from the tree of the knowledge of good and evil in the Garden of Eden.

In stage one, God could be seen as a killjoy, an ominous-appearing old man who peers over the clouds of heaven watching man for any infraction of His moral code. The God in this picture is almost sadistic in His thinking, waiting for people to slip up in the most infinitesimal way so that He may gleefully zap them. The single word best describing this stage is *fear*. Appeals to this stage include Dante's *Inferno*, Jonathan Edwards's famous sermon, "Sinners in the Hands of An Angry

God," and the histrionics of certain modern-day, hellfire-and-brimstone preachers.

How effective is using fear to convict and convert a person? How effective is fear as a weapon for goading Christians into more responsible Christian action? For most people in North America today, scare tactics are about as effective as they were when the prophets used them in the closing days of the kingdoms of Israel and Judah. Why? Because by the time the hellfire-and-brimstone preacher preaches, people have already moved on to another stage. The cutting edge of fear in their lives has been dulled.

We must be careful not to dismiss the possibility of some people being in stage one. When my wife and I had been married almost twenty years, the Lord brought a new child into our lives. When he arrived he was fourteen years old. Almost immediately we began to speak of our faith in a quiet, noncoercive manner, but he steadfastly refused to take the step of committing his life to the Lord Jesus Christ.

After more than a year had gone by and he had learned to trust us, he came to me one day and told me he was ready to become a Christian. A beautiful conversion experience occurred. Following his prayer of commitment I asked him to tell my wife what had happened to him. After he had done so, she asked him, "How do you feel?" His answer was, "Just great! I'm not afraid anymore." She questioned him further, "Afraid of what?" "I'm not afraid of dying and going to hell anymore," was his answer. Even though we had never approached him at that level of discussion, it is apparent that our son's primary cognitive orientation was one of fear and that his response to God was on the basis of that particular stage of understanding.

Is it wrong to appeal to a person for evangelistic and edificational purposes on the basis of fear? Probably not, if that's where he is in his thinking. It would be wrong, however, to try to keep a person in that stage and thus prey upon those fears in order to manipulate him.

When a person moves out of stage one into stage two, does it mean that fear no longer exists in his life? Not at all. He can continue to understand a stage of development he has already gone through. Residuals of fear remain in a person at any stage of life. Some of those residuals are built-in and God-given for the sake of self-preservation. Moving to another stage merely means that fear is no longer a person's primary cognitive orientation and no longer has an intense grip on his life.

APPLYING STAGE TWO:
THE INSTRUMENTAL RELATIVIST ORIENTATION

The one word to describe stage two people is *hedonism*. They avoid the unpleasant and major on the pleasant. The Scriptures are full of examples of people in this stage, such as the children of Israel, who escaped Egypt and then griped about the lack of culinary delights, and the people described by the prophet Haggai. "You have sown much, but harvest little; you eat, but there is not enough to be satisfied; you drink, but there is not enough to become drunk; you put on clothing, but no one is warm enough; and he who earns, earns wages to put into a purse with holes" (Haggai 1:6).

The reference is strikingly contemporary. No matter how much we have, it is never enough. We constantly crave more. If we were looking for a stage to characterize us, stage two would probably win.

A person in the Christian community may look at God with stage two eyes and view Him as the great benefactor. Perhaps he was attracted to Christianity because of what was in it for him. A highly successful tract, "Have You Heard of The Four Spiritual Laws?" is oriented directly toward stage two thinking. Do you remember how it begins? "God loves you and offers a wonderful plan for your life." How could a person miss when a deal such as that is offered? It is interesting that this particular tract has enjoyed its greatest success among college undergraduates, especially those living in dormitories and fraternity houses. Why? That group of people represents the world's largest collection of young hedonists. I believe that God gave that approach to Bill Bright to meet the needs of that audience.

A person's views toward the church at this stage: "What do I get out of it?" If he is entertained by a spectacular music program and is fed by an articulate preacher, he may stay. If not, he will seek a more comfortable pasture.

To keep a stage two person in the church on a long-term basis the church may have to provide other benefits, such as an exciting youth program, a spotless nursery, and a dynamic women's ministry. If he doesn't get all of those things, he will move on—and the church will no longer receive the five dollars a week he normally contributes.

Is it wrong to attract people on this basis? Of course not, if that's where they are in their thinking. I am convinced, however, that it is a crime to keep people at stage two, for then they will always be spectators. They will never truly get involved in the ministry of a local church. They will miss out on the joys such service brings.

APPLYING STAGE THREE:
THE INTERPERSONAL CONCORDANCE ORIENTATION

In stage three a person moves out of his purely egocentric orientation. His identity becomes bound up in the group or groups of which he is a member. He supports the group wholeheartedly and rigorrously tries to live up its ideals. He is the classical groupie.

Instead of thinking of action in terms of its personal consequences, the stage three person thinks of action in terms of how it fulfills the expectations of the group. Personal consequences are purely coincidental. At this stage real socialization occurs. A person is willing to sacrifice for the sake of his group. His rewards come from the group's approval. In order to realize those rewards he is willing to pitch in and do his share. Membership fulfills his need for a feeling of self-worth. Egotism is not completely gone, however. It appears in a more subtle form and in a more indirect reward system.

Christians are happy to sing, "I'm so glad I'm a part of the family of God." In a denominational sense, that sentiment may result in loyalty to a particular group. That loyalty is so strong in stage three people that when they move to a distant city they usually unite with a church of the same denomination.

On the surface everything seems to be joy and brightness as far as the stage three person is concerned. But there are drawbacks. Sometimes his efforts do not please the members of the group. Is pleasing others the sole criterion of what is good or bad? Surely a person's motives are important as well. What about the people in the group who refuse to play their roles? What happens if a person is a member of more than one group, each of which has differing expectations, and those expectations clash? What happens when conflicting roles cast by each of those groups demand of a person opposite courses of action? What if one of the groups to which a person belongs insists that its membership do that which is immoral or illegal?

Stage three people are wonderful to have in a congregation. They are the tireless workers a leader can always depend upon. They also tithe faithfully. On the other hand, they are already so happy with the church that they cannot be counted on to bring others into the group.

Although one would think that non-Christian stage three people would be so attracted to groups that they would seek the Savior just to be part of His family, that is not necessarily so. Many times they are already faithful members of other organizations, such as the Masons, Moose, Kiwanis (or all of these), and find their needs so well met there that they see little need for becoming a church member.

Group thinking can prove disastrous. It is difficult to estimate the number of progressive church leaders who have been run off by some "in" group in the church. Moreover, group pressures can force a person to engage in behavior he would ordinarily consider unthinkable. Witness the antics of the group in Sinai that erected the golden calf. They had progressed from stage two to stage three. How do we know? They willingly gave up their jewelry to the group so that the group's goals could be realized. Though they had moved to a more socially oriented stage of development, the results were disastrous.

Despite its drawbacks, stage three thinking is still more desirable than stage two. In stage two the "real church" is composed only of its leaders. The rest of the folks are not actually a part of the church. They just come and go and enjoy the benefits. When stage three is reached, the entity becomes the church of the people, and every part of the body is important.

APPLYING STAGE FOUR:
THE LAW AND ORDER ORIENTATION

"America, love it or leave it." "My country, right or wrong." Those might be slogans used by a stage four person. Like the stage three person, the stage four person finds his personal identity and value in the group to which he belongs. Unlike a stage three person, he views the rules and regulations of the group to be absolutely essential to keeping the group together and preserving its identity.

Because a stage four person receives his sense of identification from the group, and because he views the rules and regulations of the group as a cohesive necessity, he reasons, *If the rules are broken, the group will fall apart, and I won't know who I am.* As a result, he holds rigidly to the rules and makes sure everybody else does too. If someone breaks the rules, the stage four person will be sure to report the violator to "those in charge," even if the transgressor is one of his own family.

He sees right behavior as "doing one's duty." He will obey a law even if it is a bad law. Biblical examples of such people are plentiful. Probably the Pharisees thought this way, including their most famous ex-member, Saul of Tarsus, who experienced cognitive disequilibrium on the road to Damascus and eventually became a stage five thinker.

Current examples of stage four thinking may be found in churches that have elaborate lifestyle statements they rigidly enforce. Such lists intricately spell out dos and don'ts so that the Christian has no question as to what is or is not appropriate behavior. In some churches, the unwritten codes are just as binding as written ones.

It is not good enough for a stage four person that the Bible often paints a broad and sweeping picture. A stage four person must have everything nailed down. Once such a system has been spelled out, he is more than willing to impose it on others.

Sometimes a stage four person will remain rigidly entrenched until a member of his own family goes bad and suffers some calamity, such as divorce or imprisonment. When that occurs, the stage four person will either become fixated at that level and reject the errant member of his family, or he will be propelled into stage five thinking by the cognitive disequilibrium introduced by the calamity.

Stage four thinking is an advancement over stage three thinking in that the motive is no longer egocentric. In stage four, a person has a high moral code. He does his duty regardless of whether or not it pleases others and is accepted by the group. He receives no promise of a reward, only the inner satisfaction that he has acted the way he believes is right. His personal self-view is different from a stage three person in that instead of seeing himself merely as a member of a group, he sees himself more generally as a member of society, with certain societal obligations. A stage four person can be delightful to work with as long as the person working with him fits the same mold and has the same ideas.

To the leader who wants to see dramatic differences in the lives of individuals and in the life of a church, the stage four person may be the hardest of all people with whom he must deal. Although Jesus applauded moral behavior, He was the most uncomplimentary toward stage four people. He called them "vipers" and "wolves in sheep's clothing."

APPLYING STAGE FIVE:
THE SOCIAL CONTRACT LEGALISTIC ORIENTATION

In stage five thinking we leave the concrete, easily demonstrated categories of level one and move into the hazy, more abstract realm of what Kohlberg calls the "autonomous" or "principled" level, level two. In deference to Woltersdorff, who is critical of this level, it does seem that Kohlberg had a hard time describing this level and of differentiating the thinking belonging to the particular stages that compose it.

Kohlberg's description of a stage five individual paints the picture of a person who accepts a set of rules or laws not as something handed down from deity but as something invented by man. Since society is absolutely essential and its preservation mandatory to a stage five person, he believes that man must democratically design laws to meet society's need for order and preservation.

A stage five person will obey the laws of society, but since he does not view those laws as sacred he will constantly and critically examine the rules to determine whether or not they should be changed. If he believes change is necessary he will work hard to bring that change about. Where the law does not speak to an area of behavior, a stage five person considers himself free to make his own choices and act as he sees fit.

So far we have examined stage five in a purely secular context. If we agreed that this is all that this stage entails, then, like Woltersdorff, we would have to reject it. We who call ourselves Christians cannot concede that all law is invented by man. We have an allegiance to a law given to us by God Himself. Is stage five thinking entirely out of the range of a Christian? Most certainly, if we agree to Kohlberg's narrow definition. But if we broaden that definition, we could probably make way for a "Christian stage five."

A person in that stage would start with a basic criterion different from the standard orientation Kohlberg suggests. In the act of becoming a Christian, a Christian stage five person would have already agreed to the presence of a preexistent, universal authority whom the Christian calls "Father." He would also have agreed to submit himself to that authority. The way the Christian knows what God wants for him to do in specific areas of life is to read the Bible. The Bible is his guidebook. He voluntarily and willingly accepts it as God's word of instruction to him. Where the Bible is not explicit on a subject, he has freedom of choice. As he chooses, however, he follows guidelines such as these:

1. Is this action glorifying to God, since the major purpose of my existence is to glorify Him?

2. Is this action beneficial rather than detrimental to my body, the temple of the Holy Spirit? Is this action beneficial to the Body of Christ? As a member, I have an obligation to edify rather than hurt that body.

3. Is this action beneficial rather than detrimental to my fellow Christian? Is there a chance that it may cause a weaker brother or sister to stumble?

4. Is this action discreet and appropriate considering the circumstances involved? Is it in good taste, so that the reputation of my life will enhance the reputation of the Lord Jesus?

5. Does this action demonstrate to the world the single factor whereby I am to be identified to the world as a Christian? Is it a demonstration of love toward another Christian?

In regard to his society and his church, the stage five Christian agrees that people do construct systems of rules and regulations so that they can live together in harmony and cooperation. However, unlike a stage four person, he can look objectively at the rules and regulations constructed by people and decide for himself whether or not the rules need to be changed. Then he uses his influence to bring about the changes he believes are necessary. That is quite a different approach than the blind and rigid acceptance of rules and regulations found in stage four.

APPLYING STAGE SIX:
THE UNIVERSAL ETHICAL PRINCIPLE ORIENTATION

Those who reach stage six possess the wisdom of the ages. Imprinted indelibly on their thought patterns are general ethical principles so all-inclusive that the application of those principles always results in the proper moral behavior.

Stage six presupposes that a person has reached the point where he possesses enough wisdom to make decisions completely on the basis of his own choice without appealing to any external authority. So abstract is this stage of development that Kohlberg himself admitted that data on it were extremely rare.

Despite Kohlberg's references to the writings of Ghandi and Martin Luther King, both of whom Kohlberg believed were stage six thinkers, I believe it is impossible for mortal man to reach this stage. Only the God-man, Jesus Christ, possessed the knowledge and wisdom to be classified a true stage six thinker. That does not mean that other people cannot comprehend stage six thinking, be attracted to it, and aspire to it. One of Kohlberg's basic premises is that a person can understand and be attracted to the stage beyond the one in which he resides. Certainly the apostle Paul understood stage six thinking, as is evident in some of his writings.

However, it is hard for me to believe that even the apostle Paul reached stage six as his primary cognitive orientation. As I read other passages from his letters I see lifelong struggles in which he was not able to discover for himself the proper answers. As I look at much of what masquerades today as stage six thinking, I fear that it is merely situation ethics, which, in turn, often may turn out to be stage two thinking in poor disguise.

Although it might be interesting to have a whole church full of stage six people, I don't think that is going to happen. So, trust me, don't worry about it. How nice it would be, however, if we as leaders had stage six thoughts even once in a while.

## What Do We Do with This Information?

If Kohlberg's theory is correct, where do we go from here?

First, we do not need to accept all of Kohlberg's conclusions. He makes no pretense of being a Christian. Though his data probably are correct, he filters that data through non-Christian presuppositions, which would necessarily influence his choices. What, then, can we accept of this findings? We can accept a good deal if we approach Kohlberg's work properly. The following suggest ways a church leader can do that.

USE THE STAGES TO APPROACH PEOPLE PROPERLY

There is evidence independent of Kohlberg to suggest that people develop in stages. Probably those stages are much like Kohlberg describes them, especially stages one through four. I believe the Holy Spirit works primarily through orderly processes rather than miracles. If that is true, and if Kohlberg has been able to uncover a basic pattern through which men progress in their thinking about moral issues, Kohlberg's system may be close to the pattern the Holy Spirit follows as He intervenes in the thought processes of people. So Kohlberg's insights may help us avoid methods and content that detract from the Holy Spirit's work.

Suppose a young man aspires to the pastorate and to that end spends seven or eight years getting a "proper" theological education. By the time he completes that training he is probably steeped in stage four or stage five thinking and terminology. Yet his first professional responsibility is to a small church in a rural or suburban area where most of his people operate at stage two, or at the most, stage three thinking.

As our young "theolog" begins to relate to his people personally and in the pulpit he tends to communicate with them according to his own dominant thought pattern. As his people listen to him, they like him but cannot understand what he is saying. That is because he is conveying stage five values, whereas they relate only to stages below that level. The young pastor is unaware that he is asking his people to take giant steps when all they are capable of is baby steps. He is asking his people to do the impossible. They cannot make the growth he wants all at once.

The situation results in frustration. The leader is frustrated because he cannot see the progress he desires to take place in the lives of his people. The people are frustrated because they do not understand their leader and cannot live up to his expectations.

The situation is likely to lead to a change of leadership, a split in the church, or the young, well-trained theolog's becoming a ministerial casualty and entering secular employment.

Consider another equally sad scenario. A leader trained in Bible college or seminary finds himself ministering to a congregation made up primarily of stage two people. He capitalizes on that and initiates a program so attractive to other stage two people in his community that the church grows dramatically. A church in a major, metropolitan area hears about his success in making churches grow and decides that he is just the man for them. However, this church is made up in large part of students and faculty members from a nearby university. The predominant thought pattern here is stage four or even stage five.

Flushed by the success of his last pastorate, our hero applies to his new charge the same type of content and methodology he employed in his old situation—and falls flat on his face. His people claim that he is not feeding them the meat of the Word and that his programs are superficial and inane. The problem? His content and methods are irrelevant to the new group of people. They have outgrown what he has to offer.

Yet since his program has been attractive enough to entice some stage two people into membership, the church now has two factions. One wholeheartedly supports the pastor; the other would like to see him removed. The two groups think so differently, a ready-made situation for a church split has developed.

The secret of success in leading people is to know where they are. Then they may be led through the growth process, one step at a time, to the point of maturity the leader had hoped they would reach.

## CONSIDER THE HOMOGENEOUS PRINCIPLE

Church growth experts point to what they call the "homogeneous principle," the concept that people desire to become Christians and to fellowship in a church made up primarily of people who are like themselves. Is it not possible that homogeneity of developmental stage should be considered by a church when it plans its outreach? Could not such homogeneity be an even greater factor with which to deal than ethnic origins or the cultural or economic group to which a person belongs? Is it not possible that a church desiring to grow should explore techniques of reaching out primarily to people who are of like mind with the people already attending the church?

## MAKE STRATEGIC USE OF COGNITIVE DISEQUILIBRIUM

I have already stated that cognitive disequilibrium is the factor that propels people through the stages to increasingly mature thought patterns. If that is true, then we ought to be alert to two important matters.

First, the overall content of what is taught in a local church should contain issues that stimulate healthy cognitive disequilibrium. That is accomplished best by the faithful, objective teaching of God's Word, not by grinding theological or methodological axes. When God's Word is taught systematically and clearly, the Holy Spirit will raise in the minds of the people the issues they need to deal with. They will begin to probe their own thought patterns and may even become dissatisfied with pat formulas and seek new and more satisfying patterns of thought.

Second, we should be alert to times of trauma in the lives of our people. Those may include births, weddings, moving to a new location or job, financial disaster, disease, surgery, menopause, middle age crisis, divorce, loss of employment, and a host of other things. Traumatic events cause people to question their thought patterns and make them receptive to change.

The alert and sensitive church leader will stay close enough to his people that he will know when they are facing those crucial times. Then he will marshal the forces of the church to come to their aid, and he will concentrate on helping them make substantive changes in their lives.

## Summing It Up

If it is indeed a principal task of the Christian leader to help his people grow, how does he do that best? He does so by recognizing that people are capable of great amounts of spiritual growth but that this growth won't take place all at once. There are no quick solutions to problems of immaturity. Consequently, he will help people grow by knowing where they are in their thought processes and concentrating his efforts on meeting them at that point.

He will help people grow by using the Word of God carefully and objectively to bring about cognitive disequilibrium. He will avoid grinding his personal, theological, or methodological axes. He knows when his people are facing crisis experiences, knowing that those are the times they are most responsive to growth. He will relate to people in a crisis situation in such a way that the resulting change in their thinking is a positive one.

Detached leadership is an oxymoron. Only the leader who stays close to his people and works hard to understand his them will be effective in leading them toward spiritual growth.

## Additional Resources

Adams, Jay E. *Shepherding God's Flock.* Grand Rapids: Zondervan, 1987.

Barrs, Jerram. *Shepherds and Sheep: A Biblical View of Leading and Following.* Downers Grove, Ill.: InterVarsity, 1983.

Crabb, Lawrence J., and Daniel B. Allender. *Encouragement: The Key to Caring.* Grand Rapids: Zondervan, 1984.

Crabb, Lawrence J. *Inside Out.* Colorado Springs: Navpress, 1988.

_____. *Understanding People.* Grand Rapids: Zondervan, 1987.

Schaller, Lyle. *The Pastor and His People: Building a New Partnership for Effective Ministry.* Nashville: Abingdon, 1973.

## Questions for Discussion and Helpful Projects

1. Is there more or less an orderly pattern of human development as Piaget and Kohlberg insist? How might this pattern relate to the ministry of a church to its people? How would it relate to the role of the Holy Spirit in a person's life? How would it relate to our need as leaders to work in harmony with the Holy Spirit to minister to people?

2. If we could understand what really motivates our people, how might that change our programs of evangelism and discipleship?

PROJECT: Review the first five stages of social awareness explained in this chapter. Which stage represents a majority of the people in your congregation? What steps can your church take to make the Bible more relevant to the people in that stage? What can be done to make the Bible more relevant to people in the church who are in other stages? How are you going to best serve them?

3. Should church leaders be concerned with helping people move to a higher stage of social awareness, or should they be content to keep ministering to people in the stage they are already in?

PROJECT: Study the gospel of John and write down instances in which Jesus relates to various individuals by using methods appropriate to the stage that person is in. How many stages can you find? Can you identify instances in which Jesus helped a person move on to a different stage? How did Jesus cause cognitive disequilibrium in that individual?

4. Realizing that people cannot understand more than one stage above the one that they are in, examine the ministry of your church. Is it understandable to the people you serve? In what areas do you need to change your approach in order to bring about improvement?

# 12

# LIFE STAGES
## AND
# CHANGING
# PEOPLE'S MINDS

Though I use computers constantly, I know little about them. One day I decided to take a course to correct that deficiency. The course was a disaster as far as I was concerned, but one thing the instructor said I do remember: "Computers don't make mistakes; people do!"

Computers can work only with the facts fed to them. If they receive the wrong information, they will reach the wrong conclusions. If you program the right information into them, they will usually reach the right conclusions.

Wouldn't it be wonderful if we could program the human mind in the same way we program computers? How easy it would be to bring about widespread change in people's thinking. They would be willing to follow a leader wherever he desired to guide them. He wouldn't even have to explain his plans, actions, or motives. His people would merely respond on cue.

However, the ability to change people's minds easily might prove dangerous. What if the leader were unscrupulous? What if he wanted to bring about change only for his own selfish motives? What if he was only seeking self-aggrandizement? What if his ideas were not scriptural?

Well, thank God, the human mind is not changed that easily. However, even without that miraculous power to change minds, numerous forces today are competing with each other to program the human mind in a variety of directions. Many of them are highly successful. Television advertisers have honed this skill into a science, using ingenious means to discover what motivates people and then creating ads that influence them to buy products they don't even need. It is indeed possible to change people's minds.

As church leaders we, too, are interested in changing people's minds. So that we may do that in an ethical, effective, and biblically sound manner, I would like to examine first what the Bible teaches about changing the content of people's minds.

### CHANGING PEOPLE'S MINDS: THE WORDS THE BIBLE USES TO DESCRIBE THE PROCESS

The first of the words the Bible uses to describe the process is *nacham*,[1] describing a change of mind. This kind of change often occurs as the result of overwhelming visible evidence. A good example is in Exodus 13:17. God protected His people from evidence that would have changed their minds negatively. He kept Israel from proceeding through the land of the Philistines, the most direct route to the Promised Land, "lest the people change their minds when they see war, and they return to Egypt."

Even though the children of Israel may have been flushed with the success of their expedition so far, had they faced the superior military forces of the Philistines they would have changed their minds about going into Canaan and would have returned to Egypt instead. God kept the evidence from them so that they would not change their minds.

Among the words used by the New Testament to pick up on the Old Testament theme is the word *metaballo*. In Acts 28:6 this word indicates change in the context of turning about. As in the Old Testament example, this change of mind seems to come about as the result of striking evidence. Consequently, on the isle of Malta when Paul was bitten by a snake and the usual thing, the swelling of his hand, did not occur, the people who witnessed the event—who had at first thought of

---

1. I am deeply indebted to my former graduate assistant Douglas Soleida for his substantive research in uncovering biblical words that describe change.

him as a criminal, even a murderer—"changed their minds and began to say that he was a god" (Acts 28:6).

Visible evidence was necessary before minds would change. The leader who attempts to stand solely on the authority of his office in order to change people's minds needs to change his own mind. His people are likely to exhibit a Missouri-like stubbornness and insist, "show me." And they will be absolutely right to insist on such evidence.

Another key concept related to the changing of one's mind is what the Bible describes as the "renewing" of one's mind. In order to experience this, a person must be transformed, metamorphosed. The Greek word *metamorphoō* indicates radical change. Paul is challenging us to be engaged in the most complete change of mind possible when he writes in Romans 12:2, "And do not be conformed to this world, but be transformed by the renewing of your mind, that you may prove what the will of God is, that which is good and acceptable and perfect."

Paul also uses the word *metamorphoō* in 2 Corinthians 3:18 when he describes this grace of God working on the non-Christian to attract him to Christ, and in the Christian to bring about the process of sanctification. "But we all, with unveiled face beholding as in a mirror the glory of the Lord, are being transformed into the same image from glory to glory, just as from the Lord, the Spirit."

## Some Biblical Methods for Changing Minds

### PERSUASION

How do we change people's minds? We can do so by persuasion. There is a whole family of words to describe how this process is attempted in the Bible. The first of these, *peitho*, is found in the New Testament only. It means to bring a person to the point where he has complete confidence in something. In Luke 20:6 the people whom Jesus is teaching (with the exception of the chief priests and scribes) are completely persuaded that John the Baptist is a prophet. There is no doubt in their minds.

*Peitho* is also used in Matthew 27:20, where we are told that the chief priests and elders were able to persuade "the multitudes to ask for Barabbas, and to put Jesus to death."

Persuasion can be both damaging and successful. The apostle Paul gave witness of the positive change persuasion worked in him. Formerly he was in a legalistic stance, but now he could write in Romans 14:14, "I know and am convinced in the Lord Jesus that nothing is unclean in itself."

Through the convincing power of the Lord Jesus, Paul was persuaded to adopt a completely new value system. That was demonstrated by what may be the last words he ever wrote: "For this reason I also suffer these things, but I am not ashamed; for I know whom I have believed and I am convinced [persuaded] that He is able to guard what I have entrusted to Him until that day" (2 Timothy 1:12). Such was not a mere feeling on Paul's part. It was faith built upon observation. A complete change of mind had taken place. The evidence had been supremely persuasive.

Because of his own life and its consistency Paul could use still another word to exhort his spiritual son, Timothy, in his walk of faith, the word *plerophoreo*, which means "fully persuaded" or "fully convinced." Paul uses the term in 2 Timothy 3:14: "You, however, continue in the things you have learned and become [fully] convinced of, knowing from whom you have learned them."

Another form of this word is translated "conviction." We who live today have not experienced what the apostles did. Nevertheless, we walk by faith. The writer of Hebrews assures us, "Now faith is the assurance of things hoped for, the conviction of things not seen" (Hebrews 11:1). As Christians we are changed in mind by persuasion, responding to that which we receive on the basis of reasonable faith. As a result we become people of conviction.

In the New Testament Peter adds a further dimension to changing minds by using the word *deleazo*, "entice," to describe the tactics of false prophets who "never cease from sin, enticing unstable souls" (2 Peter 2:14). Even though the term is used here in a negative sense, can we not make a case for preaching and teaching in such a delightful and delectable fashion that we entice people to change their minds?

A similar New Testament concept is found in the word *kerdaino*, to "gain" or "win over." Our Lord suggests using this method in Matthew 18:15 where He states, "If your brother sins, go and reprove him in private; if he listens to you, you have won your brother."

How effective is persuasion as a means of bringing about change? Employed gently, kindly, intelligently, and under the right circumstances it can be a powerful weapon. And how wonderful to be able to change a person's mind and have him completely support an idea instead of trying to force him into agreeing to a decision he does not fully accept.

Want to change a person's mind? Try gentle persuasion—but be sure you get the facts right before you start! On the basis of accurate facts presented persuasively, many lives have been changed eternally.

ENCOURAGEMENT

From the earliest of Old Testament times the Scriptures suggest the use of encouragement to bring about change in people. How do you motivate a people such as Israel to stop wandering around the wilderness and conquer the Promised Land? You encourage their leaders to get on the ball and get the people moving. The Lord instructed Moses in regard to Joshua, "Encourage him, for he shall cause Israel to inherit it" (Deuteronomy 1:38). God reiterates the thought in Deuteronomy 3:28, "But charge Joshua and encourage him and strengthen him; for he shall go across at the head of this people, and he shall give them as an inheritance the land which you will see."

The word used in both passages was the Hebrew word *chazaq,* which has at its root the idea of helping a person grow firm or strong. That is the essence of discipleship. It is the primary job of the Christian leader to equip others and to help them grow firm and strong in the work of the Lord.

A prominent New Testament word denoting encouragment is the same word used to describe the Holy Spirit, *parakaleo,* "to call alongside" (or to oneself), to "urge." When the Thessalonian church was being oppressed and afflicted, Paul sent Timothy "to strengthen and encourage you as to your faith" (1 Thessalonians 3:2). In turn, the Thessalonians were to "encourage one another, and build up one another" (1 Thessalonians 5:11).

The method used by Judas and Silas to encourage the people at Antioch may not be received too well today, for we are told they "encouraged and strengthened the brethren with a lengthy message" (Acts 15:32).

In other passages, the word *parakaleo* is translated in a still stronger sense, that of urging. Paul frequently urges people to do many things. One of his more well known passages is Romans 12:1, where he writes, "I urge you therefore, brethren, by the mercies of God, to present your bodies a living and holy sacrifice, acceptable to God, which is your spiritual service of worship."

In Romans 15:30 he urges the brethren to pray for him, and in Romans 16:17 he urges those same Christians to keep their eye on the dissenters who would refute his teaching by their actions. One of his classic uses of urging is, of course, Philippians 4:2, where he urges Euodia and Syntyche to behave toward each other as Christian ladies should. For years male preachers have used this passage to castigate ladies, but I believe the warning is generic. All of us need to guard ourselves constantly and live as Christian ladies and gentlemen should.

Another New Testament word used to describe the method of encouraging or urging people to change is *parabiazomai,* which includes the ideas of the possible use of force. The word is used in regard to the two disciples on the road to Emmaus who were so struck by the stranger who walked with them that they urged, almost forced, him to stay with them (Luke 24:29).

*Sophronizo* involves encouraging or urging by recalling a person to his senses. In Titus 2:3 the older women are told that they are to be "reverent in their behavior, not malicious gossips, nor enslaved to much wine, teaching what is good." All of this is to contribute to a specific purpose: "that they may encourage [or recall to their senses] the young women to love their husbands, to love their children, to be sensible, pure, workers at home, kind, being subject to their own husbands, that the word of God may not be dishonored" (Titus 2:4-5).

The New Testament uses several other terms to discuss trying to bring about change in people through encouragement. Probably the most descriptive is *protrepo,* which means "to encourage" in the sense of turning or urging a person forward. Acts 18:27 says of Paul, "And when he wanted to go across to Achaia, the brethren encouraged him [or urged him on] and wrote to the disciples to welcome him; and when he had arrived, he helped greatly those who had believed through grace." With not only a hearty cheering section to bid him adieu but also a welcoming party to greet him when he arrived, how could Paul not be encouraged to make his mission a success!

So far we have seen that the Bible often records the use of motivational techniques to bring about change in the minds of people. But the Bible was written more than two thousand years ago. A legitimate question may be raised, "How applicable to our society today are these biblical techniques?"

There is evidence even from non-Christians that it is applicable. An article in my morning newspaper quoted a management consultant (who gave no indication of being a Christian) as saying, "The most effective managers I know seldom give direct orders. Instead they see themselves as selling a course of action. They use cajoling, persuading, bribing and rewarding far more often than direct orders."[2] What an interesting commentary on the path of action used in the Bible centuries ago.

ADMONISHMENT

The Hebrew word *ud,* "admonish," has a negative sound to it as well as a negative application. It is derived from a word that means to "bear witness," and the term includes the concept of "calling to witness." This method of bringing about change seldom has positive results. Even the Lord had problems using it. In response to His admonishment in Psalm 81:8, verse 11 notes, "But My people did not listen to My voice."

A classic example of the futility of this method is indicated in the ninth chapter of Nehemiah. The wall of Jerusalem had been reconstructed and the people were reciting their dismal past performance. When the prophets tried to admonish them in order to bring about desired change (v. 26) the people killed them rather than heed their warnings.

Even when the Lord admonished the people of Israel (v. 29), they "acted arrogantly and did not listen to Thy commandments but sinned against Thine ordinances." Again, in verse 30, the Holy Spirit admonishes them through the prophets, but the people still would not "give ear." Even their kings and priests paid no attention to the Lord's admonishments (v. 34).

Despite the apparent lack of success of this method in Old Testament times, Paul believed in using it, especially among those whose hearts had not been already hardened. Using the word *noutheteo,* which also carries with it the idea of giving instruction, he urged the church in Ephesus, "Therefore be on the alert, remembering that night and day for a period of three years I did not cease to admonish each one with tears" (Acts 20:31). Persistence sometimes wins out, especially when it is accompanied by obvious sincerity.

2. Al Bernstein, "Motivating Workers," *The Columbian* (Vancouver, Wash.), July 30, 1989, sec. C.

In Romans 15:14 Paul cites admonishment as a good method to use with one another, and in 1 Thessalonians 5:14 he urges that it be used especially among the unruly. Even in cases where a person would not heed instructions, we are told not to "regard him as an enemy, but admonish him as a brother" (2 Thessalonians 3:15).

In a sense, there is to be a universal application of this method among Christians. At least that is what we can glean from Paul's instructions in Colossians 1:28, where he writes, "And we proclaim Him, admonishing every man . . . with all wisdom, that we may present every man complete in Christ."

Finally, in Colossians 3:16 Paul establishes the element that must be present if admonishment is to be successful: it is to be done "with all wisdom." Therein lies the secret for success if there is to be any success with this method. The Christian leader must learn to admonish gently and firmly in love without grinding any axes. In the providence of God and with the help of the Holy Spirit, this method of changing people's minds will succeed in the church even though it practically never succeeds anywhere else.

APPEALING

Does an appeal to the right person do any good? Apparently it did in at least one instance in the Old Testament. Following the advice of the prophet Elisha who had restored her son to life, the Shunammite woman appealed to King Jehoram, and her property was restored to her (2 Kings 8:6). The word she used, *tsaag,* means to appeal in the sense of "crying" or "crying aloud."

The New Testament application of this method is described by the word *parakaleo,* which we have looked at before in another context. In Matthew 26:53 Jesus indicates that His communion with the Father is such that all He would have to do is appeal to God and twelve legions of angels would deliver Him from the hands of the soldiers in the Garden of Gethsemane.

In 1 Timothy 5:1 Paul advises his protégé that the way to bring about change in an older brother is not to approach him sharply, harshly, or frontally, but to "appeal to him as a father." Likewise, with men of our own age the biblical strategy is that we appeal to them as brothers.

We have lost track of this effective change technique these days. How many brash leaders, sensing the "sweetness" of what they envision as their clout, flaunt their authority before others instead of appealing to them? As a result those whom they hope to influence are completely turned off. Good ideas that should have been well received are resisted simply because the sharer of those ideas was so cavalier in his or her behavior.

Paul practiced what he preached. When he sought mercy for his friend, the escaped slave Onesimus, he appealed to Onesimus's master, Philemon, "for love's sake" instead of ordering Philemon to welcome back the slave. Paul reminded Philemon that he, Paul, was an old man appealing to him for his child, Onesimus (Philemon 1:10).

Paul was a recipient of an appeal that changed his life and ministry. In Acts 16:9 Luke tells us of a vision Paul experienced in which "a certain man of Macedonia was standing and appealing to him, and saying, 'Come over to Macedonia and help us.'" Paul did just that, and from that incident came the greatest change in the Christian church since Pentecost. Because God was able to change the mind of one man by appealing to him, not only was the man changed but the church was changed from a Jewish church to a universal church.

If God uses this method it can't be all bad! Maybe we leaders should reexamine this method and learn how to use it to change the minds of those we know who seem so set in their ideas.

SUMMARY OF THE BIBLICAL APPROACH

Notice that as we analyzed each of the methods used in the Bible to bring about change in people, none was high-handed, authoritarian, or harsh. They were gentle, loving, people-oriented, and serving. Isn't that a pretty good clue as to how we should act to bring about change?

The apostle Paul was perhaps the most authoritarian figure in the New Testament. Yet even he was gentle, loving, and gentlemanly in his dealings with people, no matter how badly they had "missed the mark of God's high calling." It is not the task of leadership to hit people over the head, threaten them, and tell them to come into line. In the entire history of the church, those methods have seldom proved effective—and they are especially ineffective today. Instead, by example the Bible teaches us that people are to be persuaded, encouraged, admonished gently, and appealed to in efforts to bring about change in their lives.

Notice, as well, that all of the biblical methods we have considered involve the appropriate use of words to accomplish their mission. The skillful use of words that are firmly grounded in the Word will always be an effective tool in bringing about change in the minds of people.

## USING EDUCATIONAL EXPERIENCES TO CHANGE PEOPLE'S MINDS

The Bible is true and reliable. All truth comes from God. Of those two points I am firmly convinced. Nevertheless, God does not reveal all of His truth through the Bible. Scriptures contain only an outline that needs to be fleshed out in every new generation. To do this, God uses a variety of sources, including the work of unregenerate people, to give us insight into many aspects of life. It is to one of those insights I would like to turn now.

If learning is the essence of change, as Martha Leypoldt insists it is,[3] then in order to bring about change, it is necessary to ask ourselves, "How do people learn?" The answer is that people learn mainly through their senses: hearing, seeing, tasting, smelling, and touching. Christians also learn through the direct revelation of truth by the Holy Spirit through the Word of God, the Bible. Even then, such revelation is usually delivered through the senses.

Since learning takes place mainly through the senses, it is reasonable to assume that the more senses employed in learning, the better the learning experience. Consequently, for years teachers have been urged to stay away from methods that employ only one human sense, such as lectures or books, and use multisense learning experiences. Through such experiences, it is reasoned, the learner can participate more actively in the learning experience.

Reflecting on this philosophy, Martha Leypoldt exhorted in her otherwise excellent book *Learning Is Change,* "Never, Never, Never lecture unless there is no other way to help persons learn. Search, Search, Search for other ways first, then if there is no other way, the lecture is for you."[4]

3. Martha M. Leypoldt, *Learning Is Change* (Valley Forge, Pa.: Judson, 1971), p. 82.
4. Ibid.

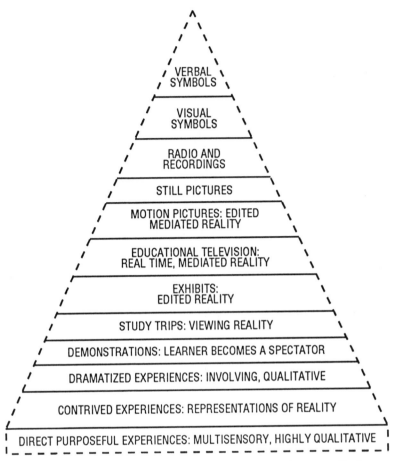

Less abstract methods are at the bottom of the cone; more abstract methods are at the top of the cone.

Fig. 3. Edgar Dale's Cone of Learning Experiences

Source:  Adapted from Walter Wager, "Media Selection in the Affective Domain.  A Further Interpretation of Dale's Cone of Learning Experience for  Cognitive and Affective Learning," *Educational Technology*, July 1973, p. 9.

The problem is that although this philosophy has been taught for many decades, it has remained untested until lately. Recently several studies of learning retention have been made. These studies have proved that in certain kinds of learning, people retain more when they are more directly involved in the learning process through multisensory experiences. As a result, perhaps reading more into the studies than was indicated from the limited results they uncovered, secular education has gravitated toward using multisensory methods whenever possible.

If such methods really worked, the quality of education should be improving. But it hasn't worked that way. Instead, during a period when teachers have been using supposedly correct methods, the quality of education has deteriorated rather than improved. Obviously something is wrong.

A look into how cognitive learning takes place suggests what might be wrong in the present approach. The relevant insights I intend to discuss come from articles in *Educational Technology* magazine[5] written by Walter Wager, who in turn makes use of insights developed by Edgar Dale and included in figure 3.

Look closely at figure 3. Dale has cataloged the different kinds of educational methods available according to their level of abstraction. At the top of the cone are the more abstract methods. They use the least number of senses. At the bottom of the cone are the more direct methods. These employ the greatest number of senses. Dale, and other educators of his day, theorized that the more direct the learning experience, the more senses used by the learner, the better the learning experience.

Dale's philosophy of learning was taught widely, but studies reported by Wager indicated that Dale and his colleagues were sometimes wrong in the conclusions they drew. For the findings reported by Wager in the area of cognitive learning, see figure 4.

Wager found that when one was dealing with little children, mentally immature persons, or unsophisticated adults, the conclusions of Dale and his colleagues were, indeed, valid. One must involve as many senses as possible to change the minds of these people. That is

5. Walter Wager, "Media Selection in the Affective Domain. A Further Interpretation of Dale's Cone of Experience for Cognitive and Affective Learning," *Educational Technology*, July 1973, pp. 9-11.

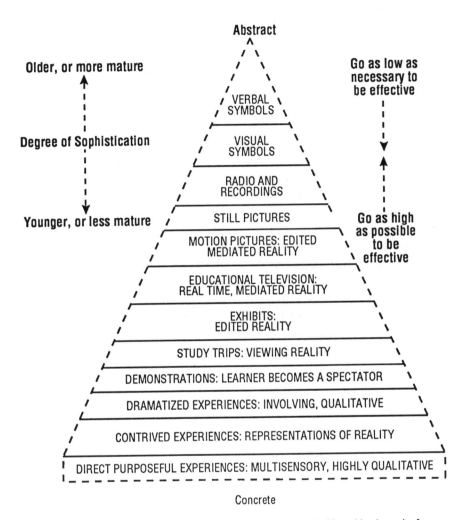

Fig. 4. Appropriate Ways to Change People's Minds [Cognitive Learning]

Source: Adapted from Walter Wager, "Media Selection in the Affective Domain. A Further Interpretation of Dale's Cone of Learning Experience for Cognitive and Affective Learning," *Educational Technology*, July 1973, p.11.

why Sunday schools have a variety of interest centers in the classrooms where small children learn.

As a leader, you have a firm, biblical obligation to "tend the flock," and that includes the "little lambs." By all means, monitor the feeding of these precious little ones and make sure their food is in palatable, digestible form. Do everything in your power to see that alternate learning experiences are provided for them during the sermon time.

Wager also found that as people grow older and more sophisticated it is not only possible but desirable to use abstract methods of educational delivery when one is attempting to change their minds.

Therefore, rather than sticking with Martha Leypoldt's advice to "Never, Never, Never" use the lecture method unless you can't use anything else, one should use the more "abstract" methods if the learners are mature adults. Contrary to popular opinion, stimulating lectures and interesting sermons along with well-written books can be effective tools for teaching content to adults. Several applications follow from this principle. First, we should secure for our adults the most gifted person possible to teach God's Word with skill, zest, and enthusiasm. The majority of this teaching can done from the pulpit, but it can also be done in Bible classes.

Second, we need to free these skilled teachers from perfunctory tasks so that teaching the Word of God can be their primary responsibility.

Third, we need to build the best church resource center we can afford and stock it with challenging books and tapes. The material should cover biblical matters and practical "how to" instruction as well. Then we need to cajole, beg, and entice people to use these materials to bring about positive change in their thinking.

How do we change people's minds? It depends upon the people! If they are small children or unsophisticated adults we employ as many of their senses as needed in the learning process. However, if they are mature adults, content can be conveyed to them successfully through such methods as lectures, sermons, and reading assignments. Depending on the degree of maturity of the people with whom we are working, we will need to vary our methods accordingly.

The right side of figure 4 deals with the elements of effectiveness and efficiency. For purposes of discussion, the two terms can be defined in this way:

*Effectiveness:* the ability to get the job done, to accomplish the intended purpose.

*Efficiency:* getting the job done with the most economical use of assets such as time, money, facilities, and personnel.

We live on an acreage in the country, and as I look out at my backyard I see numerous molehills. The task? To kill the moles so that my lawn looks decent again. To do this, I could use sticks of dynamite, well placed throughout the property. A massive explosion would take place and the moles would meet their intended end.

However, though that method would be effective, it wouldn't be efficient. It would be dangerous and expensive, and it would destroy what is left of my grass, forcing me to start all over again in planting a lawn.

The most direct methods may be the most effective for changing some people, but they may be so inefficient and expensive that it may be impossible to use them. The right side of figure 4 gives us a good rule of thumb to use in choosing methods of changing people's minds: choose those methods that are as effective and as efficient as possible.

We do not have unlimited time and resources to use in changing people's minds through the Word of God. We must be effective in what we do—but also efficient, using the resources of time, talents, finances, and supplies as economically as possible.

There is an additional point of caution here. The crucial factor in any method is the skill with which that method is employed. Boring lectures, insipid sermons, or dull books stimulate few people to the type of mind-changing experience they need to undergo if we as leaders are to bring about significant change in their thinking. We can take heart. Well-written books and well-prepared and presented sermons and lectures can have an effective impact, especially if the recipient is mature in years or sophisticated in mind-set.

How do Wager's findings compare with our biblical findings? All of the biblical methods mentioned earlier in the chapter—persuasion, encouragement, admonishment, and appealing—were verbal methods. All of them were abstract terms.

These methods were used in attempts to change the minds of people who were at least mature in age if not mature intellectually.

Similarly, the method most frequently used by the apostle Paul to change the minds of people who are geographically distant from him was the written word, certainly an abstract, efficient form of communication. How effective it was in the people who received it. It was so powerful that the early church preserved his letters for posterity.

One of the miracles of grace is that this method, this two-edged sword, is still as powerful a change agent as it was when Paul's letters were first written. This is, indeed, a testimony to the skills of the true author, the blessed Holy Spirit Himself, who is the ultimately effective teacher.

Not only are biblical methods appropriate to the type of people for whom they were used, this same biblical methodology for changing people's minds is in keeping with some of the most up-to-date findings of our contemporary social sciences.

As church leaders we have a primary target group to change if we are going to bring needed change to the church. That group consists mainly of those people who are mature in age. If this group is to make intelligent, responsible decisions in behalf of the church, it must be given the proper content base upon which to make these decisions.

Is there a biblical pattern for changing the minds of mature adults? There is, indeed, and by now I hope that pattern is clear in your own mind. To review: We bring change in the minds of mature individuals through sermons, lectures, and books that persuade, encourage, admonish, and appeal.

## Additional Resources

Egan, Gerard. *Change Agent Skills: Assessing and Designing Excellence.* San Diego: University Associates, 1988.

_____. *Change Agent Skills: Managing Innovation and Change.* San Diego: University Associates, 1987.

Fry, Thomas A. *Change, Chaos, and Christianity.* Westwood, N.J.: Revell, 1967.

Getz, Gene A. *Encouraging One Another.* Wheaton, Ill.: Victor, 1981.

Sell, Charles M. *Transition.* Chicago: Moody, 1985.

Walrath, Douglas. *Leading Churches Through Change.* Nashville: Abingdon, 1979.

## Questions for Discussion and a Helpful Project

1. Many Christian leaders have the spiritual giftedness and drive to achieve ministry success. However, their effectiveness may not always be wedded to efficiency. Explain the tension between effectiveness and efficiency. How may you work to reduce the tension between these two factors?

2. Make a list of the different age groups represented in your church. Alongside each group, list appropriate methods which may be used to change the minds of the group's members.

PROJECT: Inspect the church school curriculum used by your church. How does the curriculum for each age group compare with the list you have just made? Does the curriculum for each age take into consideration both effectiveness and efficiency?

# 13

## LIFE STAGES
### AND
## CHANGING
## PEOPLE'S HEARTS

S o far we have dealt with trying to change content and thought patterns. That is important as a foundation upon which to build constructive change. However, changing content and thought patterns does not always bring about a change in actions in the people we have targeted for change.

What is missing? We still haven't dealt with people's attitudes. In *The Human Puzzle* David Myers says that the term *attitude* "usually refers to what is inside us, especially to the intensity and direction of our feelings about something or someone."[1] Attitudes result from a complex set of hereditary and environmental factors interacting to make someone a feeling person.

Why is it that a person steeped in Bible knowledge neglects to speak of his faith? He knows better. He has been told repeatedly that he should be doing it. Yet he constantly fails to perform that task. Likewise, why is it that a pillar of the church is convicted of business fraud? He certainly knows that is not appropriate behavior for a Christian, and yet this knowledge has not affected his actions. In both cases, the violators do not lack content. They are afflicted with poor attitudes.

1. David S. Myers, *The Human Puzzle* (New York: Harper & Row, 1978), p. 93.

To what extent do attitudes affect a person's behavior? Some people think little. Allan Wicks reports that there is little relationship between attitudes toward cheating and actual cheating. Similarly, he reports that there is little relationship between the attitude of church members toward church attendance and their actual attendance.[2]

However, Wicks takes his data from what people tell him. He doesn't take into consideration the fact that people are often reluctant to express their real attitudes. Instead, they express what they think people want to hear.

David Myers sheds further light on this matter:

> People's expressed attitudes may imperfectly reflect their actual attitude for a variety of reasons including the nature of the question asked and the conditions under which the responses are elicited. This was neatly demonstrated in 1964 when the United States House of Representatives overwhelmingly passed a salary increase for itself in an off-the-record vote and later overwhelmingly defeated the same bill in a roll call vote. Potential public criticism made the overt expression a distortion of the true congressional sentiments.[3]

There are other influences, including social pressure, that keep people from expressing their true attitudes. Myers continues:

> When these other influences are minimized or when the person's behavior is averaged across many situations, an attitude can actually predict behavior pretty well. George Gallup effectively predicts voter behavior because his attitudinal measure is specific to the behavior in question, and because the anonymity of the voting booth minimizes other social influences.[4]

Why is it that people in evangelical churches who seemingly have received the correct content and who seemingly espouse the right attitudes fail to act in a biblically prescribed manner? It is likely because they have been conditioned to give the right answers but fail to value those answers personally.

2. Allen W. Wickes, "Attitude vs. Actions: The Relationship of Verbal to Oral Behavior Responses in Attitude Objects," *Journal of Social Issues* 23 (1964): 41-78.

3. Myers, *The Human Puzzle*, p. 93.

4. Ibid.

How powerful are feelings, or attitudes, in the society in which we live? Peters and Waterman have concluded that despite our sophistication, we are pretty much a feeling-oriented society. In their book *In Search of Excellence* they discuss the reason the traditional rational model of organizational effectiveness has failed in most businesses. Their conclusion? People are not rational and do not generally operate under rational reasoning. In fact, Peters and Waterman point out, businesses are full of "highly irrational-emotional human beings."[5] The "best-run" companies "simply allow for—and take advantage of—the emotional, more primitive side [good and bad] of human nature. . . . And so it goes through a wealth of experimental data, now thousands of experiments old, showing that people reason intuitively. They reason with simple decision rules, which is a fancy way of saying that in this complex world, they trust their gut."[6]

Our attitudes—our feelings—are dear to us. They are the mechanisms that help us cope with the complexities of life. They are also the instruments that make life hard for us. To maintain an unpopular attitude in the face of overwhelming pressure is the stuff of which martyrs are made. Now, martyrdom for a worthy cause is to be admired. But martyrdom for a less than worthy cause is to be pitied—and sometimes it is hard to tell a worthy cause from an unworthy one. The result is that martyrdom for a less than worthy cause is often the fate of a leader who wants to bring about change. What, then, is the first change that needs to be made in the church? The attitudes of the leaders.

How do we deal with attitudes? Sometimes we attempt to dismiss them as unworthy and move ahead with cognitive answers to our problems. A cognitive answer makes sense to a rational person, doesn't it? But if it is true that the majority of church people, like the population at large, "trust their gut" in their decision making, it is no wonder that a purely cognitive, content-based approach doesn't work in most churches. Let us, then, examine a way in which attitudes may be coupled with content to change individuals.

5. Thomas J. Peters and Robert H. Waterman, Jr., *In Search of Excellence* (New York: Harper & Row, 1982), p. 60.
6. Ibid., pp. 60, 63.

## A BIBLICAL LOOK AT HEART CHANGING

When we looked at changing people's minds it was easy to spot many words in the Bible that illustrated that kind of change. We would expect that since it is relatively easy to change a mature person's mind through the use of words. Changing a person's heart is another matter, however. Here I was able to find only a few references. In each of them direct action of some kind is applied to the person targeted for change either by God or by some human change agent.

In John 16:8, the gospel writer records the fact that the Holy Spirit is often a chief agent in changing people's hearts. He does this through a supernatural process called conviction. The word used here, *elegcho,* means to expose or reprove as well as to convict. We don't have to go about the process of changing people's hearts on our own. We will be aided by none other than the Holy Spirit Himself, who will influence the hearts of people by convicting them of their sin.

As if to reinforce this word of encouragement to us, the Holy Spirit repeats the promise in Jude 15, where He guarantees us that God will, indeed, convict the ungodly.

But how do we work in partnership with the Holy Spirit to change the hearts of people? One method the Bible suggests is the tactic of "winning over" another person. The word used, *kerdaino,* signifies "gain" or "profit." Thus, part of the strategy the apostle Paul employs in 1 Corinthians 9:19 is to assume the role of servant so that he might "win over," or gain, the greatest number of people for the cause of the Lord Jesus Christ. In subsequent verses he gives the details of this method. To Jews, he became as a Jew so that he might "win over" Jews. To non-Jews, those "without law" and weak, he personally adapted to and related to their ways so that he might win them to Jesus as Lord and Savior.

This same word, indicating "persuasion," is used in 1 Peter 3:1-2. Peter does not encourage Christian wives to nag at their unsaved husbands but instead encourages them to win over their husbands through their exemplary deportment and chaste conversation.

If I were to rate the primary requirements of a leader, certainly a winning personality would be close to the top of the list. It is an act of futility for a leader to try to change the hearts of people without first winning their hearts. People will follow a leader to the "ends of the earth" if they have learned to love and respect him.

Once again, the apostle Paul is a good example. Even when he is admonishing the Ephesian Christians in Acts 20:31 he is so loving, caring, and winning in his deportment that people repent and heed his advice. He tells us he admonished the people with tears, indicating the intensity of his message and his undeniable sincerity. Do you see what Paul is doing? He is combining actions with words. As a result, the people not only listen to the words he speaks but are also deeply involved on a feeling basis. Verse 37 reports that the people wept profusely, embraced Paul, and kissed him.

If there had been any attitudinal problems among them before this—and verses 29-30 indicate that there were—their attitude toward Paul was wholesome as he left this small group of Christians to set out on his journey. Content was channeled through feelings to bring about positive attitudinal results.

At least one more Bible word indicates a method God uses to change attitudes in His children, the word *testing*. The Hebrew word was *bochan,* and Deuteronomy 8:2 indicates that God used testing to humble and prove His people. A New Testament word, *dokimion,* records a similar story. In James 1:3 we find that testing is used effectively by God to change our attitudes. By this testing, endurance is produced within us.

To bring about attitudinal change, God often uses methods that are more action than words. When the attitudes of mankind became unbearable at the tower of Babel, God intervened directly by confusing the language of the people. Other direct means of instruction are recorded elsewhere in the Bible. Hornets were sent to make Israel willing to march to the Promised Land. Jonah was swallowed by a great fish to make him more receptive to God's command. The Babylonian Captivity was sent to chastise Judah. Indeed, Scripture offers hundreds of illustrations of God dealing with His people in a direct way, not always through miracles but often through ordinary means that are strategically timed.

Jesus, the master teacher, had a marvelous way of involving people in the learning process in order to change their attitudes. Look at His method of changing the attitude of the woman at the well. He did not preach at her but wove a web of her past activities from which she could not escape. From being surprised and indifferent, she became an evangelist who told others the good news she had learned. What a dramatic change of attitude.

## How Does Affective Change Take Place?

We have seen that cognitive and affective learning must work hand in hand if real change is going to occur in an individual. Before we take a closer look at how affective learning happens, however, I want to look briefly at the place actions have in formulating and changing attitude.

### A CHANGE IN ACTION PRECEDES A CHANGE OF ATTITUDE

If we can get people to act in a certain way, their attitudes are likely to change. Lyle Schaller makes this point in *The Change Agent*, saying, "It is clearly possible to change people's actions by legislation and apparently attitude changes as behavior changes."[7] As illustrations of this Schaller cites "fair employment legislation, open housing legislation and the legislation (usually preceded by lawsuits) which eliminated the racial or religious quotas in various educational institutions."[8] He continues:

> A lengthening list of public opinion polls and attitudinal studies indicates there has been a major change in both the openly expressed attitudes and the more reserved attitudes of the American population on a series of issues where legislation has changed behavior. While it is impossible to prove a direct cause and effect relationship, those who believe cigarette smoking causes lung cancer probably will be persuaded that legislation can change attitudes as well as behavior and that change in behavior tends to produce a parallel change in attitudes.[9]

Others besides Schaller support this position. Peters and Waterman quote a Harvard psychologist, Jerome Brunner, who said, "You are more likely to act yourself into feelings than feel yourself into action."[10] They point to an experiment carried out in Palo Alto, California, in which a number of people initially agreed to display a tiny sign in their front window supporting traffic safety. Then these people were asked if they would allow the organization to display in their yards a

---

7. Lyle E. Schaller, *The Change Agent: The Strategy of Innovative Leadership* (Nashville: Abingdon, 1972), p. 63.
8. Ibid.
9. Ibid.
10. Peters and Waterman, *In Search of Excellence*, p. 73.

large billboard supporting the same cause. Although it meant allowing outsiders to dig large holes in their lawn, most of the people who had initially agreed to display the small sign in their windows also agreed to the second step of erecting the billboard. In sharp contrast, 95 out of every 100 who had not been asked to take the first step would not allow a billboard to be erected in their yards.[11]

Peters and Waterman conclude: "The implications of this line of reasoning are clear: only if you get people acting, even in small ways, the way you want them to, will they come to believe in what they're doing."[12]

The controversy surrounding the question, "Do actions cause attitudes or do attitudes cause actions?" is something like the famous question, "Which came first, the chicken or the egg?" Common sense tells us that subjects of the experiment in Palo Alto had to be at least open to the subject of traffic safety if they were to allow even a small sign to be put up in their windows. Then as they took this first step, an even stronger attitude was formed. Undoubtedly, had the experiment gone further, people might have engaged in even more overt behavior in behalf of traffic safety.

The conclusion is obvious for those of us who want to effect changes in the church. The first step in bringing about attitudinal change is to find people who are at least slightly open in attitude to changes we want to make. The next step is to assist them in taking one small, active step in support of that change action.

From then on their attitude will probably be even more strongly supportive. If we keep on encouraging them one step at a time, and if we don't overwhelm them by asking them to take "giant" steps all at once, we may find these people becoming our most staunch allies in the change process. Like a child learning to walk, they become progressively stronger the more steps they take. Actions strengthen attitudes, which, in turn, strengthen actions.

In addition—and this thought comes from B. F. Skinner—if as each small step is taken the person taking the step is praised, encouraged, and rewarded, he will receive an incentive for further change and an enhancement of his self-image, making him feel good about himself and what he is doing.

11. Ibid., p. 74.
12. Ibid.

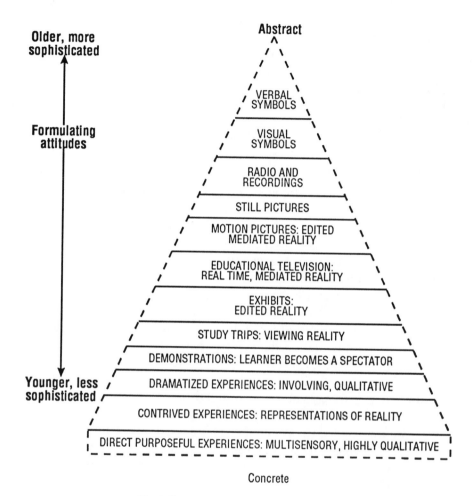

Fig. 5. How to Formulate Attitudes [Affective Learning]

Source: Adapted from Walter Wager, "Media Selection in the Affective Domain. A Further Interpretation of Dale's Cone of Learning Experience for Cognitive and Affective Learning," *Educational Technology*, July 1975, p.11.

THE PATTERN FOR FORMULATING ATTITUDES IS
THE SAME AS THE PATTERN FOR CHANGING PEOPLE'S MINDS

So far we have discussed the person who has a positive opinion, regardless of how mild, toward what we are trying to accomplish. Our next question is, "How do you get a person to act when he has not formulated an attitude on a subject and, therefore, is neither open nor closed to the proposed change?" Obviously, we must help him to formulate an attitude. But how do we go about doing that?

The work of Walter Wager provides an answer. His application of Dale's Cone of Learning Experience, "How to Formulate Attitudes [Affective Learning]" (figure 5), indicates that the pattern of learning experiences best to use in formulating attitudes is the same as the pattern best to use in helping people change their minds. Younger people and unsophisticated people formulate attitudes best through direct multisensory, "hands-on" learning experiences. Older and more sophisticated learners are best approached through abstract learning methods. Sermons, lectures, and book reading are appropriate when you are attempting to formulate attitudes in adults.

Since the majority of people we as church leaders are trying to change are older or more sophisticated learners, it is appropriate to use lectures, sermons, and books to help them form their attitudes on the subjects with which we are challenging them. Once again, the emphasis must be on quality, however.

"But my congregation varies greatly in age and degree of sophistication," you may say. Most congregations do. It is wise, therefore, to generously intersperse in your learning program experiences that are somewhere in the middle of Dale's pyramid. Those multisensory experiences will appeal to several groups of people at once. The most important lesson here is to choose the correct method to reach the targeted audience.

THE PATTERN FOR CHANGING DEEPLY HELD ATTITUDES IS
EXACTLY THE OPPOSITE OF THE PATTERN FOR FORMULATING ATTITUDES

Up to this point we have talked about formulating attitudes in people who have no strong feelings about a subject. But how does one change the attitude of an adult who is set in his ways? The right side of figure 6 indicates the best methods for changing attitudes. The formula

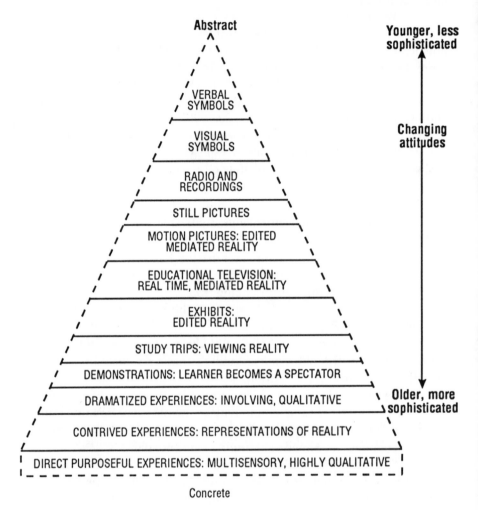

Fig. 6. How to Change Attitudes [Affective Learning]

Source:  Adapted from Walter Wager, "Media Selection in the Affective Domain.
A Further Interpretation of Dale's Cone of Learning Experience for Cognitive
and Affective Learning," *Educational Technology*, July 1975, p.11.

that applies is exactly the opposite of the one that works best in formulating attitudes.

Wager found that though abstract methods such as "telling" may be effective in changing the attitudes of young children or unsophisticated learners, the older, the more sophisticated the learner, the more direct the method that should be used. A small child with a negative attitude toward God might be able to change that attitude because of the comforting, reassuring words of his teacher. But if a mature adult is going to be convinced to change a deeply held attitude he must be involved in a direct learning experience related to that attitude.

Well-meaning people, not cognizant of this fact, have wasted much effort using the wrong methods to try to change adult attitudes. Their methods have often done more harm than good, making the learner angry instead of encouraging him to change his attitudes.

Consider a young seminary graduate about to begin his ministry in a church that has been ruled for decades by a stubborn old deacon. Through the years, pastor after pastor has attempted to bring change to this church with no results.

My friend begins experiencing success in other areas of his ministry. People are coming to Christ, and the church is growing. But this one old deacon is a roadblock to the substantive changes he and the "new order" leadership people want to bring about. One of the principal weapons in the old man's arsenal is that he is wealthy and the church cannot meet its obligations without his generous giving.

Nevertheless, like his predecessors, the young seminary graduate begins a concerted campaign to change the old man. He brings substantial biblical artillery into battle on a regular basis. All his sermons and Bible studies are aimed at changing this one man.

The result? The old deacon becomes even more entrenched in his position. He is not stupid. He knows that he is the target for the remarks being made so clearly in sermons and Bible studies. And so he mounts a campaign to get rid of the annoyance.

Nor is the congregation stupid. They realize that the pastor is training his scriptural artillery on the old deacon instead of feeding them. Though the content may or may not be applicable to the deacon, it is irrelevant to the rest of the congregation. They face other problems not being answered from God's Word. As a result, when the elderly deacon mounts his campaign to get rid of the pastor, many of the congregation go along with him. The pastor is forced to resign.

Unwittingly, the pastor was grinding an axe instead of feeding his sheep. Moreover, in an attempt to change one man in his church, he was employing a strategy that was counterproductive to its intended purpose. Moreover, in employing that strategy, the pastor was alienating others upon whom he could have depended had those people acquired proper feeding from the Word instead of receiving irrelevant material geared toward the old deacon.

My friend is currently selling insurance. The young turks with whom he had shared leadership responsibilities have all moved to different churches. Most of them are completely disillusioned and are no longer engaged in church leadership activities. The old deacon is still running things at "his" church, and he remains unchanged in his attitudes. At present another young seminary graduate is pastoring the church, beginning the process all over again and making the same mistakes made by his predecessors. He, too, is a fine man with great potential. Unfortunately his days of ministry at that church are already numbered.

How do we change the attitudes of mature adults? Thunder away at them from the pulpit each Sunday? Lay a guilt trip on them in a home Bible study? Such efforts are a waste of time and a disservice to the rest of the congregation. Worse, the targeted person almost never experiences a positive change in his attitudes through this approach. Quite the contrary, if any change is experienced it is often negative. Abstract methods such as preaching or teaching are not effective means of bringing about a desired attitudinal change in a mature adult.

We change adult attitudes by walking beside people, by getting to know them, by showing them that we genuinely care about them. Then, as we perceive any degree of openness, we help change their attitudes further by getting them involved in the learning process through the use of direct learning methods.

Let me illustrate. How many times do pastors such as myself try to lay a guilt trip on a congregation by preaching that they ought to be out evangelizing? Despite the fine scriptural discourses on the subject, the results are generally minimal. Contrast this to the methodology used by other equippers. The person who is "doing the work of evangelism" invites an otherwise timid person to accompany him on a home visit. The reluctant person observes as his "teacher" actively demonstrates how to use a little booklet to win a person to Christ. Soon the formerly reluctant person accompanies the evangelist on a regular basis.

At last, the evangelist gives his disciple a chance to participate in some small way. As time goes on the disciple is asked to take charge of more and more of the dialogue with the unsaved people they are visiting. However, he is not "dumped on" all at once. He is encouraged to assume responsibility one little step at a time. Eventually he is given the entire task of sharing the gospel under the watchful eye of his teacher.

Notice the process. The attitude of the learner changes gradually as he engages in each progressive step and is reinforced by his teacher all along the way. Eventually, not only does he become a successful soul-winner himself, he is taught to recruit a friend and begin to disciple him. Not only has the attitude of one person been changed, a chain reaction has begun that will involve other people in the change process.

What then is the proper formula to use in order to bring about the greatest change in mature or elderly individuals?

First, face the fact that the major hurdle to be overcome is the attitude that person holds.

Second, acknowledge that many of these mature people exert the most influence and constitute much of the power block in the church.

Third, recognize that if any substantive change is to take place in the church, it will happen only with the consent of these individuals.

Fourth, realize that in order for these individuals to agree to such changes in the church as we propose, a significant change in their attitudes will likely need to take place.

Fifth, remember that in formulating attitudes among the congregation nothing beats sound, attractively presented biblical teaching and preaching, but don't stop there. To change long-established, faulty attitudes involve these influence-makers in direct, involvement-oriented methods such as one-on-one discipleship techniques, role playing, and other methods that engage more than one human sense and involve the learner actively in the learning process.

Earlier in this chapter we analyzed some of the words and the methods used by God to change the attitudes of people. They are in alignment with the most up-to-date facts that research in learning theory has been able to provide for us. The answer was in the Scriptures all along. We just failed to see it.

When we work to change attitudes, change comes to a church slowly and gradually. For impatient individuals that is not soon enough, and so they chafe at the situation, lose their cool, and try to bring about change arbitrarily without waiting for people's attitudes to change.

The precipitous kind of change they envision is the kind that injures the saints and fractures the church. However, when we are patient and work gradually and steadily toward changing the attitudes of individuals, although the resulting change may be slow, it will be desired change, healthy change, and change that leaves the body intact.

Such change is part of a wholesome, innovative process in the lives of individuals. It is this kind of change which is, for all intents and purposes, irreversible. Change like this will have a much more profound and lasting effect than mere program or policy changes that are made quickly and arbitrarily. The church is Christ's bride. Handle her with great care!

## Additional Resources

Anderson, James D. *The Management of Ministry.* San Francisco: Harper & Row, 1978.

Haggai, John E. *Lead On! Leadership That Endures in a Changing World.* Waco, Tex.: Word, 1986.

Kuhne, Gary W. *The Change Factor: The Risks and Joys.* Grand Rapids: Regal Books, 1982; Zondervan, 1986.

Walrath, Douglas. *Leading Churches Through Change.* Nashville: Abingdon, 1979.

## Questions for Discussion and a Helpful Project

1. Harvard psychologist Jerome Brunner tells us that we are more likely to act ourselves into feelings than feel ourselves into action. Explain the rationale behind the strategy of getting people to act in a certain way in order to change their attitudes. In what ways might this work in your church?

2. Explain the vital role that positive reinforcement plays in both enacting and perpetuating change.

3. What means of change are instrumental in formulating attitudes in adults?

PROJECT: Together with a friend, share some experiences together whereby your attitudes have been formulated as an adult. What methods proved effective in doing this?

4. Many church leaders have made the error of trying to change adults solely through cognitive means apart from life-changing experience. Explain why experience must accompany content in order for effective change to take place.

5. Why does laying a guilt trip on people fail to accomplish the business of attitudinal change? What is usually the missing link in this often employed strategy of attitudinal change?

# PART 4:

# Circles of Influence: Organizing the Church for Dynamic Impact

# 14

# TRADITIONAL CHURCH GOVERNANCE PATTERNS

The Scriptures make clear that the church is unlike any earthly institution. It is unique in that it, alone, is a living organism. Some segments of the church seem to have lost sight of that. Organizational structures have become so complex and overbearing that in some denominations maintenance of the system takes much of the effort that should be used to do the more important tasks of the kingdom. Sometimes politics take on a scandalous dimension, as church leaders jockey for positions of power and influence within the system. Often this jockeying isn't even within the system. Ours is a day when hundreds of religious entrepreneurs are building kingdoms of their own.

Lawrence Richards has been a "voice crying in the wilderness" against this kind of organizational excess in the church. He writes, "Scripture teaches that in its essential nature the church is a living organism. We are members of a body, not an institution. Any expression the church takes must be an expression in harmony with its nature, not a stumbling copy of man's notions for organizing institutions."[1]

Richards's point is well taken. At times, however, he tends to go too far, appearing almost to abandon any form of formal organizational

1. Lawrence O. Richards, *A Theology of Church Leadership* (Grand Rapids: Zondervan, 1980), p. 37.

structure in the church. We need to remind ourselves that *organisms require organization in order to live.* We need look no further than the human body to affirm that. As an organism, we are a collection of systems that must operate in agreement and coordination if we are to live.

What is true of the human body is even more true of the church. This organism is far more fragile and far more complex than the human body—but with far more potential. If the human body, which is far less complex than the Body of Christ, needs organization, it stands to reason that the Body of Christ is even more in need of organization.

How can we reconcile the uniqueness of the body as an organism with the evident need of the body to be organized? The answer, of course, is to devise an organization that works as well for the church as the human system of organization works for our bodies. We may never completely reach that goal, but God will honor our efforts if we keep trying.

Before proposing a system that will reflect the uniqueness of the Body of Christ and its need to be organized, I should like to look at how the churches have been organized over the years. In this chapter I will look at traditional ecclesiastical systems. In the next chapter I will examine secular systems. Many times the latter have exerted far more influence over the church than the former.

Three organizational patterns have been employed in the church over the centuries: episcopal, presbyterian, and congregational. Each system has been used widely and derives its name by the most prominent feature of the system.

In their fully developed forms all three systems have a careful, built-in set of checks and balances. Unfortunately, sinful man has often found ways to get around those checks and balances, so there is no perfect system. On the other hand, each of the systems has qualities that are helpful in establishing an organizational structure for a local church.

## EPISCOPAL SYSTEMS

Episcopal systems take their name from the Greek word *episcopos,* which is translated "overseer." The term most frequently used as an English synonym is "bishop." These are the principal officers of the episcopal system. Other officials of these churches include presbyters (or priests) and deacons. Leon Morris tells us, "More Christians accept episcopacy than any other form of church government."[2]

The bishop, as the most prominent figure of this system, has general supervisory responsibilities for a number of churches. In turn, he usually works under an archbishop. In the Anglican church, archbishops report to the Archbishop of Canterbury; in the Roman Catholic church they report to cardinals who, in turn, are responsible to the pope.

In episcopal systems, power and authority rest primarily at the top and are delegated down. Theoretically, the individual church member has no authority but can only appeal to those above him. Although subordinate levels may report problems to superiors and ask for solutions that involve changes, clerics in the higher echelons are the ones who make the crucial decisions.

In recent years the practice of arbitrary, unilateral decision making by top management has been altered greatly. Even in Catholic churches, parish councils now advise the local pastor. These councils often exert a great deal of influence over decisions that ultimately affect all Roman Catholics.

Some people claim that the episcopal system is the original form of church government. Morris insists to the contrary that "the antiquity of the episcopacy is disputed. Some hold it to be the primitive form of church government, and that it is to be discerned in the NT. The evidence for this, however, is not convincing. But it had certainly made its appearance by the second century, and in time it became practically universal."[3]

It was flagrant abuses in this system that the Reformers railed against. As a result, the church governing systems of both Luther and Calvin differed considerably from the Roman church out of which they came. However, it is interesting that instead of abandoning the episcopal system entirely, Wesley adapted it to his needs. As a result, most branches of Methodism today still use a modified form of episcopacy. Utilizing this system, Methodism swept the world, bringing people to Christ and building thousands of churches where these new saints were built up in the faith. Never since the Day of Pentecost has the world

2. Leon Morris, *Evangelical Dictionary of Theology*, ed. Walter A. Elwell (Grand Rapids: Baker, 1984), p. 239.

3. Leon Morris, *Baker's Dictionary of Theology*, ed. Everett Harrison (Grand Rapids: Baker, 1960), p 184.

seen such a dramatic moving of the Holy Spirit. And it was all done utilizing a system that many evangelicals would studiously avoid.

## DEFECTS IN THE EPISCOPAL SYSTEM

Critics of the episcopal system point to the serious abuses carried on over the years by members of the Roman Catholic clergy. They point as well to the fact that in an episcopal system congregations have little say about what goes on in their own parish. Since authority comes from above, the people have had two alternatives when they disagreed with a policy: accept the dictates of their superiors anyway; or rebel, become a heretic, and be excommunicated from the church. The drawbacks of the episcopal system should not be overlooked.

## STRENGTHS OF THE EPISCOPAL SYSTEM

Nevertheless, episcopal systems do allow for churches to call upon their wisest and most godly elders for counsel. Freed from everyday pastoral duties, those leaders can act as pastors to many churches. In that role, they can lend sage advice and loving counsel to churches too traumatized by upheaval to make rational decisions. In this way, not only the local assembly practices interdependency within the assembly, but groups of churches become interdependent churches.

There is another factor to consider. Although my own preference in a North American context is for some form of congregationalism, the needs of believers in other countries may be served better by some other system. That became apparent to me when I was teaching in Africa. There, thousands of people are coming to Christ each day, but the number of adequately trained leaders is extremely scarce. As a result, one seminary-trained individual may find himself supervising the activities of fifty or more churches.

All of those churches are likely to be made up of relatively immature Christians led by individuals who have had about the same level of training as the rest of the congregation. It would seem to me that an episcopal system would be in order in this setting. A trained leader could supervise the activities of many churches, see that they do not fall into error, and concentrate his efforts on training the leaders of the individual churches. Though he could not be in fifty locations at the same time, he could gather his leaders together for training and to help them solve the problems of the churches they serve.

Another practical application of the episcopal system may be appropriate in North America. I have often thought that churches that are congregational in polity should adopt a modified episcopal system for new pastors. Somehow it is right for a new clergyman to be tested under the supervision of an experienced servant of God for a period of time before being released to operate on his own. At first, all of the authority of the pastorate would not be extended to him. Instead, he would be considered a pastoral trainee. If he did well during this period, he would be recommended for ordination and a full pastoral charge. If this were done, I believe there would be less trauma in those churches brave enough to call recent seminary graduates to a pastorate—and there might be fewer pastoral dropouts.

THE EPISCOPAL SYSTEM IN CONGREGATIONAL SETTINGS

Vestiges of the episcopal system emerge even among churches that are congregational in polity. These evidence themselves in "district superintendents," "area ministers," "state executives," and other such offices. The problem is that often none of these offices has the teeth in it to tackle the thorny problems experienced in and among churches. Though most churches hold the district executive responsible to correct problems in and among churches, seldom do they give him the authority he needs to do the job.

Although I dislike the term "independent church," I hold steady to the need for "autonomous" churches. Perhaps a better way to describe the arrangement I prefer would be to call for "interdependent" local churches. When churches vote to voluntarily associate and work with each other in a denominational or fellowship setting, they need to make certain working agreements among themselves. Those would include the surrender of some of their independence under certain circumstances. In this way, other churches and district officers would be able to step in and help a church when it is in serious trouble.

I have seen times when churches were experiencing such serious troubles that they were not able to make rational decisions. In such periods, the wise counsel of mature godly people and the objective advice of sister churches might be sufficient to keep the church from disintegrating. There are instances when even mandatory arbitration may be in order. To some dyed-in-the-wool congregationalists, this may sound episcopal and even heretical. So be it.

## Presbyterian Systems

The emphasis in the presbyterian system is upon the *presbu-teros,* the "elder," and he (and, in some churches, she) is usually spoken of in the plural. Concerning this form of plural leadership, Morris says, "At the Reformation the Presbyterian leaders thought that they were restoring the original form of church government, but this would not be vigorously defended by many Presbyterians today. It is recognized that there has been much development, but it is held that this took place under the guidance of the Spirit, and that the essentials of the presbyterian system are scriptural."[4]

Presbyterianism, in its traditional expression, utilizes a committee of elders at the local church level which is elected by the congregation. This is called the *session,* and it is able to make most of the day-to-day decisions regarding the operation of the church. Notice, however, that since the church elects its elders, it, in turn, can hold the session to a certain degree of accountability.

Over the session is a *presbytery* made up, once again, of elected representatives from several churches. In serious matters or in matters involving disputes within or between local congregations, the presbytery becomes the deciding body. Also, when a church is going through hard times and finds it difficult to make proper and rational decisions, the presbytery offers a ready-made source of help. People who at least theoretically should be more rational and objective are there to aid the church in getting over its illness.

Of course there is always the danger of self-serving, opinionated people taking over a presbytery and imposing their will on churches. In the past this has led to denominational splits among presbyterians and sometimes the abandonment of traditional presbyterianism. A result, sometimes, has been the phenomenon I call "neopresbyterianism."

### NEOPRESBYTERIANISM

In recent days many churches that have traditionally held to other governance patterns have become more and more presbyterian in appearance. But the result is seldom traditional presbyterianism with its sessions, presbyteries, and checks and balances. Instead we often find a new kind of "independent presbyterianism." Sometimes the

4. Ibid., p. 127.

model is extremely good, but in other instances it is severely lacking. Individual churches may become assertively and aggressively independent and proud of the fact that no denomination or group exercises any influence or control over them.

In some of these churches, elders are elected by the congregation. Thus, leaders are held to at least some degree of accountability. In other churches, however, the congregation has little or no say as to who their leaders will be. Existing elders elect new elders. Here the elder board becomes self-perpetuating and answerable only to itself.

Often these self-perpetuating elders put great emphasis on the fact that they are ruling elders and thus may make most if not all of the decisions. They buy, sell, and construct facilities as they wish. They hire and fire staff and spend money as they desire. Legally, they are accountable to no one but themselves.

There is no system of checks and balances in such a system. When trouble comes to the church, no objective, outside resources are available to call upon since there is no presbytery. As a result, when an intense power struggle develops within the elder board, not even the congregation can be involved in exercising discipline over the errant elders. In some cases, the elders become so impressed with their own authority that any questioning of their decisions by members of the congregation is considered insubordination and, therefore, sinful conduct.

I believe almost any reasonable system of church governance can be effective and used to bring glory to God. But remember the necessary condition—that the system be staffed by godly, selfless leaders. When self-serving, carnal leaders gain the ascendancy, all systems can, and eventually will, fail to bring glory to God.

The church can survive and even flourish under any of the three traditional systems. That is because each system has a built-in accountability system, a carefully constructed set of checks and balances. Without such built-in accountability, it is difficult for any system to survive during hard times, even if it is staffed by godly persons.

Nobody needs checks and balances under ideal conditions. The trouble is that no situation ever remains ideal. A church doesn't write a constitution for ideal times. It writes a constitution for the days of trouble. Then the constitution becomes number one on the best-seller list.

I am uncomfortable with the forms of neopresbyterianism I have just described. No matter how selfless they are, the leaders of a church place themselves and their church in a position of extreme vulnerability if the leadership of a church is accountable to no one but themselves. Under such circumstances, it is easy even for godly men to begin to consider themselves infallible and everyone else wrong or misinformed. In the past two decades, I have seen such congregations flourish wonderfully for a while. But when difficulties come, the trauma these churches experience is often terrible.

STRENGTHS OF THE CONVENTIONAL PRESBYTERIAN SYSTEM

*Multiple leadership.* The principle of multiple leadership is followed at the local level and among groups of churches. There is certainly strength in numbers when those numbers are made up of gifted, godly leaders. How wonderful when we can do the job in concert instead of as a lone ranger.

*Checks and balances.* A built-in system of checks and balances is available to aid a church in making important decisions and can bring comfort and sanity to a church experiencing chaos. This stems in part from the fact that multiple leadership has traditionally been elected leadership. Thus there is accountability integral to both the session and the presbytery. When this part of the system is properly guarded and utilized, excesses both at the local and multichurch level may be avoided.

*Completeness.* The traditional system was constructed over centuries of trial and error. The genius of the system is found in its completeness. I am concerned for churches that have adopted only a small portion of the system. That does not mean that churches that use a presbyterian system must adopt all aspects of the traditional system. It means that if they do abandon part of the system they should know why they are doing so. That may require that they study the history of the system to learn why it developed the way it did. Only then may they legitimately declare a part of the system inappropriate for their particular local context and put together a system more appropriate to their needs.

## CONGREGATIONAL SYSTEMS

Congregationalism, says Morris, "as the name implies, puts the chief stress on the place of the congregation."[5] It draws its support

5. Ibid.

from such principles as the fact that Christ and only Christ is the Head of the church (Colossians 1:18). In turn, all believers are priests (1 Peter 2:9).

Although there are many evidences of the importance of congregations in the decision-making processes of the early church, congregationalism as a system probably developed during the Reformation. Undoubtedly it emerged in part as a reaction against the excesses of episcopal domination found in the state-run churches of the day. As a matter of deep conscience, Christians separated themselves from those systems. For this separation they paid dearly, even with the loss of their lives.

Some of the most prominent early congregationalists were found among the Puritans and among some Anabaptist groups. Although it probably began in Europe, congregationalism found its most fertile ground in the spirit of democratic individualism that permeated early North America. Several denominations actually bear the name "congregational," but other groups also have adopted this style of governance. Baptists of various kinds, for instance, probably make up the largest number of congregationalists on this continent today.

As early Baptists offered the most fertile ground for congregationalism in eighteenth- and nineteenth-century America, contemporary Baptists struggle to reexamine that choice today. One of the greatest areas of examination among Baptists and other "baptistic" churches today has probably been over the question of whether to continue to adhere to traditional congregationalist patterns or to become more presbyterian in governance.

DISTINCTIVE FEATURES OF THE CONGREGATIONAL SYSTEM

*The priesthood of believers.* In a congregational system an emphasis is placed on the priesthood of all believers. In the congregational system all believers may freely go to the Scriptures and find answers to life's questions. Contrary to the practice of churches where the Scriptures must be interpreted by priests or teachers, congregationalists hold to the view that members of the congregation have access to the same Holy Spirit as do their teachers and thus can come to equally authoritative interpretations of Scriptures.

Morris justifies this approach on the basis of New Testament precedent. He reports, "Other religions of the first century required the interposition of a priestly caste if anyone wished to approach God, but the Christians would have none of this. Christ's priestly work has done away with the necessity for any earthly priest as the mediator of access to God."[6]

This strength can be the greatest weakness of the system. In its most nightmarish form, it can lead to all kinds of scriptural interpretations rendered by people who have only the most cursory and shallow knowledge of the Scriptures. Self-styled "experts" can arise and lead people astray.

It is against this kind of abuse that many pastors react today. As a result, many Baptist congregations that were traditionally creedless now have adopted intricate and detailed doctrinal statements. In turn, some Baptist pastors have come to overemphasize the teaching-pastor part of their role.

Once again, the church always seems to correct deficiencies by going to extremes. As a result, in many contemporary churches the tendency is to move back to the place where only seminary-trained pastor-teachers were trusted to interpret Scripture correctly. The danger in that, of course, is that we move back to the days when scriptural interpretation was solely in the hands of the clergy.

*Autonomy of the local church.* In the congregational system the local church is regarded as autonomous. The highest form of ecclesiastical authority is seen as resting not in groups of churches but at the local church level. As a result, no council or larger church body may impose its standards on a local group of believers. They are free to worship and function as they wish.

This feature seems to have been deeply ingrained in the practices of the early church. Morris states:

> Added to this is the emphasis on the local congregation in the NT. There, it is maintained, we see autonomous congregations not subject to episcopal or presbyterian control. The apostles, it is true, exercise a certain authority, but it is the authority of the founders of churches and of the Lord's own apostles. After their death there was no divinely instituted apostolate to take their place. Instead, the local congregations were still self-governing as we see from local church orders like the Didache. Appeal is also made to the democratic principle. The NT

6. Leon Morris, in *Evangelical Dictionary of Theology,* p. 240.

makes it clear that Christians are all one in Christ and there is not room for any absolute human authority.[7]

The autonomy of the local church is a strength in that it recognizes the biblical principle of the genius of the body working together with all its components functioning in concert with each other. This strength may become a weakness during a period of trauma. Then it is useful to have objective, outside help to aid in solving differences.

The district church-planting committee of the fellowship to which my church belongs places a limit on the degree of autonomy a "church plant" may exercise. If it is receiving monetary support from the denomination, the denominational board reserves the right to help choose its pastor and determine its polity. Only when the church is able to fully support itself is it granted full autonomy.

Again, there is New Testament precedent for an outside source exercising authority over a new or immature church. But I believe the principle should be extended to apply to older churches, too. I have a gnawing concern that we should build into our systems something to help bail out not only new churches but also established churches that have become totally confused in the midst of trauma.

*Congregational decision making.* In the congregational system major decisions are made by the congregation itself. Traditionally, it has not been the board but the congregation that approves budgets, elects leaders, calls potential staff, makes crucial doctrinal decisions, and grants large expenditures not covered in the budget.

A CRUCIAL DEFECT IN THE CONGREGATIONAL SYSTEM

The congregational system is the system with which I am most comfortable in a North American context. But there is no such thing as a perfect system. Though a congregational system gives the local church the most latitude for creative service, it also presents the opportunity for some of the greatest problems.

The chief danger is that relative democracy can devolve into a pure democracy that is akin to anarchy. You will recall the chief historical example of pure democracy, the Greek city-states. In those states the entire population gathered each time a decision was to be made. As

7. Ibid.

a result, discussion and bickering took endless hours of time. Dozens of self-styled orators had their own agendas, and few important decisions could be made.

The modern-day equivalent is the church that involves itself in an endless round of business meetings dealing with the most minute and routine decisions. In those churches little authority is given to the leadership, and leaders find it difficult to perform their assigned tasks. These pure democracies also may serve as a forum for vested interests and power brokers who want to exercise control over the congregation and see their selfish desires carried out. It is difficult to preserve any semblance of coordination and order in the program of the church when the program of the church is subject to the whims of such power brokers. Let's face it, some of these people are simply disruptive and ought to be subject to church discipline. Yet some of them have such well-entrenched kingdoms it is next to impossible to do that.

Any solution to the problem of organizational excess will include broader delegation of authority to leaders, fewer decisions on which the congregation itself votes, and far fewer business meetings.

What may we conclude regarding these three systems? Which one is the biblical system? We would be hard-pressed to make this claim about any one of them. Systems evolve over time, and yours is no exception to the rule. Be humble; the Holy Spirit is creative. He can use all kinds of systems—even some you have never heard about.

## Additional Resources

Carnegie, Samuel Calian. *Today's Pastor in Tomorrow's World.* Philadelphia: Westminster, 1982.

Gillespie, George. *Aaron's Rod Blossoming: Or the Divine Ordinance of Church Government.* Harrisburg, Va.: Sprinkle, 1985.

Harper, Michael. *Let My People Grow: Minister and Leadership in the Church.* Plainfield, N.J.: Logos, 1977.

Muller, Alois. *Democratization of the Church.* New York: Herder & Herder, 1971.

Steinbron, Melvin J. *Can the Pastor Do It Alone?* Ventura, Calif.: Regal, 1987.

## Questions for Discussion and Helpful Projects

1. The author makes the point that there is no biblically pre-scribed form of church government. He further asserts that almost any form of church government can be effective if it is in the hands of godly people with unselfish, biblical intentions.

PROJECT: List the inherent advantages of the episcopal system. In what cultural or ecclesiastical setting might this system be especially effective? What contemporary problems in North American churches could be minimized if a modified episcopal system were adopted for new pastors? Is there a biblical principle that lends support to this kind of system?

2. In democratic societies, checks and balances are fundamental instruments for short-circuiting human error. What dangers arise when a church fails to build checks and balances into its organizational structure? What are two reasons a traditional presbyterian system might be preferred over a neopresbyterian form of church government?

3. The ancient Greek city-states provide us with examples of so-called pure democracies in which the entire population gathered each time a decision was to be made. What problems germane to con-gregational forms of church government are experienced by pure democracies?

# 15

---

# SECULAR
# GOVERNANCE
# PATTERNS

Having looked at three traditional ecclesiastical types of church governance, I want now to examine three secular models. Before I begin, I must include a disclaimer: ecclesiastical and secular forms of governance have influenced and built upon each other for millennia, and it is impossible to find a system that is purely ecclesiastical or purely secular. Many systems of governance and management are in current use, but in this chapter I will draw your attention to three that I believe have impacted the church the most.

## THE BENEVOLENT DICTATOR

At the heart of autocratic systems is a person who is in charge. He dominates the entire system and exercises general, overall control. About such a person, Mark E. Hanson writes:

> The leader holds a high position because he or she is an elitist of sorts—superior in mind, knowledge and experience. The leader possesses, as Barnard observes, the ability to "bind the wills of men to the accomplishment of purposes beyond their immediate ends, beyond their times." Therefore, no one else is more qualified to sort out the tangles of problem situations and set the organization back on the

track of maximum efficiency. In pursuit of this task, the leader is supported by the full weight of the formal organization hierarchy and all the power, information and resources that the hierarchy can bring into focus.[1]

In such a setting there is absolutely no question as to who is the boss. The person at the top is clearly in charge, and he calls the signals for the rest of the organization. He may or may not call upon subordinates for ideas and may or may not choose to accept those ideas when they are offered.

This is the kind of church leader who wants to make every major decision and be kept informed of every minor one. He wants to be on top of every situation and is upset when surprises come his way. By and large, nobody does anything without his knowledge or permission. If anyone does, he is labeled rebellious and carnal.

Does any of this sound familiar? Have you ever seen a church that works this way? Though I have described a stereotype, elements of the pattern appear in many churches today. Church growth literature seems to promote this style of authority by insisting that the churches that are really growing are those which "enjoy" strong leadership. Pastors and church leaders who long to act like dictators point to church growth literature for authentication so that they can legitimately practice the style.

When the pastor is the "boss" in this model, he may be dubbed either a "benevolent shepherd" or a "self-serving dictator" depending on whether or not people agree with him. Often the latter title is given to him by other pastors who are jealous of his apparent success.

Sometimes it isn't the pastor who exercises the primary control in a local church. A "tribal leader" or group of "tribal leaders" may reserve this dominion for themselves. Trouble arises when a pastor is unaware that he is not in charge or *is* aware and tries to wrest control from the tribal leaders. Unless the pastor has been able to muster a great deal of clout ahead of time, sparks fly high and he usually looks for another church.

1. Mark E. Hanson, *Educational Administration and Organizational Behavior* (Boston: Allyn & Bacon, 1985), p. 181.

### A BENEVOLENT DICTATORSHIP IS NOT ALWAYS APPROPRIATE

Is this pattern necessarily always wrong? Of course not, but it isn't always appropriate either. To succeed, the model demands a special kind of leader and a congregation willing to follow such leadership. Under those circumstances, it can be a viable form of church governance. In some cultural settings, it may even be the only model under which a church can effectively operate.

Church planters often adopt a centralized model and find it successful until the church grows mature and begins to develop other skilled leaders. Then the church planter finds himself out of sync with his congregation. As a result, he either changes his style, moves on to plant another church, or stays to see his good work disintegrate.

This style is often highly inventive and creative. In some settings it is extremely effective and productive. Sometimes the worst problems with this leadership style make themselves apparent when it is, at last, time for the leader to leave. The church then finds that the remaining leadership is incapable of making decisions. The church was really a one man church. Perhaps it would have been best for the church to disband when it was time for the "benevolent dictator" to leave.

### A BENEVOLENT DICTATORSHIP IS NOT NECESSARILY BIBLICAL

Is this style biblical? Outside of the founding apostles, I see no New Testament example of such a leadership style. Neither do I see any clear prohibition. I believe that godly men whose hearts are pure before God and aim to bring glory to Him may use this style effectively. The catch is that they need exceptional strength of character and personality to pull it off, and they must exercise this strength within the proper context. I am convinced that there are people who do not want to make decisions for themselves. Such people will often gladly and blindly follow an autocratic leader.

### A BENEVOLENT DICTATORSHIP HAS MAJOR DRAWBACKS

Although a benevolent dictatorship may be effective with the right leader and the right kind of people, it has drawbacks.

1. *It is potentially the most dangerous model of all because it draws attention to the authority of a person.* Also, it has the tendency

to glorify a person instead of God. If that person slips, the damage to the church, to individual Christians, and to the secular community can be immense.

The possibility of such authoritarian leaders falling and the disastrous aftermath of such a fall have been vividly painted for us by the secular media. They have had a heyday because of the antics of fallen preachers. The good image evangelicals once had has been irreversibly tarnished. The higher the prestige, the higher the amount of unbridled authority, the greater the chance for a mighty fall. I would be wary about setting myself up for that kind of a fall.

2. *The style can be extremely dangerous when a leader slips theologically and begins to insist that his people accept his pet ideas as being absolutely authoritative.* Destructive cults have often resulted from such thinking.

3. *People who buy into such systems often become and remain incapable of deciding and acting on their own.* Instead of exploring all of the exciting things God may have for them, they become robots who respond as their leader dictates. Congregations of "clones" may act according to the direction of a leader instead of experiencing the diversity of their spiritual giftedness. Creativity among church members is de-emphasized, and eventually the entire church suffers because of its one-sided philosophy of ministry.

In writing to the adverse impact a dictator may have upon his followers, James Means writes, "Authoritarian leaders have often produced feeble followers. A church filled with submissive people is not a worthy goal. To make matters worse, sometimes leaders mistake compliance for unity, acquiescence for cohesiveness. Good leaders produce strong, contributing people, not weak, compliant people."[2]

An additional problem may arise when a person in leadership imagines himself to be a strong leader when he isn't. Without really knowing what makes his congregation tick, such an individual may think that all he has to do to solve his problems is to set up a dictatorial system. He is often unaware that such a system is inappropriate for and unacceptable to his congregation. Worse, he is unaware that even if the system were acceptable, he would not be the person who could pull it off.

2. James E. Means, *Leadership in Christian Ministry* (Grand Rapids: Baker, 1989), p. 154.

As a result, both the system and he fail. When that happens, often it does not occur to him that it was he, not the congregation, who was guilty of the greatest error.

Unless you are an extraordinary person and operate under unique circumstances, avoid this kind of leadership pattern. Even if you believe you are the right person and the circumstances are ripe for this model, seek the counsel of many godly people to confirm or contradict your own limited impressions. Remember, rare is the individual who can succeed using this system.

## THE BLESSED BUREAUCRACY

To analyze the bureaucratic system adequately, it is good to look back to early organizational theory. About three decades into the twentieth century, the work of Frederick W. Taylor and Max Weber began to dominate thinking about the so-called progressive workplace. Rational behavior and predictability were the name of the game. Taylor and Weber sincerely believed that in a scientifically run bureaucracy "rational authority is projected throughout the organization in such a way as to directly control human activity to the points of high predictability and maximum efficiency."[3] So popular were the optimistic views of the early social scientists concerning bureaucracy that their ideas penetrated all layers of our society, including the church.

In a bureaucracy authority originates at the top and filters down to the bottom in a pyramidal fashion. The "top" may be a board or a person. In a typical bureaucracy, the bureaucrats, or people in the various echelons of authority, become well entrenched. As a result, they are often the ones who actually call the signals. A chief example of this is the government of the United States. There, entrenched bureaucrats have had their way for decades. It doesn't really matter who is in office, Democrats or Republicans. Despite the efforts of a well-intentioned, reform president, he soon learns that he cannot change the system appreciably.

### THE BUREAUCRATIC STYLE EXACTS A HEAVY PRICE

We need look no further than many average North American churches to find a ponderous, slow-moving bureaucracy complete with

3. Hanson, *Educational Administration and Organizational Behavior*, p. 7.

bureaucrats (some of whom are power brokers), endless committees, and tedious methods of initiating any kind of change.

Some churches survive like this for years. Sometimes the only note of dissatisfaction is expressed by the young people, who survey the hopelessness of the situation and check out in droves. Those with vested interest in the bureaucracy see the situation differently. The *real* problem, they say, lies with impatient newcomers who try to initiate change overnight. They don't see these newcomers as creative, idealistic, and innovative leaders who bring a glimmer of hope to a bad situation and are working to make things better. The result of the clash is that defeated, disillusioned, but creative leaders leave the church and are reluctant to exercise leadership anywhere else for a long time.

## THE BUREAUCRATIC STYLE
### WORKS AGAINST INITIATIVE AND INDIVIDUALITY

Since the bureaucratic system is so pervasive, it is legitimate to ask, Are there any redeeming qualities to such a system? Supporters of such a system would probably list at least two. The first of these is that *a bureaucratic system is a relatively efficient way to carry on routine operations and preserve the status quo.* Hanson writes:

> Bureaucratic structure and administration are designed to routinize problem solving—to treat incoming questions and issues in a programmed, systematic way that will draw upon a minimum of human and material resources. If each issue or personal problem and organization were treated as unique, . . . then the problems of planning, coordinating, and controlling would require massive amounts of time and resources. By routinizing the processes of the organization, the myriad competing demands on the system can be dispatched quickly and efficiently through established standing operating procedures. Hence, the multitude of round holes are created into which pegs of all sizes and shapes must fit.[4]

But is this really such an advantage? If we look at the other side of the coin, we see that though orderliness and routinization may prevail, the price for that orderliness is sometimes paranoia in the leadership regarding those under them. In *Barbarians to Bureaucrats* Miller writes, "The bureaucrat corporation is in the process of losing its pur-

---

4. Ibid., pp. 61-62.

pose and health."[5] As a result, intricate systems of rules and regulations are formed to cover every minor procedure. A good indication of how bureaucratic a church has become is the size of its constitution and bylaws. The more bureaucratic, the larger the document. In a bureaucratic church, following procedures slavishly often is more important than reaching the church's principal goals.

The bureaucracy tries to anticipate any deviance and establishes procedures to keep the organization on course and to deal with deviance when and if it arises. Since the procedures are so well established, a bureaucracy is a difficult system under which to initiate changes. Its byword is "We have always (or never) done things that way."

Supporters of a bureaucracy would say, "We must do things with decency and order. People are so unpredictable these days that we have to keep close controls on what they are doing. After all, the program of the church must be considered foremost." At this point people such as Richards would fairly scream, "People are individuals and each new situation must be handled intuitively and individually, not routinely. Remember, we must first meet the needs of individuals, not always worry about the program." I would agree.

Those who call for "decency and order" have a point. There is a sense in which certain procedures must be routinized even in the church. That is why it is good to have a carefully worded (but not necessarily overly long and totally comprehensive) constitution and by-laws. It is also necessary to have policy manuals that indicate orderly, established ways of handling such things as finances, administrative duties, selection of personnel, business meetings, and other such details. It is not sufficient to do these things "as the Spirit moves," or to fly by the seat of one's pants. Among the agencies that will hold us accountable for orderly, routine procedures is the Internal Revenue Service.

At the same time we need to build into an orderly system a consideration of the needs of individual people. After all, we are in the people business. So although it is good Christian stewardship to practice sound management principles in matters of finances and other routine matters, we must avoid forming a bureaucracy. A bureaucracy will hinder us from productive, creative ministry to and in behalf of people. It will take a workable management system and turn it into something

5. Lawrence M. Miller, *Barbarians to Bureaucrats* (New York: Clarkson N. Potter, 1989), p. 111.

the scribes and Pharisees would have admired. If bureaucratic rule and "red tape" characterize your church's governance pattern, your system needs drastic overhauling. As long as bureaucracy prevails, that church will accomplish little for Jesus Christ.

THE BUREAUCRATIC STYLE
ENCOURAGES THE GROWTH OF FIEFDOMS

The second advantage of bureaucracy its proponents champion is that *a bureaucracy permits many people to exercise strategic leadership ministries within the church.* The reasoning is that if many people exercise their leadership gifts in the right context the chance of an overall dictatorship's developing is lessened.

Supporters of bureaucracy forget that it is possible for bureaucrats to establish fiefdoms of their own. How many long-term organists have controlled the music programs of churches for decades? A constant exercise of power keeps the church from moving forward and reaching its full potential. Sometimes it keeps the church stale and stodgy, which, in turn, deters growth.

THE BUREAUCRATIC STYLE
ENCOURAGES THE PETER PRINCIPLE

There are further dangers. One is that the Peter Principle takes over. The Peter Principle—"a person is likely to be promoted to his level of incompetence"—works especially well in a bureaucracy. If a person hangs in there long enough, he is likely to be elevated on the totem pole. But since he is more likely to be promoted on the basis of his loyalty to the system instead of his creativity, often small-minded people with little vision come to dominate the system. Then, when creative people with imaginative vision long to see something done, loyal bureaucrats crush them by sheer weight and clout. The creative people either give up and succumb to the system or move on to another church. In both cases the church loses the creativity it desperately needs.

THE BUREAUCRATIC STYLE
BOGS CREATIVE PEOPLE DOWN IN ROUTINE PROCEDURES

In still another case, creative people may be viewed as good prospects to incorporate into the bureaucracy. But when they find themselves in office they are confronted with an overwhelming barrage of routine duties. Sitting on endless committees, engaging in tedious paperwork, and fulfilling the demands of ceaseless procedures soon dominate all of their time. Thus their creativity and effective labors are lost to the church. In a bureaucratic system we can hinder getting the work done by making chiefs of hardworking Indians.

THE BUREAUCRATIC STYLE
ACTS AS A DETERRENT TO SERVING PEOPLE

A bureaucracy will lead to the death of effective ministry in a church. So the lesson to be learned here is: realizing that some procedures must be routinized, we must still do everything in our power to keep a bureaucracy from forming in our church. We must build into our church safeguards against a bureaucracy's forming. These safeguards will include limitation of tenure, which guards against kingdom building.

We must examine our church's system of governance continually. Is the efficient functioning of the system becoming more important than the people the system serves? If the system acts as a deterrent to serving people, it is probably well on the way to bureaucracy. Renovate the system as soon as you can. Do it before it becomes deeply entrenched.

If you are a new, idealistic leader facing an unwieldy, resistant bureaucracy, go slowly. Remember, a bureaucracy is the hardest system of all within which to initiate change. Bureaucrats guard their positions jealously. You are on shaky and dangerous ground, so be alert! Be advised, as well, that you may well have to change the bureaucrats before you can change the system.

Most of all, hang in there! Rome wasn't built in a day, and neither was the bureaucracy of your church. It will take more than a day to correct the problems the system presents. Is your church worth it? If the answer is yes, then it is also worth the effort to bring about the changes the church needs if it is to move ahead. Beware of bureaucracy.

## LIVING SYSTEMS

Recent thinking concerning organizations has arisen from the field of biology. As biologists have recognized living organisms as collections of interdependent and interrelated subsystems, social scientists have applied the analogy to institutions. In institutions, not only are there formal subsystems, there are also informal subsystems that are just as important and influential. For example, a certain Bible study in a church may not exercise a role in the formal governance structure of a church, but as an informal center of influence it may actually exercise greater decision-making power than the official board. A friend of mine in the pastorate knows how true this is: he claims that it was a Bible study group in his church that was the impetus for forcing his ouster from the pastorate!

Hanson illustrates such a collection of interrelated subsystems in figure 7. In describing this diagram he writes:

> An organization like a school system is made up of a multitude of subsystems that are interrelated. Each subsystem is a part of a greater subsystem, which is part of an even greater system. For example, the two Spanish teachers form a subsystem of the language department which is a subsystem of the humanities division which is a subsystem of the high school which is a subsystem of the school district which is a subsystem of the state legislature. The action patterns of any one of these subsystems cannot be fully understood independent of its immediate linking subsystems. For instance, the actions of the history department cannot be understood independent of the constraints and demands placed upon it by the policy of the high school or by the expectations and needs of various groups of teachers.[6]

When I read Hanson's description, my thoughts are drawn to the average local church. The same paragraph could be written using church terms instead of school terms, and it would apply perfectly.

AN OPEN SYSTEMS INSTITUTION IS DYNAMIC

In "open systems" theory the institution is dynamic, or "living," instead of static, or "dead." The open systems approach insists that an institution is not entirely self-directed. Strong external stimuli dramatically affect it as much as its component parts do. Put another way, when we talk about an open system we are talking about a collection of interdependent subsystems that together resemble a living organism in the way the entire system functions. An open system is

6. Hanson, *Educational Administration and Organizational Behavior*, p. 61.

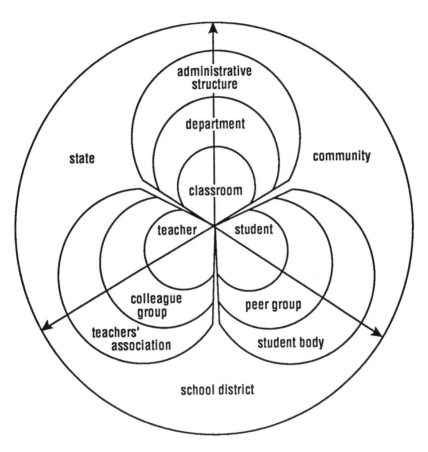

Fig. 7. Subsystems

Source: From E. Mark Hanson, *Educational Administration and Organizational Behavior*, 2d ed. Copyright © 1985 by Allyn and Bacon. Reprinted with permission.

greatly affected by the interaction of its component parts and is also significantly influenced by many external pressures.

Does this pattern resemble anything you have read about in the Scriptures? How about the description of the church as a body in 1 Corinthians 12? The social scientists seemed to have borrowed a metaphor from the Bible.

There is a difference in the church and other organizations, however. Whereas other institutions may resemble a living organism in some ways, the church is the only true organism. Therefore, the analogy of an organism, though imperfect in describing other institutions, fits to a "T" at least one biblical description of the church.

AN OPEN SYSTEMS INSTITUTION AND
AN EFFECTIVELY LED LOCAL CHURCH HAVE MUCH IN COMMON

What other comparisons can be made between an open system and an effectively led local church? Hanson lists at least thirteen characteristics of an open system. I believe that at least twelve of these apply to the church; I have listed them below.

1. It is characterized by interlocking cycles of events within the subsystems.

2. Power is diffused into the subsystems, which must differentiate and integrate their activities.

3. The demands and needs of the environment give direction to events.

4. Communication follows a system-wide information network designed to integrate the activities of subsystems and to establish linkages with the environment.

5. The managerial subsystem must function in support of the needs of other subsystems.

6. Conflict is inevitable and can lead to positive change through creative management.

7. There are many ways of performing a task that are equally satisfactory.

8. The institution focuses on the way it *does* function instead of the way it *should* function.

9. It is open and responsive to the environment through input-output exchanges.

10. It is characterized by dynamic rather than static relationships.

11. Its chief leadership is often subject to events that are not of their making and are beyond their control.

12. Equilibrium in environmental-organizational exchanges gives order to the institution.[7]

The social scientists have discovered something valuable to us as church leaders. Using some of their insights and building upon the biblical text, it is possible to construct a biblically viable system of church governance. Notice, however, that systems theory is a whole different way of looking at institutions rather than a distinct and different organizational pattern. It does not discard the benefits of strong leaders or helpful routinizing. Neither does it say that the best points of the episcopal, presbyterian, or congregational systems must be discarded. It intimates, instead, that these ecclesiastical and secular systems must be subservient to the fact that the church is the Body of Christ. As any human body has definite needs, the church has even more complicated needs.

Any governing system a church adopts must be subservient to the needs of the church and must contribute to the church's reaching the goals of evangelism and edification. Where governing structures hinder the reaching of those goals, the system must be overhauled or discarded. Discarding the system may be tantamount to killing the sacred cow. Impatient leaders tend to move rapidly in this direction, hoping to find a quick fix for the church's problems. Generally the results are anything but desirable. On the other hand, overhauling the system is much harder and more time-consuming, but it can be done and will bring about results that are much less traumatic and much more lasting and far reaching.

7. Ibid., pp. 146-47.

## Additional Resources

Atkins, Stanley, and Theodore McConnell. *Churches on the Wrong Road.* Chicago: Gateway, 1986.
Haeffner, Arden Dean. *The Pastor as Motivator.* Master's thesis, Dallas Theological Seminary, Dallas, 1977.

## Questions for Discussion and a Helpful Project

1. PROJECT: List the three types of secular governance mentioned in this chapter. Review the history of your church. Which of the three types has impacted your church over the years? List the good ways and the bad ways it has done so. Are you currently living with a system that hinders rather than helps your church accomplish its mission? In what ways can this problem be corrected?

2. What advice is given in this chapter to the leader who is contemplating using the autocratic model of church leadership? In what instances may this model be appropriate?

3. Someone has declared that the seven final words of a dying church might be "We've never done it this way before." Explain why a church that subscribes to a bureaucratic framework runs the risk of falling into this category.

4. The genius of a bureaucratic system is its capacity to accelerate efficiency by decentralizing decision-making power. However, this chapter states that "a bureaucracy will lead to the death of effective ministry in a church." What kinds of problems are invited when too many people occupy strategic leadership positions in a church?

5. What are some of the features of an open system? How could some of the insights social scientists have discovered about organizations be integrated with a local church's philosophy of ministry? What important items must be kept in mind when one is contemplating the integration of secular systems theory with a church framework?

# 16

# DYNAMIC CHURCH GOVERNANCE PATTERNS

How does a church leader move his church from a static, one-dimensional church organization to a pattern that is dynamic, multidimensional, and effective in ministry? He does so by following a three-pronged method of attack: he works to make his church multicelled in its social organization and ministry teams; he simplifies its formal leadership structure; and he engages the congregation in creative goal-setting. All of this he undertakes in the context of principles that underlie a sound and biblical church organizational system. The first two of these elements, developing a multicelled church and simplifying its organizational structure, will be discussed in this chapter; creative goal setting and principles of a sound church organizational will be discussed in the next chapter.

## DEVELOPING A MULTICELL CHURCH

In his book *Growing Plans*[1] Lyle Schaller points out that the problem with many change-resistant churches is that they are what he calls "single cell" churches. This pattern locks the church into organi-

1. Lyle E. Schaller, *Growing Plans* (Nashville: Abingdon, 1985).

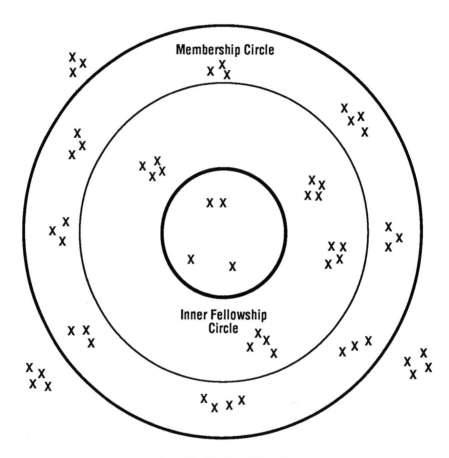

Fig. 8. The Single-Cell Church

Source: From *Growing Plans—Strategies to Increase Your Church's Membership* by Lyle E. Schaller. Copyright © 1983 Abingdon Press. Reprinted by permission.

zational paralysis and makes it almost impossible for new leadership coming into the church to bring about needed change or to mobilize the church for performing the tasks of the kingdom.

Figure 8 describes a single-cell church. It consists of an inner circle, or nucleus, and two surrounding rings. The inner cell is what Schaller calls the "fellowship" circle, the "in group," the people who are really in charge and have been for a long time. When they refer to the church and its operations, they "use pronouns such as 'we,' 'ours,' and 'us,'" Schaller says.[2]

The outer circle is what Schaller calls the "membership circle." People in this circle "often use pronouns such as 'they,' 'theirs,' and 'them'" when they speak about the inner workings of the church.[3] They have joined the church and may even occupy church offices, but they do not hold power in the true decision-making process of the church.

Sometimes a pastor or gifted lay leader does not understand this point and makes the mistake of assuming that because he has been called or elected to office by the congregation he is necessarily a part of the power structure of that church. Not so; it may take him years to reach that status. Moreover, when a pastor or lay leader attempts to bring change to a single-cell church he may find that he cannot do so because he is not included in the inner, or fellowship, circle of the church. The power structure is so well defined that any attempts he makes to initiate new programs or renovate old ones are quickly rebuffed.

Schaller initially tended to believe that only relatively small churches could be classified as single-cell churches, and I agreed with him until I observed that the phenomenon was also present in much larger churches. My own background includes exposure to many churches of ethnic origin that still identify closely with their roots. In addition, I have observed many churches that were born out of a split with another church or because their church separated itself from a major denomination with which it could no longer agree doctrinally. My observations of these ethnic-formed and problem-formed churches lead me to believe that often they remain single-cell in mentality even when they have grown relatively large and are separated by many years from their origins.

2. Ibid., p. 26.
3. Ibid.

It is possible also for a church to have a single-cell mentality even when several fellowship circles exist. In this case the fellowship circles are distinct from one another and do not cooperate; instead each exercises considerable clout and vies with the others for power.

Schaller insists that churches that remain single cell in mentality will never advance. They are sedentary and probably have grown as big as they will get. The only hope for instituting change in such a church is to turn it into what he calls a multicell church.

When the new leader has been in position at least a year and has "tested the waters" concerning the church's openness to the changes he wishes to make, he takes his first steps in moving his church toward becoming a multicell church. He does not move quickly. As a first requisite, he targets people from the fellowship circle to become his special disciples. He does that because significant change in a church cannot be made unless members of the principal power group of that church cooperate. They are the people who will legitimatize any change. Initially he focuses on members of the fellowship group with whom he can relate and who seem open to the attitudinal changes he wishes to bring about. Even a person who is slightly open to change is a better initial target than the person whose attitudes are set in concrete. He will not attempt to crack the hardest nut at the beginning, for that kind of relationship will take some time to develop.

Through the use of involvement-type learning experiences he disciples these people, leading them step by step as they identify some area of ministry interest that is appealing to them. Suppose it is the objective of the leadership to initiate a ministry of "care groups" within the church, but that such a plan has met with initial resistance. The wise leader pulls back and targets people in the fellowship circle whom he finds are open to and even eager to start caring groups. He encourages those people and, with the help of one or two of them, forms his first care group.

Figure 9 describes in schematic form what the leader is doing as he forms the caring group. He has recruited one or two of the fellowship circle to give this ministry legitimacy, and at the same time he has added a number of interested people from the membership circle and even some individuals from outside the membership of the church altogether. A two-cell church now exists.

After sufficient time has elapsed and the smoke has cleared, he repeats this process with other ministry areas, such as women's Bible

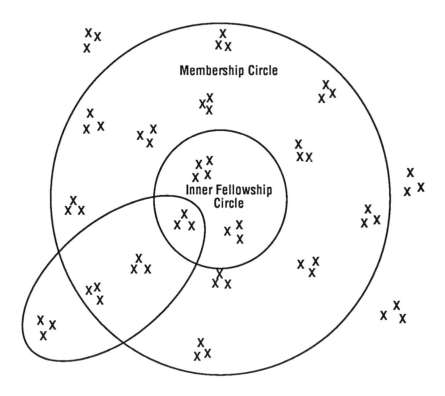

Fig. 9. The Two-Cell Church

Source: From *Growing Plans—Strategies to Increase Your Church's Membership* by Lyle E. Schaller. Copyright © 1983 Abingdon Press. Reprinted by permission.

studies, senior citizens' activities, or other ministries he believes are germane to meeting the needs of congregation. The church now becomes a multicelled organism (figure 10). Instead of being organized around a central power nucleus it has become ministry oriented. The leadership of the church have become encouragers, facilitators, and coordinators of the many important ministries that are now involving so many people of this church in such a meaningful way.

When the church becomes a multicelled organism, says Schaller, the "old single core no longer has the visibility or power it once had, and most members are not sure who is in the center circle—and many do not care."[4] The tyrannical power of church bosses is then at an end, and positive change becomes much easier to initiate.

## THE POWER OF THE FELLOWSHIP CIRCLE

Let's backtrack for a moment and analyze why we start this process with members of the fellowship circle. We do so because that's where the clout is. If members of the fellowship circle are not enlisted, the church will remain a one-cell church, and no substantive, long-lasting change will take place.

Sometimes the change agent ignores this principle, bypasses the fellowship circle, and is able to initiate changes by utilizing members of the membership circle. These may even be far-sweeping changes. But if the changes brought about by this means antagonize or alienate the people in the fellowship circle, not only may those changes be short-lived, the change agent himself may be out of a job. He will be squeezed out by members of the fellowship circle, for they hold the controlling interest in the one-cell church, whether or not they occupy an official office, and will resent any competing focus of power.

So the wise change agent selects members of the fellowship circle whose attitudes have changed for the better and who have the potential to work patiently with other people. He talks with them about the need to change the attitudes of other people in the congregation, and he enlists them in the program. He tells these members of the fellowship group how to go about enlisting new participants, and he includes them as observers as he does just that. Soon, under his watchful eye, they begin the process itself with other people. After consider-

4. Ibid., p. 31.

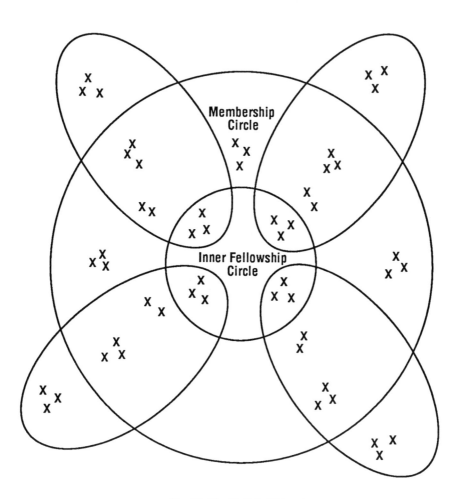

Fig. 10. The Multi-Cell Church

able practice, they, too, become skilled at the process and are able to launch out on their own. Always, there is constant, careful communication between the fellowship group recruits and the leadership of the church.

What this amounts to is a "one-on-one" discipleship program where as people's attitudes are changed, they, in turn, are employed in changing the attitudes of others. Such a program can become contagious and eventually may help to change the attitudes of the entire church.

## Dealing with Alienated Fellowship Circle Members

There is still one significant problem area to deal with. Schaller warns that when such changes take place in a church's power structure, often it finds itself left with people he calls "angry alienated ex-leaders." Sometimes these people realize what is going on in plenty of time to cause a great deal of discomfort to the new leadership. At other times they do not realize what is happening in time to do anything. As a result, they find themselves cut off from the mainstream of church life, begin to attend church infrequently, or even spend portions of the church year away from home, perhaps in a semiretired status. Schaller believes that this development is unavoidable.

It is at this juncture that my spirit rebels. If the church is truly the Body of Christ and if all parts of the body are necessary for its health and proper functioning, I cannot be content with ex-leaders merely dropping out. Their experience, maturity, and wisdom may be just the factors lacking in its newer group of leaders.

So let me issue a challenge to those who read this book. When your church is involved in the change process, some dropouts may result. But do not accept them as inevitable. Review the chapter of this book that discusses the words the Bible uses to refer to the process of changing people's minds. There you will find such terms as *appeal, persuade, urge,* and *encourage.* Those are the tactics to be used with people after deep personal relationships have been established and you have earned the right to be heard.

Then review the chapter that tells you how to change the attitudes of mature people. Remember, adults must be exposed to direct learning methods. Lecturing won't work. Undoubtedly, this will involve the concentration of the resources of a church leader in the direction of one particular individual for what may seem to be a relatively long period of time. If this doesn't result in a positive change, some energy will have been wasted—but if it does work, look what the church has gained! We are not talking here about enlisting the halting services of a novice, but enlisting the support of a seasoned veteran whose heart and mind have been changed. Here is a leader who is now able to draw upon all his accumulated spiritual resources and the experience of his years to bring about substantive, mature, and relevant change to the church of Jesus Christ. In my estimation, to be able to reclaim such an individual is one of the primary objectives that the wise change agent should be pursuing.

### Translating an Informal Multicell Organization into a Formal Church Structure

In chapter 2 the mission of the church, to glorify God, was broken down into six goals under the headings of evangelism and edification (figure 2). Were we to build a traditional church governance structure using those goals, that would be for most of us a great improvement over what we have had in the past. At least the structure would tell us what our church hopes to accomplish.

Figure 11 illustrates a traditional system using the church's basic goals as a guideline. This system is an improvement over the structures used by many churches. A good quality of this structure is that overall authority is vested in the congregation and the board is responsible to the body as a whole. This structure also has the virtue of indicating who is in charge and some of their responsibilities. That is important, for whatever organizational system you devise, it is essential that you spell out clearly the relationships of the pastor, the board members, and the congregation. Means writes to this point, saying:

> The most crucial questions concerning church leadership include the following: Are church leaders placed among members or are church leaders placed over members? Are leaders to control the church and make decisions for the church, or is the church to participate in making major decisions? Should the church defer to its leaders' determination of the will of God, or should leaders defer to group determina-

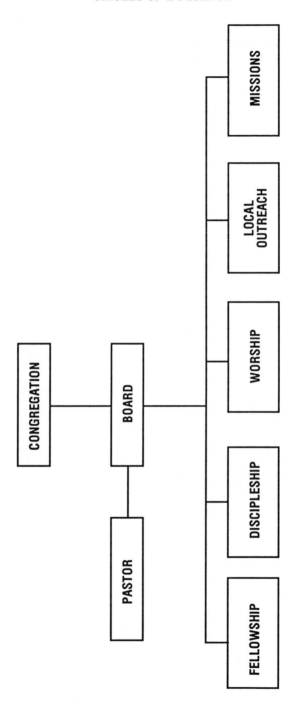

Fig. 11. A Traditional Church System

tion of God's will? Answers to these questions determine how leaders actually conduct themselves in their ministries.[5]

There is another benefit in the system pictured in figure 11. It indicates a single board system rather a multiboard nightmare. Yet even this system has weaknesses and limitations. One of those drawbacks is that it is a hierarchical system. The underlying philosophy is that authority comes from above and is directed downward through the system. A defect of the traditional system is that it makes the pastor an appendage not answerable to the congregation. He appears to work directly for the board, something that seems most unwise. Though the pastor should be open to seeking and receiving the counsel of board members, the pastor should lead the board rather than being directed by it.

Still another drawback exists in the system represented by figure 11. The board appears to be directly responsible for the program and activities of the church. Granted, the work may be divided up among the board members, but in the diagram no one individual appears to be providing overall coordination to the ministry. This lack of coordination will make it impossible for a board to act effectively. The principle of responsibility applies here as well as elsewhere: When everyone is responsible for everything, specific things seldom get done well.

Moreover, the practical workings of such a system often involve countless hours where board members sit in session discussing how each program of the church should run. Those are often wasted hours when greater work of the kingdom should and could take precedence. When so much detailed discussion must precede any substantive action, there is often little time to carry out the action itself. Without an efficient way of making decisions and initiating action, no wonder so many churches lumber along.

What should the proper church organizational structure look like? It should be a multicell structure similar to the organizational pattern discussed earlier in this chapter (figure 10). The system should be "open" in that it takes into consideration the needs of the society around it and responds to those needs. It should not be a self-serving, stagnant organism but a vital, functioning one. It should have a single

5. James E. Means, *Leadership in Christian Ministry* (Grand Rapids: Baker, 1989), p. 43.

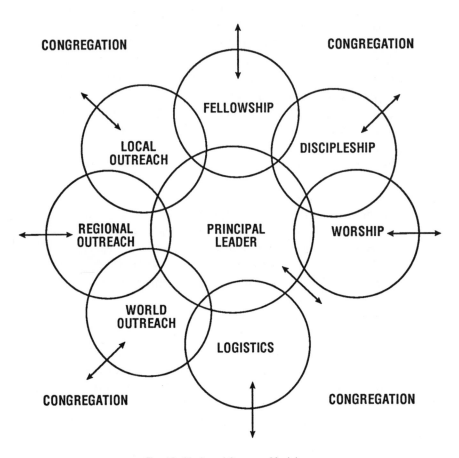

Fig. 12. Circles of Concern Model

coordinating source, the pastor, who is a servant to both the board and the congregation. Yet, as servant, he is responsible for directing and coordinating the entire operation of the body.

In such a system the ministries are intertwining and interdependent. Strictly speaking, a chart cannot effectively convey this idea. In reality, every circle intertwines with every other circle, something that cannot be fully expressed two-dimensionally. Each ministry interfaces with all the others. All must work in harmony so that the church may be balanced and biblical.

The congregation surrounds everything and is impacted by all the ministry areas. In turn, it is equipped for service by all of the ministry areas. As a result, the body ministers inwardly through the edificational ministries and outwardly through the evangelistic ministries. What should result is a living, dynamic organism, truly a circle of concern (figure 12).

## TRANSLATING THE "CIRCLES OF CONCERN" MODEL TO THE LARGE CONGREGATION

I am convinced that the coordinators for each of the seven ministry areas should be considered members of the ministry staff, whether they perform their ministry full-time, part-time, or as volunteers. I also believe that most churches should have only one board. In a smaller church, where a majority of the ministry staff members are volunteers, it is fitting and proper that the various ministry coordinators be members of that board.

But at some point a church will become so large that a one-board system is no longer effective. When a church is so big that it is able to staff most of its ministry positions with full-time paid coordinators, there needs to be an additional level of governance. Whether we like it or not, paid staff members will always be looked upon by some church members as employees. Consequently, if paid staff members actually run the church, both real and imagined "conflict of interest" questions may arise.

The Acts 6 model is helpful here. You will remember that the apostles were bogged down in the machinery of trying to do the mechanical details of the ministry. They were not able to properly engage in prayer, the teaching of the Word, and general strategizing as to how the new church should carry out its mission effectively and efficiently.

Therefore, they appointed seven capable administrators to coordinate the ministry programs of the church. The apostles were then freed to perform those things important to them and to act as a policy-making body.

We notice something akin to this in secular corporations today. A board of directors represents the stockholders and establishes policies for the firm. The president, as chief executive officer, carries out these policies through his various vice presidents. Notice, however, that in a well run company members of the board of directors do not dabble in the actual operation of the corporation. They leave that to the president and his assistants.

Many churches do not follow this pattern. In them the policy board also carries out the details of supervising the various ministries. Sometimes the board does this in virtual disregard of the pastor, who is trying to supply overall leadership to the church. I believe a church needs to have a body of people who focus on policy making. In a small church, the congregation can serve as that body. Ministry coordinators, in turn, who are, by and large, volunteers, can stay close to the congregation and sense its wishes.

In a larger church, however, a separate group of individuals is needed. This group becomes the real board of the church, with the ministry coordinators serving together as a "ministries council." This board is made up of "elder types" who will agree to work with and pray for the pastor as he supplies overall leadership to the church. This board becomes the eyes and ears of the ministry team (figure 13).

In such a system the function of the policy group is different from that of the ministries council. Its task is to listen to the congregation and its wishes. In addition, it has a prophetic function: to "see visions and dream dreams" of what the Lord has in mind for the expanding ministry of this congregation. Each of the members of this group pledges to be mutually supportive of the other members, and each promises to fully support the pastor both in prayer and in action.

This group becomes the pastor's advisory council and, in rare cases, if the pastor requires discipline, it becomes the first-line disciplinary group. If further action is required, the matter is then referred to the congregation.

This group should not exceed six or eight in number. Moreover, a member of the group should serve only on this group and not on the ministries council. Members should, of course, be free to carry on

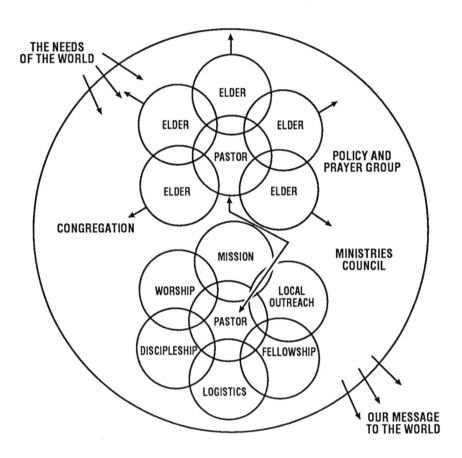

Fig. 13. A Proposed Governance Structure for a Larger Church

other ministry responsibilities such as teaching or singing in the choir. However, they should consider their first priorities to be as follows:

1. Prayer. Whatever they have to do to "free up" their schedules, they must remind themselves that prayer is their most important ministry.

2. Fellowship among themselves. Their fellowship pattern should be a model for the rest of the church.

3. Close contact with the church members. This enables them to discern general levels of satisfaction and dissatisfaction and how well ministry roles are being met.

4. Bible study. Through serious and concentrated study in the Word, God reveals to them His great plan for His church.

5. Study of church-related materials such as this book, which will help them in their task of providing guidance to the church.

6. Special care of the pastor and his family. These are the folks who sense when the pastor is tired and needs to take a few days off. Likewise, if he is not performing as well as he should, they are the people who find out why and try to help him correct that situation. This group also looks after his physical welfare, encouraging him to get the proper amount of both exercise and rest. In turn, they make sure that the church provides generously for his financial needs.

One final disclaimer in all of this: The illustrations I have used in this chapter are for the stimulation of your thinking. No one can possibly foresee the staffing needs of every church. However, I hope and pray that these ideas will serve as fruitful stimuli for discussion and that your church will begin to think of staffing in creative ways.

## Additional Resources

Anderson, James D. *The Management of Ministry.* San Francisco: Harper & Row, 1978.

Blanchard, Kenneth, Patricia Zigarmi, and Drea Zigarmi. *Leadership and the One Minute Manager.* New York: William Morrow, 1985.

Dale, Robert D. *Pastoral Leadership.* Nashville: Abingdon, 1986.

Egan, Gerard. *Change Agent Skills: Assessing and Designing Excellence.* San Diego: University Associates, 1988.

————. *Change Agent Skills: Managing Innovation and Change.* San Diego: University Associates, 1986.

Fry, Thomas A. *Change, Chaos, and Christianity.* Westwood, N.J.: Revell, 1967.

Gangel, Kenneth O. *Leadership for Church Education.* Chicago: Moody, 1970.

Goodwin, Dennis. "Using Job Assignments to Get Added Value from Church Staff." *Church Administration,* November 1989, pp. 9-10.

Kuhne, Gary W. *The Change Factor: The Risks and Joys.* Grand Rapids: Zondervan, 1986.

Lindgren, Alvin J. *Management for Your Church.* Nashville: Abingdon, 1977.

Lueke, David S., and Samuel Southard. *Pastoral Administration: Integrating Ministry and Management in the Church.* Waco, Tex.: Word, 1986.

Mickey, Paul, and Gary Gamble. *Pastoral Assertiveness: A New Model for Pastoral Care.* Nashville: Abingdon, 1978.

Mitchell, Kenneth R. *Multiple Staff Ministries.* Philadelphia: Westminster, 1988.

Peck, Terry. "Building Positive Relationships Among the Staff." *Church Administration,* November 1989, pp. 16-18.

Schaller, Lyle E. *The Change Agent: The Strategy of Innovative Leadership.* Nashville: Abingdon, 1972.

————. *The Multiple Staff and the Larger Church.* Nashville: Abingdon, 1987.

Sell, Charles M. *Transition.* Chicago: Moody, 1985.

Sheffield, Jimmie. "Ways the Staff Develops into a Team." *Church Administration,* November 1989, pp. 6-7.

Stamey, Judy. "How to Build a Team of Volunteer Leaders." *Church Administration,* February 1990, pp. 15-17.

Thomas, William C. *The Pastor and Church Administration.* Wheaton, Ill.: Conservative Baptist, n.d.

Wiersbe, Warren, and David Wiersbe. *Making Sense Out of the Ministry.* Chicago: Moody, 1983.

## Questions for Discussion and a Helpful Project

1. What two requirements must be met in order for change to be a legitimate goal of the church? What advice would you give to a leader who insists on implementing change before those requirements have been met?

2. What are the biblical standards that should be adhered to before change is initiated?

3. What are the principal reasons it is so difficult to bring about needed change in many churches?

4. List the ingredients of change, and describe how each of these plays an integral part in the process of change.

5. A common error committed by church leaders seeking to implement change is that of trying to change the church single-handedly. What are some of the inherent problems of the lone ranger approach to ministry? In what way can a church leader effectively enlist the aid of his people in the effort of change?

6. In what ways do pastors frequently err when dealing with problem people in their church? What approach could be taken to better facilitate the use of these problem people?

PROJECT: Along with other (sympathetic) leaders develop a strategy for relating to a "domineering deacon" in your local church.

# 17

---

# GOAL SETTING
## AND
# PRINCIPLES
### OF
# ORGANIZATION

Most of us cannot start with brand-new churches. As a result, we have to start with what we've got, a church likely steeped in tradition and full of warts. Is there hope for such a church? Absolutely. Can such a church make drastic changes? Certainly—but not immediately. We start with the people and the structure we have. Then, as we have seen in the previous chapter, we work patiently to build a multicell church. At the same time we involve as many people as possible in the goal-setting process, the subject of the first part of this chapter. All of these activities are carried out in the context of sound principles of church organization, the subject of the latter portion of this chapter.

## A GOAL-SETTING PROCESS FOR A LOCAL CHURCH

The goal-setting process proposed in this chapter involves all of the members of the church. It should result in the church's setting for itself goals that are dynamic, spring from the deep-felt wishes of the congregation, and result in newly invigorated ministry.

1. *In a series of youth and adult Sunday school classes or evening services, teach a biblical philosophy of ministry to the people.* Instruct the people as to what the church is all about, what its local and

global mission is, and how leaders are to aid in accomplishing its mission. If you have already presented the circles of concern model (figure 12, chapter 16), use it to outline what the church should be doing; if your church hasn't yet reached the stage where it is appropriate to present that model, use a modified form of the diagram to make the same points.

2. *Turn the congregation into a corps of dreamers.* Ask them to answer this question in writing: "If there were no shortage of money, personnel, or other resources, my fondest and most extravagant dreams for this church would be: _____." That step alone should whet their appetites and get their artistic juices flowing.

3. *Divide the congregation into groups, and encourage them to share their dreams in brainstorming sessions.* Stress that there is no room for any kind of negative comment in these sessions. Excite them concerning the great fun of thinking in open-ended terms. Have them visit shut-ins, listen to their ideas, and bring those ideas to the group as well.

4. *Ask the groups to refine their dreams into goals, write them down, and hand them in to the church secretary, who will sort the proposed goals into the seven ministry categories of the circles of concern model.* Eliminate duplications, and publish a proposed list of goals for each of the seven ministry categories. Distribute the list to all of the members of the church, and ask for their feedback.

Give the congregation a deadline by which to interact with this information and provide the feedback you have requested. By now you will probably find that most of the congregation is excited about the goal-setting process.

5. *Taking into consideration the written and oral feedback you receive, publish revised lists of proposed goals for each ministry category.* Call the congregation together for a well-publicized evening service. After a stirring inspirational service containing a short, motivational message, assign the people to their choice of one of seven groups (representing, of course, the seven goal categories).

Each group should be led by a member of the present leadership team who has interest and/or supervisory responsibilities in that particular area of concern. Encourage the people to have a good, rousing time of discussion. Remember, negative comments are not allowed. Have each group prioritize their list of goals according to importance and the church's needs. Lead each group in selecting an ad hoc committee that will assist the leaders in constructing objectives for each of the goals.

6. *Teach each committee how to construct objectives.*[1] Although there is not room to consider this process in depth at this point, here are a few observations.

A good objective has the following qualities:

    a. *It is acceptable.* People do not react harshly against it but feel that it is something with which they do not mind identifying. Sometimes they may even strongly identify with the objective and claim ownership. Then you are well under way toward reaching that objective.

    b. *It is reachable but not too easy.* An objective needs to be attainable but not so simple that people will not be challenged in meeting it. If an objective is too easily met people never fully appreciate it; on the other hand, an objective must be within the realm of possibility.

    c. *It is measurable.* There must be some tangible way of measuring whether or not the objective has been reached. However, some things are easier to measure than others. One can readily measure actions, such as evangelistic visits, but attitudinal changes are much harder to gauge. About the only hint we have that those are reached is when a person's outward behavior changes. If Joe Brown was always reluctant to witness but now volunteers for service on an evangelism task force, we have a measurable indication that his attitude toward witnessing has improved.

Constructing objectives is a difficult job, and you may need assistance in learning how to do it. The church education faculties of Christian colleges and seminaries may be good sources of help, as may be denominational church education specialists. If the church is small and has no denominational resources, a larger church across town may

---

1. A classic book on this subject is Robert F. Mager, *Preparing Instructional Objectives* (Belmont, Calif.: Fearon, 1962). In addition, Gospel Light Publishers and their subsidiary, ICL, have published a number of books that deal specifically with preparing objectives for the church.

be willing to lend you their church education staff member for this task.

I have already intimated that we are interested in good objectives that bring about changes in people. The changes I have in mind have to do with content and attitude. It is good to maintain a balance between cognitive (content) and affective (attitude) objectives and to see to it that the two work hand-in-hand. Learning how to write good objectives is the first step toward reaching those objectives.

7. *When you have learned how to construct objectives, lead the ad hoc committees in doing so, prioritizing those objectives and publishing them for the congregation.* Request feedback from the congregation. From that feedback have the committees further refine the objectives. Publish this final set of objectives, and propose it to the church for formal adoption.

8. *Charge the committees with the responsibility of examining the present programs of the church.* Which programs currently help the church reach its objectives in the category with which that committee has been working? Does the ministry of that program overlap with some other category?

9. *Present members of the church board should then reorganize the board.* Board members will be assigned the supervision of ministry areas illustrated in the circles of concern model. They will assume responsibility for the programs the committees have assigned to those areas of supervision.

At this point, the question might arise about the source of personnel for this system when the church is small. In a small church, it is not unusual for a leader to double up and take the responsibility for more than one of these areas. Chapter 18 will speak in more detail regarding creative staffing patterns designed to meet the seven kinds of church goals.

Remember, no system is perfect. Neither is any process. Only the Holy Spirit can effect the changes that need to be made in the church. Depend on Him completely. Remain His humble servant and *pray, pray, pray*.

## Basic Principles of Sound Church Organization

Five principles of church organization should undergird the work you do to revitalize the structure of your church.

PRINCIPLE #1:
KEEP THE STRUCTURE AS SIMPLE AS POSSIBLE

Citing the need for simplicity in organization, Gene Getz writes, "If organization is to be functional it must be as simple as possible. Complicated organizational patterns frequently become 'ends' in themselves."[2] Many of us have found his words all too true in the churches with which we have worked.

The church adopted organizational simplicity from its beginning. Often we look at Acts 6 to show that a local church needs different levels of management. What we seem to forget is that early church leaders did not establish those levels until it was absolutely necessary.

Keep in mind how many believers we are talking about. The church got a big start on the day of Pentecost when three thousand believed and were baptized. Since many of those converts were from out of town, undoubtedly they left Jerusalem and shared their faith with the people back home. Nevertheless, just a few weeks later, in Jerusalem alone there were five thousand male believers, according to Acts 4:4. Add women and children to this number and you get a very large figure. The church in Jerusalem was huge.

But it didn't stop there. Acts 5:14 reports, "And all the more believers in the Lord, multitudes of men and women, were constantly added to their number." Acts 6:1 indicates that this was an ongoing process. The number of people coming to the Lord was so large the apostles appointed another echelon of leadership to assist them.

Note why they did so. Though meeting the physical needs of its members was an important part of the church's ministry, the job had become so big the church was not operating properly. Moreover, the huge task of meeting physical needs was diverting the energies of the apostles from their principal task, ministering from the Word.

In view of the huge size of the church, notice how simple and uncomplicated the new organizational structure was. I am not saying that the problems faced by contemporary churches are identical to those of the first century, but the example of the early church sets a precedent for keeping organizational structure as simple and uncomplicated as possible. This is especially significant when it is contrasted with what I see in some contemporary churches of seventy-five mem-

2. Gene A. Getz, *Sharpening the Focus of the Church* (Chicago: Moody, 1974), p. 157.

bers or less. Often these small churches have an organizational pattern that vastly exceeds that used by the megachurch of the first century. So much of the church's energy is diverted to maintaining the structure that little of the work of God actually gets done.

*One board is usually enough.* How should simplicity demonstrate itself in church management? For a start, it is difficult for me to imagine a church of under one thousand in membership that needs more than one board. Moreover, I cannot visualize a church board that needs to be composed of more than eight members, including the pastor. My position on this goes along with my belief that an organizational structure should be built around accomplishing goals. Later on in this section, we will look at the makeup of such a board.

*Limit the number of standing committees.* Not even the largest church imaginable has need for more than seven standing committees. Those committees should be composed of principal, coordinative leaders rather than people who are elected at large by the church.

*Use ad hoc committees widely.* Although the number of standing committees should be kept as low as possible, ad hoc committees should be used liberally to enable the church to meet special needs. Ad hoc committees by definition are formed to accomplish a specific task and then be disbanded when the specific job is accomplished. Building committees and pulpit committees are examples of ad hoc committees established to complete a special task. Investigative committees could be created periodically to determine how well a church is accomplishing its mission in certain specific areas or what kind of new organizational structure is needed for the church.

Does your church have special meetings such as Bible conferences, revival meetings, or missionary conferences? Is there a special anniversary on the horizon? Is there a need to survey the community to determine its unique needs? All these and dozens more are fit candidates for the work of ad hoc committees. A few of the chief benefits of an ad hoc committee are these:

1. Ad hoc committees address themselves to specific tasks instead of having dozens to accomplish. If people have only one task to do, they should be able to do it better than having to juggle the responsibilities of many tasks.

2. Ad hoc committees lend themselves to a definite time frame. Instead of requiring a prolonged, ongoing period of labor, a task can be accomplished in a reasonable period of time.

3. Instead of keeping people tied to the committee for long periods, ad hoc committees enable them to accomplish an assignment and move on to some other involvement if they wish. Busy people are refreshed by knowing that they are committed to a single task, not to a lifelong career on a church committee.

4. Ad hoc committees enable church leaders to discover competent people who can be recruited later for more prolonged leadership roles. If people do not perform well on a temporary level, they may need to mature more before they can be given other, more enduring tasks.

5. Ad hoc committees can become valuable information sources, bringing to the church board information that would not be available through ordinary channels. This is possible because ad hoc committees concentrate their efforts on only one area.

6. Ad hoc committees offer the possibility of wider participation of members in the leadership process. Creative but busy people are able to lend their efforts to leadership. This is a good way to utilize people who are creative, gifted leaders but do not meet the biblical requirements for top leadership positions in the church.

PRINCIPLE #2:
ASSIGN AUTHORITY COMMENSURATE WITH RESPONSIBILITY

This basic rule makes sense in any area of life. Even in the church we see people who are hungry for and jealous of the authority they have been able to accumulate through the years. They are reluctant to give up this authority for any reason. An effective organization cannot operate in this manner. All authority cannot be concentrated only in the hands of a few. Authority must be shared in order to get the job done properly.

Olan Hendrix puts his finger on another important aspect of this principle. He writes: "Decisions should be made on the lowest possible level, as near as possible to where the work is actually per-formed."[3] Even in the church, there are principal leaders who reserve the right to make any decision, large or small. That attitude deprives the church of forward momentum and demoralizes capable workers who want to get on with God's redemptive program.

Picture the scene. A company hires a president, and each stock-holder has in mind specific expectations for him to meet. Yet the presi-dent is given no authority to fulfill his responsibilities. "Ludicrous! Ridiculous!" we are quick to say. Yet this is exactly the game played by thousands of local churches across North America. No wonder the church lumbers like a giant tortoise instead of marching like a mighty army. Who can get anything accomplished under such circumstances?

How do we avoid such a situation? First, we write a well thought-out philosophy of ministry. After this philosophy of ministry has been presented to the church and the church accepts it, we teach it to our people through every vehicle possible. It should be the subject of Sunday school and Bible study classes for everyone older than junior high people. It should present clear guidelines for the leaders' expecta-tions of their congregation and the congregation's expectations of its leaders.

Second, we construct carefully written job descriptions for each church leader. This may be a tedious task, but in the long run it will save time and energy because it will eliminate needless confusion. The job description will list the responsibilities of the office and will specify the authority relationships (both up and down) involved in that function.

Third, we spell out the limits of the office. We specify exactly what kinds of decisions that leader may make and what decisions he should refer to a higher level of authority. We circulate that job de-scription among the church members. We ask for feedback and request a congregational vote. Once the congregation has agreed to the job de-scription, we will have recourse to this document should disagreement arise.

As leaders of the church, we have a covenantal responsibility to one another and to the church at large regarding these matters.

- We covenant together to defend one other and support the other's job description if disagreements arise.

3. Olan Hendrix, *Management for Christian Leaders* (Grand Rapids: Baker, 1989), p. 85.

- We agree that if trouble arises we will correct the problem as soon as possible and initiate redemptive action immediately under the guidelines listed in Matthew 18. We will carry out any necessary discipline impartially.

- We will develop a careful budgeting procedure integrated with all job descriptions. The leader will formulate a yearly budget, planned together with the people serving with him. The board will consider that budget in light of the overall needs and anticipated income of the church. The leader, in turn, is told at the beginning of the year what the budget is for his area of responsibility. He is also appraised of any limitations set on the expenditures he may make. All limitations should be reasonable and clear, and a carefully written procedure should be in place for approval of expenditures that exceed the budget.

- All of this is to be done in an orderly way: authority will be commensurate with responsibility, and checks and balances will be in place. In that way authority is free to be used but not abused.

PRINCIPLE #3:
MAKE SURE THAT LEADERSHIP IS SHARED

A lone ranger mentality is not a wise mentality. Even if you are a good leader, you are not good enough. You cannot possibly do the job alone. This is not your church. It is God's church. The principle of shared leadership is often encountered in the New Testament narrative, especially the book of Acts. This principle of shared leadership is appropriate for today.

Volumes could be written about the wisdom inherent in what the book of Proverbs calls "a multitude of counselors." I have never met a rational person from whom I could not learn something. When you as a leader come to believe that you need not learn anything more, do the church a favor and resign from your position.

Although shared leadership is desirable and even essential, that does not mean a church should build a top-heavy organizational structure where nearly everyone is a chief and there is a crucial shortage of indians. It is true that the key to good leadership is communication that travels from the bottom to the top as well as the other way around, but a few good leaders at the top usually are enough to direct the efforts of a church of any size.

Are there not enough biblically qualified leaders to do the job? Use the leaders you have. Don't be in a hurry to give them titles that may make them proud. Some of them may never meet the biblical qualifications for elder or deacon. Nevertheless, these are the people you have available to act as leaders. Remember the words of 1 Corinthians 12. It is God who has constituted your local assembly. It is He who put those people there, knowing that they would have to serve as leaders with some shortcomings.

Nurture, instruct, and equip each other the best you can and leave the rest to God. Moreover, remember that discipling is always a two-way street. As you disciple someone else, be aware of the areas in which he or she can train you. Listen to these people. They may not have a Bible college education, but many times God has given them wisdom that can never be found in a formal theological education.

Be aware also that women exercise significant leadership roles in the church, whether your church formally recognizes that or not. Just because you are a man, don't deprive yourself of the marvelous knowledge and wisdom women bring to accomplishing the mission of the church. Be grateful for the insights your wife can give. Thank God for these marvelous partners He gives us. Outside of the gift of salvation, there is no greater gift.

PRINCIPLE #4:
PLACE SOMEONE IN CHARGE AND LET IT BE KNOWN WHO THAT PERSON IS

Here we build upon principles 2 and 3. At the same time we affirm the principle of shared leadership, we need to acknowledge a fact of life. When everyone is responsible for everything, specific things seldom get done well. In order to get any job done properly, qualified people must be given supervisory responsibility to see that it gets done. Moreover, principle 2 insists as well that they be given commensurate authority to accomplish their mission.

That does not mean that they should be given unbridled authority. Nor does it justify leaders' acting in a dictatorial manner. It acknowledges that they have been chosen because of their known competence and are therefore given the latitude they need to do the job to which they are appointed. Support these leaders with the necessary authority and funding. Don't dabble in their areas of responsibility unless you see glaring weaknesses. Make it apparent to everyone in the church who is responsible for supervising or coordinating a given area of endeavor.

Another factor applies here. Although I have solidly supported shared leadership, there is no such thing as equality of leadership. Someone always ends up in charge. That's the way life is. Just as each area of responsibility in the church must have a coordinator, the church itself needs a top coordinator. That person gives overall guidance and supervision to the program and activities of the church. In most cases this top supervisor turns out to be the pastor, for most people naturally hold him responsible for the overall guidance, direction, and coordination of the church's program. However, it is not enough for some people to merely take for granted that the pastor exercises this responsibility. Instead, it must be clearly stated and communicated to all of the members of the church that the pastor not only is held responsible for this function but is also given sufficient authority to carry it out.

Why is it that this function normally falls to the pastor? Because he often has the most formal training and experience. He is also the most public leader of the church. Since he is the one who instructs people from the Word, most people think that he is the logical one to lead in other matters. Please understand that I am not talking about pastoral dictatorship. I am referring to coordination and supervision, the essence of what is implied in the word *episcopos*, overseer.

Should the pastor always be the one to exercise primary leadership? There are cases where the pastor still has insufficient experience in the ministry to be given this tremendous responsibility. Then a mature layperson should be placed in charge. He should be instructed to take the inexperienced pastor under his wing and disciple him. In that particular church setting the pastor may never come to the point of taking over the primary leadership. That may have to wait until he gets to his next church.

In rare cases the pastor may be capable of great preaching and teaching but incapable of carrying out the primary leadership capacity. With the consent of the pastor, the church may think it advisable to retain the pastor for his preaching and teaching ministry but to remove other responsibilities from him. In that case, there would need to be a clear understanding between the pastor and the ministry coordinator.

Also, the actual role of the pastor would have to be communicated clearly to the congregation.

You will note that I am writing in rather nebulous terms at this point. That is because I have never seen an arrangement like this work. Maybe you will be the pioneer who plows new territory.

PRINCIPLE #5:
CHURCH GOVERNMENT SHOULD BE COMMITTED TO REACHING BIBLICAL GOALS

Of all the principles we have discussed, this last is probably the most important. A church must have a clear focus. Its leaders must know that they have been chosen to accomplish a specific mission within the kingdom of God. This principle is of vital importance to you as a leader so that you do not flounder in confusion, wondering what you should be doing. Means indicates that floundering describes all too many present church leaders. He writes:

> Many church leaders are fuzzy about their mission, their place and their responsibilities. Consequently, they typically do what necessity and urgency seem to demand, what they feel most pressured to do at the moment. They lack focus, direction, and clarity about their task and function. Leaders scurry to plug gaps, pump up programs, meet a variety of apparent needs, and produce statistical results—all without a clear concept, a theoretical model of what they are and what they should be doing.[4]

Establishing the leadership framework of the church according to the biblical goals of the church aids greatly in curing this ill. It will give church leaders a clear picture of what they should be doing and will let the church know what results to expect from its leaders.

There is another practical reason your church's governing structure should be organized around reaching the church's goals. It keeps those goals fresh in the minds of the people. In *Management for Christian Leaders* Olan Hendrix draws our attention to what he calls the "radic" group. This he defines as a group in which "the level of group concern is greater than the level of personal concern."[5] It is Hendrix's contention that the church always was designed to be a radic

4. James E. Means, *Leadership in Christian Ministry* (Grand Rapids: Baker, 1989), p. 45.
5. Hendrix, *Management for Christian Leaders*, p. 82.

group. Essential to a church's being such a group, according to Hendrix, is its commitment to accomplish the Lord's goals. Hendrix writes:

> What holds the radic group together? It is the goal. The more we are obsessed with the goal, the more we are willing to tolerate individual differences within the organization. The less we are obsessed with the goal, the more we need to have personal conformity within the organization. Somebody comes to you and he does not say things just the way you would say them. If we are goal-oriented, we say, "This man has something to contribute and we will endure much from him because he is going to help us reach our goal."[6]

There is only one legitimate reason for a church to construct an organizational system. It is to help the church reach its biblical goals. If the organization per se becomes supreme and hinders the church from reaching those goals, the organization must be drastically changed or even discontinued.

## Additional Resources

Alexander, John W. *Managing Our Work.* Downers Grove, Ill.: InterVarsity, 1975.

Anderson, James D. *The Management of Ministry.* San Francisco: Harper & Row, 1978.

Bradford, David L. *Management for Excellence: The Guide to Developing High Performance in Contemporary Organizations.* New York: Wiley, 1984.

Hendrix, Olan. *Management for the Christian Leader.* Milford, Mich.: Mott, 1981.

_____. *Management for the Christian Worker.* Libertyville, Ill.: Quill, 1976.

Powell, Robert R. *Managing Church Business Through Group Procedures.* Englewood Cliffs, N.J.: Prentice-Hall, 1964.

---

6. Ibid., p. 84.

## Questions for Discussion and Helpful Projects

1. "When everyone is responsible for everything, specific things seldom get done well" is a common truism. How does this principle relate to the inability of a church board to efficiently manage its affairs without a competent leader coordinating their activities?

2. Any system may look good on paper, but the "proof of the pudding is in the eating." The value of any system lies in the impact of its application. With this thought in mind, what do you think is the key to good church government?

3. Goal setting must be a top agenda item for a leader who intends to accomplish anything significant for God. What programs may church leaders implement to cultivate fertile soil for goal setting among the people?

4. A model has been given in this chapter for constructing a goal-oriented church governance structure.

PROJECT: Adapt that model to the specific needs of your church. How would the board structure appear? What is your proposed division of responsibilities? Under what headings would each of your church's ministries appear? What would the agenda for board meetings be like?

5. List the basic principles that should underlie a sound organizational structure for your church.

PROJECT: Analyze how well each of those principles is being applied in the programs of your church. Where and how can improvements be made?

6. What kind of benefits accrue through the use of ad hoc committees?

PROJECT: List the tasks currently being performed by standing committees in your church that could be handled better by ad hoc committees.

7. In his book on management Olan Hendrix says that decisions should be made at the lowest possible level and as close as possible to where the work is actually performed. Why is it paramount that the principles of "assigned responsibility and commensurate authority" be enacted in the church? Can you recall trauma that has resulted in your church when those principles have been ignored?

8. Why is it necessary for a church to have a chief coordinator? Why is it important that everyone knows who is in charge of what and the amount of authority that person has to get his job done? In what situations should the senior pastor not be given the role of chief coordinator?

9. Olan Hendrix proposes a leadership ideal that mandates that group concerns take precedence over individual concerns. Explain the biblical rationale for the radic group concept Hendrix propounds.

# 18

## STAFFING CREATIVELY FOR KEY LEADERSHIP NEEDS

One the most refreshing features of the first-century church was its ability to think creatively and to produce original solutions. Unfortunately, from that time on, creative church thinking seems to have gone downhill. Maybe that is one reason, with a few wonderful exceptions, the North American church is no longer as effective a force in winning society as was the first-century church.

When you consider staffing your church, don't be a copycat. Don't try to duplicate either the New Testament church or a successful contemporary church. Consider the reasons these churches were successful. Discover their principles rather than adopting their methodology. Then, after surveying both your needs and your assets, be creative in establishing your own patterns. Here are some principles you may find helpful.

### Go Back to Your Basic Goals

Suppose your church is large enough to support a full-time pastor. What action should you take? "Why, look for a pastor," you may respond. Wait a minute, you are already ahead of the game. Before you even ask the question as to whether or not you should call a full-time staff member, you need to take some preliminary steps.

The first thing to be considered is this: Have you established goals in each of the seven areas mentioned earlier in this book? If you have not, you need to do so before making any decisions concerning staffing. If you have established goals, you need to take them out, dust them off, make any revisions necessary, and spend quality time in prayer over them. Then keep them on the front burner in all considerations of staffing.

## Remember Your Target Groups

Next, ask yourself, "Have we, as a church, been realistic in identifying the principal target groups we can effectively reach?" If you have not yet identified your target groups, you should do so before considering any staff choices. If you have identified target groups, you need to review the characteristics of those groups and their specific needs.

Then backtrack a bit. Ask yourself, "Are we being overly optimistic? Can we really expect to reach each of these groups, or all of these groups? Should we concentrate our efforts on fewer types of people?" On the other hand, you may want to ask, "Have we been too conservative? Are there other groups we should add to our list? Are there people already in our midst we are overlooking? Should we be improving our ministry to them and reaching out to other people like them?" Last, we need to look hard and realistically at the particular areas in which we need professional leadership.

The leadership needs that will be discussed in the rest of this chapter correspond to the seven ministry areas and the coordinator's position mentioned in chapter 16 and described in figure 12, "Circles of Concern," and figure 13, "A Proposed Governance Structure for a Larger Church." A ninth area, responsibility for youth programs, is also discussed.

## Leadership Needs for Overall Ministry Coordination

The first place we need to consider for professional leadership is in the area of overall ministry coordination. In chapter 16, which discussed the circle of concern model, the pastor was described as the person most likely to hold this role, but that need not be the case. Whether we select the pastor for this role or someone else, we need to ask several questions before we fill the position.

Could an untrained volunteer coordinate all the ministries of the church and keep all of them in balance and working in harmony with one another? Probably not, because that is a specialized kind of ministry and that would probably eliminate an untrained person. Could we choose a person with potential giftedness in the area and procure the proper training for that person? Certainly, but that will take a great amount of time, and meanwhile our key needs are not being met. In addition, ministry coordination is a time-consuming ministry. People engaged in it have to be available at all hours of the day and night to meet and deal with individuals and committees.

It would appear, then, that one of our primary needs would be a ministries coordinator who could stay on top of things and keep the ministry of the church moving ahead in a coordinated fashion. This is a key person because he becomes the axle around which the entire program of the church revolves. But should this task represent the sumtotal of his full-time ministry? Probably not, except in large churches.

As a result, a smaller church will have to look for a person who can also serve as the coordinator in one or more of the seven individual ministry areas for which it has established goals, or it will need to look to the pastor to fulfill this role.

## LEADERSHIP NEEDS FOR LOCAL OUTREACH

This is the area where many churches put the least emphasis. They are often content to hire staff to meet the edificational needs of the established flock. However, the employment of an evangelist seems to be far from their thinking. As a result, the saints tend to stagnate and build up a fortress mentality, and the church struggles merely to maintain the status quo.

To be healthy, every local congregation needs to establish and preserve the proper balance between evangelistic and edificational emphases. However, it doesn't always work out to be a fifty-fifty proposition. Sometimes, a congregation needs a shot in the arm in one direction or the other. So it must constantly consider: "Have we been unbalanced in our approach? Do we need to have a renewed emphasis in a certain direction?"

I have seen sedentary churches combine the role of evangelist with that of ministries coordinator to produce a "pastoral office." As a result, the primary emphasis of the church for that period tended to be outreach. I have a problem with calling such an individual "pastor," since many of the pastoral-type responsibilities are often given a low priority under such a ministry. Maybe if we didn't call him pastor, we would see that we need a pastor in addition to this person.

However, sometimes a church will find a rare combination who can both "do the work of an evangelist" and still carry on the shepherding functions effectively. If you find one, hold onto him tightly. He is a rare jewel. Moreover, make sure that he doesn't spread himself too thin or overwork himself. You need to keep him around for a good long while.

However, a local outreach coordinator must be more than a soul winner. To function biblically as an evangelist, a prime emphasis according to Ephesians 4 must always be to equip the saints for the work of evangelizing. Moreover, it is not enough to merely hire a person who is skilled in evangelism and in training others for evangelism. In addition, we need to ascertain if this person is able to relate to the target groups we hope to evangelize. If he does not relate well to those groups, he is the wrong person for the job.

Another point needs to be remembered. It is good to "give a cup of cold water" in the Savior's name. It is even better to accompany it with a clear, palatable presentation of the gospel. The evangelist must also keep this phase of his outreach ministry in mind. However, be realistic. He will probably not have the time to carry on this ministry personally. As a result he will need the skills to select and train others who will perform this Christian task in a sensitive and loving manner.

We have considered combining the function of evangelist with either ministry coordination or the pastoral office. However, the person whose specialty is evangelism may not be especially adept in either of those two areas. He may, on the other hand, have the necessary skills to add the position of "discipleship coordinator" to his evangelistic duties.

Be creative in putting together combinations. Survey the needs, find out who is available to meet those needs, and then tailor the combinations to the people. But don't think that it is always mandatory to combine functions in order to create full-time, paid positions. It is probably a good idea to do that in the case of the ministries coordinator, but there is nothing wrong with meeting the rest of the church's staffing needs with part-timers if they are available. Even a part-time evangelist may be a valuable member of a church's staff.

## LEADERSHIP NEEDS FOR REGIONAL AND WORLDWIDE OUTREACH

Today there is a wealth of skilled people available to help a church develop a consciousness of missions. Is yours a denominational church? Its representatives will often lend their services free of charge. If yours is an independent church, you may depend on "faith missions" to aid you in planting churches and sending out missionaries to foreign cultures and lands. These groups, too, can provide valuable resources and people to help a church meet its regional and worldwide outreach goals.

The trick is to remember to use these valuable resources. And that takes someone at the local church level to coordinate a missions education program that keeps challenging Christians. The needs in this area are threefold.

The first is to constantly alert people to the missionary opportunities available in their own country and overseas. Here people need to be constantly reminded not only of our Lord's directives but also about the urgency of the hour.

The second challenge is to inspire people to give money to support missionaries. This may be done in many creative ways.

A final challenge involves the need to identify people in a congregation who should be missionaries. But the responsibility of a congregation does not end there. A church should be prepared to help potential missionaries receive the training they need. That may involve a substantial monetary commitment on the part of the church.

Except in the largest churches, the task of coordinating this ministry, as important as it is, may be done by a volunteer. In fact, sometimes people with unusual skills and experience may be called upon to serve in such a volunteer capacity. A large church in Portland employed a retired missions executive as a "dollar a year" man to direct the missionary outreach program of the church. He was effective in formulating a missions policy and a missions budget each year and in keeping the church alert to its missionary opportunities.

It isn't too important how you staff this position. More important is that you not neglect this vital area of your church's ministry. To merely give a few patronizing dollars to missions is not enough. Your people need to be spiritually and emotionally involved in the task of spreading the good news. This will not happen automatically. It takes a creative and persistent individual to see that it is done properly.

## LEADERSHIP NEEDS FOR WORSHIP

True worship is the facilitator of all of the church's other ministries. I have repeatedly insisted that worship planning and execution must be done extremely well. That does not happen automatically. A skilled coordinator is needed not only to plan and supervise worship programs but to train the participants.

This means that the "visible" worship leaders, such as song leaders, choir members, instrumentalists, and ushers, need to be trained appropriately. But it also means that worshipers must be educated as to the reason they are doing certain things and the spirit in which those practices should be done.

The preaching or teaching of God's Word is, of course, an integral and important part of a worship service. That is usually a function of the person bearing the title of "pastor," since a vital part of a pastor's role is "feeding the sheep." In settings where the pastor is knowledgeable in the area of worship, he may also wish to serve as worship coordinator. However, there are times when he has neither the necessary sensitivity or skills to do that.

Sometimes there are gifted musicians in a congregation who make excellent worship coordinators. In that case, it is necessary for that person to work in close cooperation with the pastor so that his work complements, rather than competes with, the pastor's. Musicians, however, may not be able to train sound technicians or ushers. Since those services play an important part in facilitating worship, the worship coordinator may have to call in reinforcements to help with their training.

A church with a successful worship program in Portland employs a woman part-time as worship coordinator. She directs the choir, coordinates the instrumentalists, trains ushers, plans music, chooses Scripture passages, and utilizes methods that ensure worship participation by parishioners.

She selects everything with a dual purpose. First, does it facilitate the worship of Almighty God? Second, does it complement the pastor's sermon topic? That demands that she work in close cooperation with the pastor. She is worth far more than the wage she is receiving.

Once more, we are presented with two kinds of staffing possibilities. The first is to combine worship coordinating with other responsibilities and utilize a full-time person. There are many creative ways of combining the tasks under one person.

The second alternative is to employ a part-time person or a volunteer. In smaller churches, if the worship coordinator is limited to this one task, a volunteer will usually be able to handle it effectively. However, regardless of how you staff this position, remember that it is an important job. Nothing is strategically more important to the health of the church than worship that is well done.

## LEADERSHIP NEEDS FOR FOSTERING FELLOWSHIP

I include under "fellowship" all of the "caring" activities that accrue to members and friends of a local church. These include visitation and counseling as well as the fostering of genuine *koinonia* between people. They also include meeting people's physical and financial needs. In many churches there is no organized plan to meet this array of needs and, as a result, vital ministries are often overlooked. In this area of ministry we can't let things "just happen." Careful planning and coordination must go on constantly to see that people and their needs do not fall through the cracks.

In many churches the pastor or other staff members are expected to do the majority of counseling and visiting. Rarely is there a good, effective system where deacons bear a major responsibility for these tasks. Sometimes that is because a handful of deacons are given the responsibility for both running the church and providing care for a number of families. Those kinds of expectations place more responsibility on deacons than they have the time or energy to accomplish well.

In many churches, the ladies are given the task of creating social occasions where people can meet and where friendships can begin. However, once again, these activities are seldom part of a coordinated program where Christians are charged with the responsibility of fellowshipping with one another and providing care for one another.

My conviction is that a church should establish a "deacon pool." That is done in stages. First determine how many men and women in the congregation meet the biblical requirements for the office of deacon. Next, ascertain their willingness to serve in this office. When doing so, we must emphasize that becoming a deacon involves a lifetime commitment to a deacon type of ministry. Be careful to specify that this will not necessarily entail service on the deacon board if your church has one. Then provide the necessary training for the new deacons. Deacons used in the fellowship-caring program of the church will need training in at least three skills: effective visitation, counseling, and fellowship fostering.

### THE ART OF EFFECTIVE AND SENSITIVE VISITATION

With a few pointers given in class and some on-the-job training, many people can become effective visitors. This kind of ministry will be primarily edificational rather than evangelistic. Sometimes evangelistic opportunities will present themselves even in routine visits to homes, hospitals, and nursing homes. Visitation deacons must be alert to these openings. If they find that they cannot evangelize effectively themselves, they will need to know where to find reinforcements to help do the job.

Older, retired people are often excellent at visitation ministries. Unfortunately, in our emphasis on youth, we have often encouraged people to remain on the shelf once they reach retirement age. That waste of their talents is of great detriment to the church. We must reverse this trend. Their age, wisdom, and experience should make them excellent prospects, as older women begin visiting and instructing younger women, and older men do the same for younger men.

### COUNSELING

I am disturbed that such a mystique has arisen around the subject of counseling. Believe it or not, people have been counseling in an effective manner since the beginning of the world. In contrast, psychology as a science has only existed for about one hundred years.

I strongly believe that 95 percent of the counseling needed by church members can be accomplished by other church members who have received a minimal amount of training. That training may be provided by a pastor or other staff member who has counseling skills. Or a church may bring in a professional counselor to provide counselor training for its people. Counseling often begins as a fellowship function and leads to discipleship.

There are at least three points where skilled training is needed. The first is in the area of effective and careful listening. Those who would counsel need to be slow to render an opinion. They need to be careful to hear what the other person is really saying.

The second area is the ability to draw answers from the Scriptures and to help a person apply those answers to his or her problems. Here the emphasis must not be on a counselor's taking the other person's burden on his own shoulders. That will never accomplish anything lasting. Instead, the counselor must learn to help the hurting person discover his own answers and take definitive steps to solve his own problems.

The third area of expertise is to know when one is in over his head. The counselor should be taught certain danger signals and know when, where, and how to refer a difficult case to a person with greater skills. Especially is this true if there is any hint of mental illness or even the slightest threat of suicide.

FELLOWSHIP FOSTERING

It is my conviction that deacons should keep track of the families assigned to them, making sure that there is at least one contact each week. That contact may be by telephone, in person at a church service, or through some fellowship occasion.

Also, the fellowship deacons should use a variety of ways to stimulate genuine *koinonia,* not only between themselves and the families or individuals they serve but between the families themselves. A deacon might organize potlucks where several families get together or might exercise the gift of hospitality by periodically inviting two or more families or singles to dinner or dessert in his (or her) own home.

Do not take for granted that deacons can "just naturally" perform these services. In most cases, careful training will be necessary. Moreover, emphasize to the deacons that theirs is not only a serving role, it is also an equipping role. Just as they have received training to perform these services, they must teach others to do likewise. A primary task for deacons should be locating and developing others who are potential deacons. May I emphasize that if deacons are made responsible for the care of people they should not be assigned principal administrative tasks in addition.

Here, as in all the other goal areas we have covered, there is a need for someone to coordinate and supervise the ministry. It has been lack of overall planning and coordination that has rendered many church fellowship programs ineffective. Since many of the ministries carried on through this program are akin to pastoral-type ministries, the pastor may wish to retain overall coordination of this program himself. In that way, he can place the proper emphases where they belong and can ensure that the people working with him in the program have the proper training. He can also hold them directly accountable to himself and thus make sure that the job is getting done properly and effectively.

However, if your church has already given the pastor all of the tasks that he can effectively accomplish, you will need to choose someone else to coordinate this important program. This is a case where the individual will be required to work closely with the pastor. The pastor, in turn, should be an important and integral member of the fellowship committee.

Sometimes it will work out well for the fellowship coordinator to direct discipleship ministries also, since the two ministries often operate hand-in-hand. The assignment of these two responsibilities—fellowship and discipleship—to one individual will provide more than enough work for a full-time staff person.

In smaller churches, coordination of a fellowship program could be done by a volunteer. Sometimes a mature deacon and wife are an ideal team for this ministry. Other churches may choose to utilize an active, healthy retired person. This is such an important and vital ministry that the volunteer should not bear any other responsibilities.

## LEADERSHIP NEEDS FOR DISCIPLESHIP

Discipleship has been defined as the sum total of the church's instructional programs, including teaching delivered from the pulpit. This kind of definition demands a program that differs markedly from the typical church education program. As a result, it presents a number of challenges.

First of all, this is, by necessity, a carefully coordinated program. In contrast to the typical church education program, it is a planned, coordinated meal rather than a potluck. So that it can be properly coordinated, the director of the discipleship program will need to know months and even years (if possible) ahead of time what the primary thrust of the pastor's messages will be. He then builds the rest of the instructional program around the pulpit instruction, complementing and supplementing that ministry.

Thus the pastor must learn to depend on the Holy Spirit to help him plan for the future as well as for the immediate present. If you are a pastor, there is no biblically valid excuse for not planning ahead. When you do that, your congregation will have the best chance of getting a balanced and healthy educational program.

There is a second challenge faced by using this kind of coordinated system—the need for using a variety of instructional methods so that teaching may be accomplished effectively and efficiently. Therefore, do not start by considering programs. Instead, look to your desired objectives first. Then find out what kinds of methods will best help you reach those objectives. Remember that reaching cognitive objectives will require different methods than reaching affective objectives. Consequently, appropriate types of instructional methods are chosen in relation to the overall needs of the church, the needs of an individual, and the needs of the task for which the person is training. That may be the chief challenge a discipleship coordinator faces.

Third, a discipleship coordinator must remember that he is part of a ministry team. That team is intent on accomplishing two kinds of goals and objectives: evangelistic and edificational. He must be careful to see that the training given his people is balanced between the two goals.

The discipleship coordinator must pay attention to his job title. He has not been selected to be a jack-of-all-trades, carrying on a perpetual juggling act. His is first and foremost an equipping and coordinating task. He must constantly work to disengage himself from nitty-gritty tasks, and he must learn that the details of running a program should be placed squarely in the hands of the person who takes over the direction of that program.

He will learn, for example, not to involve himself with ordering supplies and recruiting teachers for the Sunday school. That is the job of the Sunday school superintendent. The discipleship coordinator, instead, supervises the selection of curriculum and the training of teachers. Instead of actually doing the work of his program directors, the discipleship coordinator is there to encourage them and give aid as needed.

Who should carry on these wide coordinative responsibilities? Because my own interests lie in this area, as a full-time pastor I served as my own discipleship coordinator. In keeping with that task I also offered teacher-training classes on a regular basis. Not all pastors will be able to do this, however. Some come out of seminary with the barest hint of how to run a church education program. Others don't even want to be involved in coordinating such activities as children's clubs.

If that is the case with your pastor, bring someone competent alongside to work with him. This need not be a full-time church education director. It may be a paid, part-time worker or a full-timer who carries on leadership functions in one or more of the other six basic ministry areas.

It may be that the pastor has great interests in this area and a great desire to learn. In that case, the church may want to import an expert for a designated period who would train the pastor. Eventually, of course, this is such a large job that, when the church grows big enough, it should be a full-time position. Until then, all kinds of creative alternatives can be explored. I know of a church, for instance, that shared a church education minister with two other congregations in the area. Teachers from all three churches were trained simultaneously, and the professional worked with the lay leadership of each church to ensure that individual needs were met.

## Leadership Needs for Logistics

In one of the churches I pastored, a lady exclaimed, "What a relief to work with you. With [your predecessor] it was worse than working for a CPA." Although that was meant as a compliment, what she was really pointing to was my weakness in the area of logistics.

Rarely will a church find a pastor who is proficient in this area. As a result, it will usually entrust its financial and building needs to a committee. Where there is "elder rule," the deacons may get this job. Where the deacons are the "top dogs," the trustees generally handle these matters. It really doesn't matter what you call them. The end result is usually the same.

I have to admit that committees are necessary to coordinate ministries, share mutual prayer concerns, and help each other find solutions to tough questions. However, they are an inefficient way of getting things done properly and in a timely fashion. That is best done by using a responsible person.

Of all areas of the church's ministry that need dedicated coordination, this area probably needs it the most. Yet, in many churches, logistics is the area that most often functions without such coordination. Since this is such a neglected area in so many churches, let us look for a few minutes at the responsibilities a church should give a logistics coordinator. As we do this, we need to consider, as well, what kind of a person we are looking for to carry out this kind of ministry.

Logistics is necessarily a means to desired ends. Thus it is a subsidiary, or support, ministry. As such, it is important that the coordinator never become impressed with his title but continually consider himself a servant of servants. A servant mentality should prevail in all of his or her services.

This person also must be scrupulously honest since he will be managing the total assets of the church. It is wise that he and certain others serving with him be bonded for the safety of the church's assets as well as for the reputation of those who minister in this way. In addition, the logistics coordinator must be fiscally level-headed. Rather than the pastor, this is the person who should work with the other ministry coordinators to formulate the annual budget. Moreover, he should learn to do so on the basis of good, hard facts and realistic projections.

Why exclude the pastor from such a function? It has been my experience that many pastors, myself included, tend to be people of great imagination and vision. Thus, they have a tendency to allow their faith to devolve into fantasy when it comes to projecting a church budget. How often is this done? How many churches do you personally know of that are not meeting their budgets? It becomes a source of defeat and anguish to a church. It is far better to underestimate the budget and then be surprised when surplus funds result. In the kingdom of God, there is always a needy work in which to place surplus funds. How nice to have extra money for those needs.

A logistics coordinator should be flexible, and the church budget should reflect that kind of flexibility. Some church budgets look as if they were constructed by a representative of the IRS. Every small category is defined and the funds are locked in tightly to the details of each category. Lack of flexibility in a budget can thwart the church's ability to function effectively. A certain amount of latitude must be built in by the person formulating the budget.

Sometimes people can get so bogged down in budgets and procedures that these become an end in themselves. We must employ a person in this position who can keep the real end—the ministry of the church—in mind. He or she must also be cognizant of the church's goals and be committed to helping the church reach those goals.

He must be a "people person" with experience in managing people. He may be working with temperamental volunteers. The problem is that such people are often irreplaceable. Have you tried to recruit church treasurers or financial secretaries lately?

A logistics coordinator must be able to computerize all of the perfunctory fiscal functions necessary for the work of the church. Today, both computers and comprehensive church management software are readily available and relatively inexpensive.[1] When a computer can perform a service efficiently, easily, and quickly, I think it is a sin to tie up Christian servants in performing that function manually. Free your people for more creative Christian service.

Details are an important part of a logistics coordinator's life. It is he who must keep track of church equipment and project an equipment replacement schedule. He is also the one who will keep track of such things as expected carpet life so that budgetary plans may be made for its replacement. In my extensive ministry, I have seldom found a church that programmed for a new roof, a paint job, or replacement of such things as a furnace or electrical system. In most cases, those items were left to deteriorate to the point that someone had to push the panic button. At that point, there was usually no money available for such necessary repairs, and it put extraordinary pressure on people to give "above and beyond" their abilities. That is a poor way to carry on God's business.

No one should expect a logistics coordinator to perform all these functions himself. Instead, he should find competent people to work with him, assign them tasks, and keep them accountable in accomplishing those tasks. Able-bodied retired people are often good prospects for these helpers.

1. The finest comprehensive, integrated program for church management that I know about is produced by Computers for Churches. Their current address is P.O. Box 42-8069, Evergreen Park, IL 60642.

In large churches, a logistics coordinator's position will usually be a full-time paid position. However, smaller churches can do nicely with a part-time person or even a volunteer who has sufficient time to devote to this ministry. At times during the church year, it will be a busy position. At other times, it will be relatively quiet. This, then, is a good position for a hard-headed, warm-hearted businessman who retires (perhaps early) and agrees to serve the Lord through the use of his business expertise. The job usually is such that he can spend a few hours each week in the church office and even take off a few weeks to go to Palm Springs in the winter time. Even though this is a support service, it is a vital, needful ministry in every church.

## WHAT ABOUT YOUTH MINISTRY?

I must confess that I have a great aversion to hiring a youth director as the second full-time staff member. To do so concentrates a great deal of finances on a relatively small percentage of the congregation. Before we seek an alternate solution to hiring a youth director for a small church, let's dispel a myth. It is not necessarily true that a church that fails to hire a full-time youth director does not really care about the needs of its young people. Indeed, the hiring of a full-time youth director may actually be a disservice to the youth of the church if he is an ill-equipped person or one who considers his ministry only a stepping stone to the pastorate.

What are we looking for in a youth ministry? The average youth program probably centers on discipleship and fellowship. Upon examining what we ought to be doing, however, most people would admit that evangelism should be included. Therefore, what we may be looking at is two separate ministries. One of these would be the primary responsibility of the discipleship director. He would be responsible for selecting and providing training for adults who serve young people not only as teachers but as fellowship facilitators. The church's fellowship coordinator would help these adults foster fellowship not only among the youth but between the youth and other age groups as well.

Because youth ministry is somewhat specialized, both the discipleship and fellowship coordinators might find it necessary and helpful to draw on professional help for the training process. A given church might consider the following three options for such a position: a part-time, paid youth coordinator; a volunteer who has sufficient time to devote; a professional whose services are shared by several churches.

It would not be the principal responsibility of the professional to "play with the kids." This may be left to the volunteer youth sponsors. Instead, he or she would be expected to be a idea person, a trainer, a consultant, a coordinator. Anyone who has ever been associated with a successful youth program knows that the major factor in the success of that program is good, volunteer sponsors. However, that does not mean that the professional will be completely detached from the young people. Only in knowing them as individuals and participating in their activities will he gain their confidence and be able to construct a program to meet their needs.

But what about evangelism? Since youth are often designated as one of the target groups a church wishes to reach, there should be an evangelistic program geared to youth. This should be as well planned and orchestrated as the edificational youth program. Here, the person responsible is the evangelism coordinator. He, too, may want to ask someone with some appropriate training to help him. In addition, he must operate in close cooperation and coordination with the person directing the edificational youth program, since it will be that program into which the new Christians will be funneled.

Who are the best individuals to reach young people for Christ? Many feel that the youth themselves do the best job. Therefore, mature young people who have been nurtured in the edificational program can be utilized in the evangelistic program. Notice, I am not suggesting that every young person get into the action, only those who have proved themselves to be dependable.

## A Brief Review

I am firmly convinced that many churches cripple their ministry by attempting to put all of their "eggs in one basket." It is unrealistic to think that a church can select a pastor who is capable of fulfilling all of their expectations. And they soon find that out. Then, when he fails to live up to their expectations, the church may put itself in a financial crunch by hiring the second staff person.

However, even here, many times the church is tied to a traditional staffing pattern that it observes in other churches. Thus, the second staff member is rarely employed in areas that are likely to prove most beneficial to the church—those equipping ministries that result in church growth.

This chapter has been designed to say to local church leadership, "When looking for leadership staff, survey the real needs of your church, extricate yourselves from the box of traditional staffing patterns, think creatively and look around at who might be available to meet your needs." Perhaps in doing so you may decide that the traditional pattern is right for you. On the other hand, you may opt for other patterns, perhaps staffing the church largely with bi-vocational people, gifted volunteers, or retirees. Maybe you will find that there is no ongoing need for a paid staff member in a certain area. Instead, you may decide to contract for the services of a professional for a given period of time who will train your people for volunteer service in this ministry.

Sometime, you may even agree to share the services of a professional with another church in your community. Or you may pool resources in some other way so that each congregation works to enhance the other's ministries.

Perhaps the greatest areas of stress in the ministry today arise out of the unrealistic expectations a congregation has of its professional leadership. In turn, the staff—well aware of its own limitations—may feel frustration because it has been made aware of those expectations. There are few people around who can begin to be "all things to all men." Unfortunately, conventional staffing practices tend to promote such a demand. As a result, congregations suffer and able people are turned into dropouts. Creative staffing promoted among churches may work wonders to preclude this from happening.

## Additional Resources

Anderson, James D. *The Management of Ministry*. San Francisco: Harper & Row, 1978.

Blanchard, Kenneth, Patricia Zigarmi, and Drea Zigarmi. *Leadership and the One Minute Manager*. New York: William Morrow, 1985.

Dale, Robert D. *Pastoral Leadership*. Nashville: Abingdon, 1986.

Gangel, Kenneth O. *Leadership for Church Education*. Chicago: Moody, 1970.

Goodwin, Dennis. "Using Job Assignments to Get Added Value from Church Staff." *Church Administration,* November 1989, pp. 9-10.

Lindgren, Alvin J. *Management for Your Church.* Nashville: Abingdon, 1977.

Mitchell, Kenneth R. *Multiple Staff Ministries.* Philadelphia: Westminster, 1988.

Peck, Terry. "Building Positive Relationships Among the Staff." *Church Administration,* November 1989, pp. 16-18.

Schaller, Lyle E. *The Multiple Staff and the Larger Church.* Nashville: Abingdon, 1987.

Sheffield, Jimmie. "Ways the Staff Develops into a Team." *Church Administration,* November 1989, pp. 6-7.

Stamey, Judy. "How to Build a Team of Volunteer Leaders." *Church Administration,* February 1990, pp. 15-17.

## Questions for Discussion and a Helpful Project

1. List the reasons it is often unproductive for a contemporary church to try to adopt the early church as a detailed blueprint for ministry.

2. What is a typical contemporary church staffing pattern? Why may such a pattern prove detrimental to the church? What steps may be taken to change this unproductive pattern?

3. Discuss the mentality that often takes place when a church decides to hire its second staff member. What are some ways in which you can help your church change its mind and staff more effectively?

PROJECT: With a group of other leaders, list the major goals of your church. Imagine for a moment that your church has no professional staff at present. Devise a number of creative ways in which you could staff in order to best meet your goals. Draw up a proposed job description for each of these staff members.

4. Why is the position of logistics coordinator so important? What kinds of qualities would you look for in a candidate for that position?

# 19

# ACCOMPLISHING
## THE
# TASK
## THROUGH
# COMMITTEES

Through years of ministry, I have served on a variety of committees. In most cases, their meetings were exercises in frustration. Why? The committee took tiresome hours considering endless problems that could have been solved by competent leaders if they had been given sufficient authority. This book calls for a different kind of committee, where each member is assigned a job to do and given the necessary authority to carry it out. Committee meetings are freed up so that members may:

1. Engage in genuine Christian fellowship, share victories and burdens, and pray for one another.
2. Encourage, aid, and share ideas with each other; help each other discover answers to problems that seem insoluble.
3. Keep each member informed as to what is going on in everyone else's area of responsibility.
4. Discover how this overall area of ministry is doing in meeting goals and objectives established for it by the church.
5. Coordinate programs so that they work together to reach the church's goals.

In order to do all of this well, each leader must know how to perform as a team player so that all team members enhance each other's ministries. Here are some suggestions for building and utilizing a team spirit in committees.

### Recruit Amiable People

"Movers and shakers" can get things done, but they often ride roughshod over the people with whom they are working. Nothing thwarts forward progress more decisively than utilizing people who can't get along with others.

### Form Them into a Team

Promote fellowship to help build team spirit. If people fellowship often with others, they will get to know, appreciate, and trust one another. Maximize fellowship opportunities especially in the formation stages of the team. Work to foster fellowship among people who need to work the closest together.

Practice what you preach. As their leader, fellowship often with them—individually, in small groups, and with the committee as a whole. Most important, get to know each leader personally. Of all the people in your church, concentrate the most attention on members of your leadership team.

### Disciple Your Team Members

Intimate Christian fellowship offers the best possible opportunities for discipleship. It breaks down barriers humans have toward one another, allows people to express themselves more sincerely, and gives the leader an idea where his people need training the most. Invest and build yourself into your team members. Encourage them to do the same for you. Emphasize that they need to be constantly building up one another.

### Be Warm and Human

Every time you meet with them, express your appreciation for the job that they are doing. Find out their pains, both personal and ministry related. Then find out their hopes, plans, and dreams for the future. Be knowledgeable about their ministry. Know if there is any further monetary or personnel support that they need to get their job done. Go to bat for them.

Make sure that they are not overworked. If you detect "battle fatigue," suggest that they take time off. Finding a suitable replacement is your task, not theirs. They already have enough pressures and worries.

Teach through example. Establish a genuine friendship with that person. Let him know that he is of worth to you as a person, not just as a means of getting a job done. Take an interest in his family, his hobbies, his concerns. Train him to do all of these things with the leaders whose programs he coordinates, and his peers on the committee you head.

## USE COMMITTEE MEETINGS WISELY

### DURING COMMITTEE MEETINGS SPIRITUAL PRIORITIES SHOULD BE PLACED FIRST

When you assemble your team, begin each meeting with a time of sharing personal victories and needs, followed by a time in which those needs are brought to the Lord. Then give each person the opportunity of sharing what is going on in his ministry area, the success or failure of present programs and past events. Encourage each person to share his dreams for the future and the plans and events that will make those dreams become a reality.

### COMMITTEES SHOULD RARELY MAKE DECISIONS

Individuals are better decision makers than committees. Individuals are helped to make appropriate decisions through proper training and the assignment of sufficient authority to get the job done, means which are cited often in this book. When leaders are equipped in this manner, they rarely need to ask for a committee's help in decision making. However, let's explore some possible occasions when committee help is required.

*Use a committee for help in scheduling.* Normally, at the beginning of each church year all committees of the church get together, individually establish their plans for the coming year, and set tentative dates for the "special events" that help them carry out these plans. Then the board of the church meets, lays out all of the proposed events and coordinates the year's schedule so that events complement rather than compete with each other. From there on, only as a substantive program or schedule change is needed does the leader need to ask his committee or the church board for a decision.

*Use a committee to establish or alter budgets.* Each year, leaders of individual programs bring budget requests to their committee. Having received general budget guidelines from the board of the church, the committee members then "hammer out" how that budget will be divided. Under normal circumstances, each leader will be expected to function within his budget limit.

However, sometimes unexpected occasions arise which are marvelous opportunities for ministry but have not been previously budgeted. In addition, a specific program may succeed so well that the budget is not sufficient to serve the great numbers of people enjoying that program. This is another occasion when a committee can aid the leader in requesting and receiving additional funds. Sometimes other committee members will have budget surpluses that they can share. At other times, the committee as a whole will need to make a budget request to the church board. When a committee rather than an individual makes such a request, the church board will be more apt to approve the request.

COMMITTEES SHOULD WORK TOWARD CONSENSUS

On those rare occasions when a committee must make a decision, it is important that they take the time necessary to reach a consensus. James Means discourages the use of voting to accomplish this. He writes, "Good leaders recognize that voting rarely, if ever, contributes to consensus; it usually polarizes a group of people and is antithetical to group cohesiveness."[1]

Working toward consensus often requires that a person be ready to compromise his position along the way. I am not talking here about doctrinal or convictional compromises. Rather I am referring to compromises as to methodology. Here the committee head must be certain that if he expects his committee members to compromise, he must be willing to do so himself.

---

1. James E. Means, *Leadership in Christian Ministry* (Grand Rapids: Baker, 1989), p. 146.

In order to reach proper compromises, he needs to teach his people that compromise, in some cases, may be a sign of extreme strength rather than weakness. Means states:

> Solving problems and reaching decisions demand a kind of give and take where positions are at stake and where it is impossible for everyone concerned to be equally right all the time. But having to give way or alter a position in the face of compelling argument is no loss. The executive who can develop a position, believe in it, support it to its fullest, and then back down is a strong person.[2]

Means then cites Ted Engstrom, who reminisces:

> When we are young, we refuse to compromise. As we grow older, we realize we have to compromise. Perhaps in our thirties, we learn to compromise. By forty, we are willing to compromise. Sometime in life we (it is hoped) we learn that our "ideals" are less than ideal when placed alongside those of others. "Our goals" turn out to be more desirable than "my goals."[3]

In striving for consensus, there is an additional consideration. Remember, a solution to a problem may appear to be logical to you and most of your committee members. However, one or more members may be "tracking" in the area of feelings instead of facts. Feelings are important. When strong feelings are expressed, back off from making the decision and help a person change his feelings through the methods I discussed in part 3. Then the path to consensus may be "on track" once again.

## RESOLVING CONFLICTS

But what about instances where the leaders you supervise simply do not get along either with you or with each other? As a result, it is difficult to work as a team and nearly impossible to reach consensus on anything. Do not despair! As usual, the Scriptures have some profound answers.

2. Abraham Zaleznik, *Human Dilemmas of Leadership* (New York: Harper & Row, 1966), p. 36.
3. Ted W. Engstrom and Edward Dayton, *The Christian Executive* (Waco, Tex.: Word, 1979), p. 59.

### APPROACH CONFLICT WITH A HUMBLE SPIRIT

We find the first of these in Numbers 11. Here Moses is faced with a rebellion engineered by his own family members, Aaron and Miriam. Interestingly, before the Scriptures reveal his solution to the problem, they give us something of his character which describes why he acted that way. Numbers 12:3 records, "Now the man Moses was very humble, more than any man who was on the face of the earth." Does that give you a clue as to the kind of person who can settle conflicts effectively?

### ATTACK CONFLICT WITH PRAYER

Moses' response to this conflict was to turn to the Lord. This is always the best first step for us to take. If we are bitter about the conflict and the person, we should take it to the Lord until His sweet presence dispels that bitterness and helps us once again to love the individual who is causing the conflict.

### WHEN FACED WITH CONFLICT, SEEK THE ADVICE OF OTHERS

Again we turn to Moses as an example. In Exodus 18, we note that things are getting out of hand. Moses' scope of authority is too broad, and he is losing control. As a result, he seeks the older and wiser counsel of his father-in-law. Moses follows that advice, and the conflict is solved amicably. We are wise when we follow his example. Often the best counselor is one of the church's mature prayer warriors.

### EFFECTIVE CONFRONTATION IS BASED ON SOUND RELATIONSHIPS

It is difficult to resolve a conflict by approaching a person "cold turkey." Usually he or she will not really listen to us unless we have established a meaningful, mutual relationship. In Galatians 2, we note that a serious conflict has arisen between Paul and Peter. Before considering Paul's solution to that conflict, however, keep in mind Paul's relationship with Peter. In Galatians 1:18, Paul writes, "Then three years later I went up to Jerusalem to become acquainted with Cephas, and stayed with him fifteen days." This was not a chance acquaintance. Peter and Paul spent considerable quality time together. Not until you really know a person and have showed him that you care for him, will you have earned the right to lovingly confront that person.

## DEAL WITH CONFLICTS OPENLY

Conflicts are never solved by sweeping them "under the rug." In Galatians 2:11, Paul writes about how he handled this conflict with Peter: "But when Cephas came to Antioch, I opposed him to his face." Let's look at some concrete steps we may take in order to deal with conflicts properly.

## APPROACH PEOPLE INDIVIDUALLY

If there are two people involved, we first approach each one separately. We do so at a "neutral" site where the discussion can be more relaxed. Many of us have utilized a luncheon engagement as the standard setting for such a mission. If you do so, select a restaurant where you can find a private, secluded spot.

After lunch and exchanging "pleasantries" with the individual, state the reason for being there in clear, nonthreatening terms and then ask that the two of you pray together. If possible, suggest that both of you pray audibly.

Next, tell him that you are going to explain the problem as you see it. Ask him to listen to you and tell you where he feels you are right and wrong in your impressions. Then state the problem as objectively as possible, being sure not to attack him personally or make him overly defensive.

Give him ample time to comment and express both his thoughts and his feelings. Listen respectfully and comment as positively as possible. Let him know that you respect both him and his feelings even though you may not agree with him.

Ask him to outline for you a proposed plan whereby this issue may be resolved. You may find that he is right on "target" and that the problem is already as good as solved.

In other cases, you may discover that this person has severe attitudinal problems. Then you may want to institute a process similar to the one outlined in section 3 to help change that person's attitude.

If the conflict is not between him and you but between him and another person, you need next to approach the other "gladiator" and follow the same steps as you did with the first person.

After you have approached both people individually, bring the two "contestants" together at lunch. Once again, follow a similar format, exchanging pleasantries, praying, stating the problem. This time, also ask each of them to state the problem (objectively) as he sees it, asking each to comment as to what he thinks is the accuracy of the impression expressed by the other person. Sometimes, right at this point, misunderstandings will be aired and people will finally begin to understand and appreciate each other.

Ask them to propose a solution to which both of them can agree. If they can't, and both of them are at fault, you will need to proceed with your attitude-changing process. If at all possible, program the process in such a way that the two are going through the steps together. By doing so, who knows, they may even grow to like each other. However, even if just one of them is at fault, it is not too bad an idea to include the "innocent party" in the process. Familiarity, in this case, does not necessarily breed contempt.

If you discover that an individual engages in conflict almost continually on almost every issue that is raised and perpetually has difficulty getting along with the other members of the committee, you may determine to take other action. Undoubtedly there is a serious personality problem that may have serious spiritual overtones. As a result, you may elect to take some of the following steps.

1. You may ask the individual to resign. After all, you have other things to do than to concentrate such huge portions of time helping this person with his attitudes. If the individual does resign, try to assign him to someone who can disciple him. If he refuses such help or engages in subversive behavior, then steps of church discipline may be in order.

2. If the individual will not resign, you should have the power to dismiss him/her since you were probably his or her recruiter. However, for your own protection, do so with the knowledge and approval of the church board.

   Again, after dismissal, try to enlist this person in a discipling program. Whether or not he agrees to discipling, if he promises to behave himself and does not engage in divisive action, then leave him alone for a while and see what develops. If he does not keep his promise to act biblically, then he is a candidate for church discipline.

3. You may decide that this person is simply a "fish out of water." Maybe he should be doing something other than supervising a church program, especially where he has to work as a member of a committee. It could be that he would do better as an "Indian" rather than a "chief." Work with him to try to discover an area of service in which he can find fulfillment rather than frustration. Gain his agreement to resign his present position and serve in the suggested area. If you cannot, then you probably need to take either step one or step two above.

So far I have said much about the area of church discipline throughout this book. Let's see now how it works as applied to a church leader.

### DISCIPLINING A LEADER

If you are a Christian leader, you need to continually remind yourself that you are not above the requirements for purity and holiness that you would impose on your congregation. If anything, there is a higher and more demanding/exacting set of standards placed upon you. Do not ever think that discipline is inappropriate for you. If anything, you should be subject to more stringent discipline than other members of the congregation.

Earlier in this book we discussed discipline as an underlying rule of life within the church, an everyday occurrence to take care of little things before they become big things. In some detail, we examined together Matthew 18, and I stressed the need to follow the pattern as specified. Above all, I insisted, we are not to neglect the first stage of that pattern, the one-on-one approach. This must be a primary consideration, as well, when disciplining a leader.

Now, since we are dealing with a congregation in which every believer is also a priest, be aware that it is legitimate for every one of those believers to approach a leader on a one-on-one basis to engage in this kind of discipline. Don't be surprised when it happens. Expect it!

On the other hand, parishioners need to know that there is a biblically prescribed pattern for disciplining a leader. They are not ever justified in merely "blowing their top," giving vent to pet prejudices and airing their rage. In dealing with one another, but especially in dealing with leaders, the key is found in 1 Timothy 5:1, which says, "Do not sharply rebuke an older man, but rather appeal to him as a father." Even though the leader may not be older in age, he is "older" in the sense that the church has selected him for an important office. By virtue of his occupying that office, I believe he should be given the respect the Bible indicates is due an older person.

However, as leaders, we also need to listen to the concerns of every believer and take them seriously. If expressing the concern does nothing else, it may indicate to us an adverse spiritual condition with which he needs help. Moreover, if the concern has been expressed improperly, we need to help the person learn the process of expressing future cares in a biblically acceptable manner.

So far we have been discussing the common, "every day" kind of discipline which, I believe, needs to be practiced regularly by the church. Now let's look at a more stringent disciplinary situation. Earlier I discussed in some detail the kinds of problems that disqualify a leader because he is no longer "above reproach." Add to these a person's unwillingness to cooperate as a member of a leadership team or his inability or unwillingness to get along with people. Such sins not only indicate spiritual immaturity but often cause serious disunity in the church.

Again, the Matthew 18 pattern would insist that the person who personally observes a serious problem of any kind deal first on a one-on-one basis with the alleged offender. It is not biblical for a leader to act on the basis of a rumor or second-hand information. Carl Laney warns of the ease with which Christian leaders may be maligned by false accusations. Pastors whom he surveyed warned: "You must have reliable witnesses"; "Act on facts, not hearsay or rumor"; "Make certain of the accuracy of the charge"; "Get the facts straight before initiating action."[4]

Laney further cites the warning of Homer Kent, who writes, "No person is more subject to Satan's attack in the form of gossip than God's servant."[5] In like fashion, R. C. H. Lenski insists, "The honor due the office demands protection, for even a charge of which an elder

---

4. J. Carl Laney, *A Guide to Church Discipline* (Minneapolis: Bethany, 1985).

5. Homer A. Kent, Jr., *The Pastoral Epistles* (Chicago: Moody, 1958), p. 185.

is acquitted nevertheless damages his office and his work to some degree."[6]

If, when the rumor is tracked down, it is found to be untrue, then it is mandatory that we initiate the steps of Matthew 18 against the accuser. Moreover, it is vital that we inform the accused. Thus he will be prepared to defend himself against those who accept and spread the rumor as fact.

If the rumor is found to be factual, the person discovering the facts should first approach the accused. However, since the accused is a leader, there is a prescribed pattern that differs slightly from the Matthew 18 formula.

Let's suppose that you are the person who will initiate disciplinary action against a fellow leader. If that person has sinned against you, you need to approach him first on a one-on-one basis. Usually, however, his sin is not specifically against you, and you need additional information. Speaking to such a situation, 1 Timothy 5:19 says, "Do not receive an accusation against an elder except on the basis of two or three witnesses." Again, make sure that these witnesses have first approached the alleged offender individually and personally.

Next, approach him with these witnesses and allow him to defend himself. If there is no viable defense, he, along with the witnesses, should be brought before the church board for further action. If he is proved guilty beyond a shadow of a doubt or the evidence is substantial enough to destroy his credibility as a leader, he must be removed from office immediately. Make sure that your church constitution has provisions to do this. The reason for his removal (but not all the gory details) should be reported to the church.

At this time, remedial action may be taken if he is willing. If he is truly repentant of his sin, then the restoration process should begin. He may start by confessing his sin and asking for forgiveness, first with the board and then with the congregation. Other prescribed remedial measures should follow. Responsible members of the board or other mature Christians will oversee this. Together with the offender, they will devise a plan and a timetable for restoring him to fellowship with the church.

6. R. C. H. Lenski, *St. Paul's Epistles to the Colossians, Thessalonians, Timothy, Titus and Philemon* (Minneapolis: Augsburg, 1961), p. 684.

If he is not repentant, then the words of 1 Timothy 5:20 are clear. "Those who continue in sin, rebuke in the presence of all, so that the rest also may be fearful of sinning." We are to "lay it on the line," preferably in his presence with the whole congregation being present. If he refuses to be present, we will prudently explain the situation to the congregation and take action to remove him from both membership and fellowship.

In these days when so many people are "litigation crazy" we must be doubly certain that we have explicit provisions in our constitution and bylaws that specify which kinds of sins and conditions warrant this type of discipline. We must also be certain that we carry on the public phase of the disciplinary process in the most discreet fashion possible. However, even after doing so, be prepared for a lawsuit. It may well be a price that a church must pay in order to discipline biblically. In that light, does your church have malpractice insurance? This is a "must" these days!

What does disfellowshipping mean? It does not mean avoiding all contact with the offender. It does not mean excluding him from attending church services. Such a practice would certainly be declared illegal. Disfellowshipping certainly would include withholding the Lord's Supper from the person. It would also mean that fellow Christians not of his own family should avoid sharing meals with that person and avoid other "fellowship activities," even such things as handball or golf.

At all times, Christians should be open and willing to meet with this person and discuss his spiritual condition. However, it should be made plain to him that this is meant to be strictly a remedial occasion to help that person back to fellowship.

Even when the offender has agreed to and taken all of the remedial steps, however, be appraised that the desired end product of Matthew 18 is restoration to fellowship but not necessarily to leadership. Considering the sin and its impact upon the congregation and the community, that person may never again be deemed "above reproach." It is a shame, but there are sins that have such horrendous consequences that the talents and giftedness of an individual may be lost forever. This, however, is the fault of the individual, not of the disciplining church.

In other cases, after a sufficient amount of time has lapsed, a church may decide to first entrust the disciplined person with "lesser" positions of leadership than that which he formerly occupied. Eventually, he may aspire to the leadership position from which he fell. However, again, this depends upon whether sufficient time has elapsed so that he is, once again, considered "above reproach." Sufficient time, in my estimation, may mean five or ten years away from his former kind of ministry. Certainly it should be more than the one year which some churches are using as an arbitrary figure these days.

In this chapter we have traced an unfortunate route—from committee assignment to conflict resolution to harsh church disciplinary measures. We would pray that it would not go that way but that God's leaders will learn to live and serve together amicably as a team. Hopefully, this chapter has presented some constructive ways which you, as a leader, can put into action to help see that this happens.

## Additional Resources

Bennis, Warren G. *Why Leaders Can't Lead: The Unconscious Conspiracy.* San Francisco: Jossey-Bass, 1989.

Bradford, Leland P. *Making Meetings Work: A Guide for Leaders and Group Members.* La Jolla, Calif.: University Associates, 1976.

Clarke, Jean. *Who Me? Lead a Group?* Minneapolis: Winston, 1984.

Hestenes, Roberta. "Turning Committees into Community." *Leadership* 10, no. 3 (Summer 1989): 46-52.

Johnson, David. *Joining Together: Group Theory and Group Skills.* Englewood Cliffs, N.J.: Prentice Hall, 1987.

Lawson, Leslie Griffin. *Lead On! Complete Handbook for Group Leaders.* San Luis Obispo, Calif.: Impact, 1982.

Leas, Speed. "Inside Church Fights." *Leadership* 10, no. 1 (Winter 1989): 12-20.

Madsen, Paul. *The Person Who Chairs the Meeting.* Valley Forge, Pa.: Judson, 1973.

Schul, Bill D. *How to Be an Effective Group Leader.* Chicago: Nelson-Hall, 1975.

Yancey, Philip. "The God Who Delegates." *Leadership* 10, no. 1 (Winter 1989): 64-66.

## Questions for Discussion and Helpful Projects

1. Imagine that you are responsible to lead a church committee. What responsibilities do you have toward the committee members? Name ways in which you can help them accomplish their mission.

PROJECT: Devise an agenda for either an actual committee or an imaginary committee over which you would preside. What would be your specific duties as the leader of that meeting?

2. The author has advocated a model for a committee that requires a minimal amount of decisions to be made by that committee. In view of that model, on what occasions and under what circumstances should committees be called upon to make decisions?

3. Search your knowledge of the Scriptures. List some biblical examples of conflict resolution.

PROJECT: From those examples, draw up a list of principles for resolving conflict in the church today. What are the specific kinds of situations in which those principles may be applied?

4. Why is the matter of church discipline for leaders so much more serious than the discipline of ordinary members? What additional guidelines does the New Testament give for the discipline of a leader who persists in sin?

5. What stipulations would you make for the reinstatement of a fallen church leader? Explain the distinction between restoring a fallen leader to fellowship and restoring him to leadership.

# 20

## SELECTING PROGRAMS
### TO MEET
## BIBLICAL GOALS

S uppose the past could be erased and your church had a chance at an entirely new beginning. What is the irreducible minimum of programs it would choose? Some will respond, "We don't even talk about programs until we review our goals; our programs must be built on goals and objectives in order to be effective," and you would be right. Let's look at some general guidelines for selecting programs to reach goals.

### WORSHIP: THE "MISSING JEWEL"

Worship should be the best thing we do as a church, for it is our special offering to God.[1] This is no place to employ amateurs or learners. Unprofessional conduct on the part of a worship leader distracts rather than enhances a person's ability to worship. In *The Effective Pastor* I wrote at some length concerning the conducting of a worship service.[2] In this book I have been and will be discussing additional thoughts on the subject.

1. The book by Ronald B. Allen and Gordon L. Borror, *Worship: Rediscovering the Missing Jewel* (Portland, Oreg.: Multnomah, 1982) is, of course, the inspiration behind the heading immediately above and is well worth careful study.
2. Robert Anderson, *The Effective Pastor* (Chicago: Moody, 1985), chap. 13.

The church needs a serious, substantial service designed specifically for worship. That service could be held at almost any time on Sunday or during the week. "Praise choruses" are not enough for this service. It is the place to explore the grand musical heritage of the church, beginning with substantive hymns ascribing glory to God. Solid, in-depth Bible teaching should incite the Christian to the deeper aspects of the Christian walk.

Through the years, a rich liturgical library has been built up for the church, including prayers that may be recited as a congregation, confessions of faith, confessions of sin, and other corporate readings. You can lead a horse to water, but you cannot make him drink. Likewise, you can lead a person to a worship service, but you cannot make him worship. But at least you can provide the vehicles that will help him worship.

Some of my own most significant times of true worship have been during the serving of Communion. Communion seems to have been at the heart of the worship of the early church. Communion may not have been observed every day, but it was observed at least weekly (Acts 20:7). I believe that Communion should be observed each week as the heart of the worship service. It should not be tacked on to the service. It should be an integral, unhurried, important part of a worship service observed to the glory of God.

Just because Communion is served does not mean that the teaching should be curtailed. The people who attend the service should plan ample time to give themselves as an offering to God. They should also worship God through sacrificial giving. I believe it is important for a congregation to participate publicly in this exercise and bring the money forward as an act of corporate dedication.

Read the resource materials at the end of this chapter for ideas to help make your worship service special to the glory of God. The worshiper should not leave the service asking if he received something from it but instead should be asking, "What did I do for God in that worship service?" for worship is to be dedicated solely to God. Participants should worship so intensely that they come away from the service tired as well as blessed. Individual worshipers and the corporate body of believers should expend major effort in planning, conducting, and participating in the worship service. If worship is fully practiced, many other important areas of the Christian life will come into line naturally.

Christians need to be involved in individual worship, too. This practice should grow out of their moment-by-moment fellowship with God. It is more than just observing a quiet time, though such times should be a high priority for the Christian. Dozens of times a day the believer can praise, thank, and adore God. He can marvel at the sunset and share his life with a child. During such times he can express his praise—sometimes quietly, sometimes vocally, sometimes privately, and other times corporately with other Christians.

Sometimes when we are with Christian friends the presence of God is so evident it is natural to engage in worship together. That worship may take many forms. It may express itself in the singing of a hymn or praise chorus. It may take the form of prayer. In some Christian circles, it is even permissible to celebrate Communion together in a home when it is evident that God has visited in a special way. The form of worship is not important. What is important is that you not miss the opportunity. Some of my most precious times of worship have been those special times with Christian friends.

Each ministry area is inextricably bound to the other. Worship can arise out of times of fellowship; sweet fellowship can evolve out of worship. Proper discipleship is built upon a foundation of fellowship, for the discipler has earned the right to be heard; discipleship training is an integral part of a worship service. In turn, discipleship, done properly, should result in local outreach and a vision for worldwide ministry. As we consider constructing programs for each of these areas, we need to keep in mind the effect each program will have on all the other areas of concern.

## DISCIPLESHIP: THE EQUIPPING TOOL

Discipleship is the sum total of the church's educational efforts. It is an equipping task involving three emphases: one-on-one, one-on-a-few (Bible classes and study groups), and one-on-many (the pulpit teaching ministry).

A discipleship program should provide equipping for every member of the church. It should be a coordinated program integrated into the fiber of the church and run by an individual given the responsibility of its coordination.

At the heart of any instructional program is the teaching of adults from the pulpit. All other teaching should revolve around that teaching and complement it. Notice that I said "adults" in relation to the pulpit teaching ministry. It is wrong for adults to force children to sit through pulpit presentations that are unintelligible and boring to them. God's inerrant Word is so precious that it is a crime to use it in an uninteresting way.

Though it may be profitable to include children in the rest of a worship service, it is detrimental to insist that children sit through the pulpit teaching. It is better to dismiss them at some point during the service to an instructional time in which the pulpit subject, or something like it, is broached in terms children can readily understand.

Should the church have a Sunday school? Not if the Sunday school is designed to be the primary teacher of biblical truths to children. Sunday schools have devolved into a time of primary teaching, but from its inception Sunday school was designed to be an evangelistic tool for reaching out to unchurched kids. The task of teaching spiritual truths to Christian children has always rested on parents, though most contemporary Sunday schools allow Christian parents to skip that responsibility.

If we hope to raise children who are scripturally grounded, parents must become the principal teachers of their own children. In scriptural and theological teaching for kids, "home schooling" is not an option. It is a necessity. Moreover, since there are so many families who are unwilling to take on that responsibility, willing Christian families should "adopt" other children for this training and include them in a family instructional program.

I know of no truly good curriculum geared to parents who send their children to public or private schools but wish to home school their children in scriptural truths. If there are evangelical curriculum publishers reading this book, may I challenge you concerning this great need? We also have a great need for adult home schooling curriculum that will teach adults how to feed themselves on the meat of the Word. It is absurd for an adult Christian to insist that he be constantly spoon-fed.

Sunday school should be an outreach ministry. It should also be a time for developing fellowship among the participants and for reviewing and codifying what people have learned during the week through their home schooling curriculum.

Sunday school should contain enough solid teaching so that those who are intellectually and spiritually lazy will get some spiritual food to digest. The Sunday school curriculum should be tied to the overall, coordinated discipling plan of the church. It may be difficult to use currently produced curriculum for that purpose, since those are usually general in orientation. Your church may need to write its own curriculum or to adapt commercial curriculum to meet its special needs.

The timing for Sunday school is important. Some young families are exhausted after an hour of Sunday school, a fifteen-minute interlude, a long worship service, and the inevitable fellowship time after the worship service. As a result, many churches have gone to a Sunday evening or a midweek church school. Other churches have eliminated adult classes altogether. Instead, Bible studies are conducted at various times and in a variety of locations during the week.

Sunday school for children is sometimes conducted during the regular worship time or during "junior church." Many churches following this practice have at least two worship services. As a result, families can attend both the worship service and Sunday school, and Sunday school and junior church teachers also are able to attend a worship service.

Besides instruction that is primarily biblical or doctrinal in nature, each church needs to offer special kinds of equipping classes. Those may be of short duration or extended over a longer period of time as needed. They may be in response to certain ministry needs, such as training people to be church leaders or Sunday school teachers, teaching people how to share their faith, or teaching them to cope with a pressing problem they are facing.

Such classes may be offered during the Sunday school hour, but they will usually meet the needs of more people if they are scheduled at other times during the week. A church with limited staff and resources will find it helpful to enlist the help of resource persons from other churches to teach the classes; in turn, churches with large resources find blessing in sharing their resources with less fortunate churches.

Increasingly, churches are being challenged to undertake teaching ministries that speak to some contemporary moral problem. Many "support groups" are being formed for recovering addicts, single parents, bereaved adults, and others with specialized needs. Sometimes those programs are conducted as a joint effort of two or more churches working together to meet the special needs.

Resist the temptation to be "all things to all men." Jesus did that and Paul tried, but you don't have a chance! If you have to choose between many instructional options open to you as a church, do a few things at a time and do them well. Be sure that those special training opportunities are designed to equip the church to reach your primary target groups. And, of course, make sure that they contribute directly to reaching the goals and objectives your church has established.

So far, I have referred to the one-on-many and one-on-a-few aspects of a discipleship program. Yet to some people such programs do not represent discipleship at all. To them, only one-on-one instruction denotes "real" discipleship. At this point, it might be helpful to look at a more biblical picture of discipleship.

The word *discipleship* per se is never mentioned in Scripture. We are told merely to "make disciples." In the early church, that was an "all hands on deck" proposition. The total resources of the church were concentrated on the one project. It must be so today as well. The total job of making disciples is far too large and complex a job for one person.

When we concentrate only on one-on-one methods, we risk establishing a "guru" mentality in the minds of the disciple and the discipler. Through the years I have discipled many people on a one-on-one basis, but I have always done my best to avoid making anyone "my" disciple. Even the thought terrorizes me. We are only to make disciples of Jesus Christ. Only He is truly worthy of being followed on a consistent and prolonged basis.

Where does the one-on-one discipleship method work the best? It is a necessity with new believers. Usually, the best person to disciple a new convert is the one who led him to Christ. That is not always possible, however. Sometimes the most "unlikely" people act as evangelists. In that case, the evangelist may need someone with more competence to help him disciple the new convert. However, at least in the early stages of the discipling process, it is good for the evangelist to meet with the disciple and discipler.

It is not the task of the discipler to make the disciple dependent upon him. His challenge is to disciple in such a way as to make his role obsolete. Just as a child is taught to be more and more independent as he approaches adulthood, so a disciple should be weaned away from his discipler. The discipler then becomes a lifelong friend and resource, and the disciple is freed to take the necessary steps toward Christian maturity.

Other prominent candidates for one-on-one discipleship are people who are facing severe troubles or who have habits they find hard to overcome. Even here, it is not the role of the discipler to establish a life-long dependency relationship. That is ultimately harmful to the disciple.

Teenagers respond well to one-on-one discipling. Often a "neutral," more objective adult can help a teenager through a difficult period with greater understanding than can his parents. Sometimes another adult can see potential in a teenager that his parents fail to see. The discipling of teens often may result in the teen's committing his life to a church vocation.

It is helpful for responsible adults to establish discipling relations with single parents or children of single parents. In most cases, it is proper only for the discipler to disciple someone of his same gender.

Brand-new pastors may want to be discipled by a godly saint who has had a great deal of experience with the integral workings of the church. Of course, one-on-one discipling is never one-sided. Both the disciple and discipler are constantly in a learning mode.

What about curriculum for this kind of discipling? Organizations such as The Navigators and Campus Crusade for Christ have discipling materials useful in teaching people the basics of the Christian walk.

The amount of formal curriculum used will differ markedly with the situation. Before prescribing more content, we need to ask ourselves, "To what sources of content is this person already exposed? How extensive is this content? In what essential areas is the content weak?" On the basis of that assessment we will vary the amount of content assigned to the disciple. If he is already being bombarded with content, little more is needed. Then the task of the discipler is to help the disciple apply what he is studying. On the other hand, if the content is incomplete and deficient in some vital area, the discipler will want to supplement that content.

I have already stated my conviction that really successful discipling is built upon a fellowship base. Sometimes the role of the discipler will be principally that of fellowship. Out of that fellowship will arise vital questions. Then the discipler can exercise his most effective role.

## Fellowship: The Sustaining Blessing

"If I weren't a Christian, I don't know how I would survive a time like this. My Christian brothers and sisters have been wonderful." How often have you heard someone say something like that? At the core of the benefits realized through the Christian life are precious relationships among Christians. Those relationships need to be encouraged and nurtured by each church. That needs to be done on a systematic, coordinated basis so that nobody "slips through the cracks."

The church fellowship program also needs to include a shepherding system that keeps close tabs of people. We are responsible for our people. We need to know their needs so that we may minister to those needs. The world says, "Don't get involved with people," but the Christian must become a "holy busybody," for he is, indeed, his brother's keeper.

In addition to the array of social occasions churches use to foster fellowship between people are two other important vehicles for building close relationships: (1) the made-to-order structure that emerges naturally out of the boards, committees, and ministry tasks in which a church engages and (2) the effective fellowship structure that emerges from the common tasks Sunday school teachers, AWANA or Pioneer Club leaders, youth sponsors, church ushers, and others share. These natural groupings will not automatically produce deep relationships. The church must deliberately build into every board and committee of the church a fellowship emphasis. Board or committee members should also be taught to assume a certain degree of responsibility for fellow members and should begin to look out for each other's needs. The same should be true of persons engaged in special church tasks. Since they have similar interests, they should be encouraged to build deep, lasting relationships among themselves.

Other ready-made fellowship opportunities may be found among adult classes, "special need" groups, church athletic teams, ushers, and those who attend church repair days. Some churches construct intricate care group systems or home Bible study groups that function as care groups. Such groups are fine for those who are not ordinarily involved in some kind of ministry activity, but problems arise when people are expected to relate to those groups in addition to serving on boards and committees. High worker turnover results. The church is simply wearing out its people by imposing unrealistic expectations.

To avoid placing unreasonable demands on people, build a fellowship foundation on existing groups. Then consider those who are not yet involved in a group and make a number of group options available to them. Another word of warning. Don't expect everyone automatically to flock to home Bible studies or care groups. Some people simply do not like such activities. Remember, also, that substantive learning and fellowship may occur even through such "extraordinary" groups as softball teams. The trick is to program deliberately to see that this is done.

A number of tools facilitate fellowship. Unfortunately for those of us who gain weight easily, food is one of the best. Many times when food is served in connection with some routine meeting of a committee or other group, it greatly enhances the possibility of genuine fellowship occurring. Don Bubna muses, "For as long as I can remember, I have had the idea that eating with people is a great way to make friends. Some of my happiest memories from childhood are of a steady stream of guests at our table."[3]

In addition to its ready-made opportunities for fostering fellowship among people through groups, the church should take formal steps to encourage one-on-one fellowship. It might survey the congregation and find people with common interests and abilities and then devise ways of bringing those people together in meaningful relationships. Many people too shy to be a member of a group will blossom when they find a close personal friend. What better place to find that friend than in the church?

Earlier I discussed the need for the church to make use of "holy busybodies" so that fellow Christians may be aware of the needs of people. To do this, I suggest the employment of "deacon people." These people need not necessarily be members of the deacon board. In fact, it is better if they are not.

A member of the church board, however, should coordinate the activities of these deacon-type people. He should meet with them regularly to find out which members and friends of the church they would like to be responsible for. Then he can assign a reasonable number of people to each deacon's shepherding group. The groups may vary in size according to the time each deacon has available, though five families is probably the maximum number that should be assigned to any deacon. If a deacon experiences difficulty communicating with an individual, that individual should be assigned a different deacon.

The primary responsibility of the fellowship deacons (both male and female) is to look for the welfare needs of the congregation but par-

3. Donald L. Bubna, *Building People Through a Caring Sharing Fellowship* (Wheaton, Ill.: Tyndale, 1978), p. 47.

ticularly of their assigned people. They should be required to contact each family or individual for whom they are responsible at least once a week. They may do that in a conversation at church, through a phone call, or in a personal visit. If a person on their list is a shut-in, a personal visit is especially appropriate.

As their people identify needs, the fellowship deacons should take steps to meet those needs. If they have the necessary resources to meet the needs themselves, they should do so. Otherwise, they should call in reinforcements through the director of fellowship ministries. Nobody should be allowed to fall through the cracks. There should be continual contact with all the members of the church on a regular basis. The fellowship deacons become the heart of the church's counseling program.

As extraordinary needs surface (hospitalization, for instance), they should be brought to the attention of the pastor so that he can minister in his special way, visiting the persons experiencing the need and and praying for them. The deacon, in turn, should call on the extended resources of the church body to provide for the family's physical needs while their loved one is in the hospital. When the counseling need is over his head, the fellowship deacon seeks the resources of someone with more training. Counseling needs often arise in fellowship occasions, and many times require discipleship to satisfy those needs.

Christian fellowship should be one of the greatest fringe benefits of the Christian life. Yet many Christians do not experience that kind of fellowship because no one in the church makes it happen. Let your church be a sterling exception to this neglectful condition.

## A Cup of Cold Water in Jesus' Name

So far we have looked at edificational goals. Before I move to evangelism I want to consider an area toward which the edificational and evangelistic resources of the church should focus: ministry to the poor. Christians are becoming aware that our Lord places a great responsibility on us to minister to the poor, and evangelicals in particular have been criticized by some for ignoring the plight of the poor. Fortunately, this is an unfounded allegation. In a conversation with George Gallup, Jr., some time ago, he told me that evangelicals have a far better record of ministering to the poor than do the liberals. It may be that whereas the liberals are vocal about the needs of the poor, they believe that government should be the great benefactor. Evangelicals, on the other hand, may not talk about the subject much but give their alms in secret, knowing that the Rewarder sees.

Because evangelicals are faithful to this responsibility does not mean that they have arrived. There is plenty of room for us to step up our activities to meet the needs around us. Our first responsibility is to the poor within our midst. Again, the key is for an effective deacon system through which special needs can be identified.

It is inexcusable for a church to have a family in its midst that does not have adequate food and shelter. Those are the basics. The church needs to take any steps necessary to remedy the situation. There are sensible ways of approaching the problem. Some people are in desperate need because they have acted unwisely. As we help them it is important that we not encourage them to continue to act unwisely. Here we can use the talents of financial counselors to help people put their fiscal affairs in order. The best advice they may need is to drive an older car, live in a less prestigious house, or prepare less costly but nutritional meals. If they are unemployed, perhaps the church can call upon its collective resources to find employment for them.

The church probably has a special maintenance fund, but instead of doling out money to people, it may want to ask that the people they are helping take temporary employment at the church. They do not need to be given a "grungy," janitorial job. Use their gifts and talents. If they are capable of office work, let them help in that way. In most churches there is plenty of backlog. Carpenters, plumbers, landscapers, counselors, painters—you name the vocation, and there will probably be a need for it. Some people can even be used effectively as visitors to shut-ins and those hospitalized.

At times, aid may take the form of temporary housing provided by a member of the church. However, there should be a clear understanding that this is to last only so long. Meanwhile, they will be expected to make new arrangements.

A principal need may be for temporary transportation or babysitting services while the parents look for a job. A more desperate need may be for someone to pay the rent or the utilities bill for a month or so until the family gets on its feet financially. Each church should have special funds set aside for that purpose. This is not an option. We are given the responsibility to take care of our own.

Our church takes a "deacon offering" after every Communion service. However, often needs exceed funds, and additional financial appeals are directed toward our congregation. Sometimes one of our own is in need, and we don't even hear about it. Some "anonymous" person pays the rent or utility bill, or stocks the family with groceries. We also maintain a "closet" where clean, attractive clothes are available to people in need.

In our city a group of churches has pooled available skills. When a member of any of those churches needs help but cannot afford it, he calls the coordinator of the program. Carpenters, plumbers, electricians, car mechanics, and numbers of other kinds of specialty people are on call. Often those artisans and craftsmen are retired people who want to use their skills to the glory of God.

Most important of all is food. In no case should anyone go hungry. Surely with everything the Lord has given to us, we can find enough money to provide food for those in need. It doesn't have to be T-bone steak as long as it is tasty, filling, and nutritious. Many churches in Portland maintain food pantries. Periodically church members are asked to bring certain kinds of food to restock it. Other churches maintain food funds. As needs surface, they direct people to certain food markets where the church has accounts. People are given a certain limit to spend and are allowed to select the foods they want.

But this is not only the responsibility of the church. Each Christian should ask the Lord what is expected of him individually. During my childhood many of the homeless were called "bums" or "hoboes." Some passed through our community on a regular basis. Word seemed to have got around that our house was a place to get a free meal, because frequently we would find one of these people knocking on our door. Despite the fact that we were poor ourselves, my mother never turned anyone away hungry. She always prepared a simple but nutritious hot meal for them. I wonder how many times we fed the Lord in disguise.

Earlier in this book I spoke to the issue of ministering to the aid of the unsaved poor. When a "cup of cold water," food, or shelter is given in Jesus' name, the person receiving it should have no doubt in whose name it was given. When a person comes to us for material help, we should share the gospel without being pushy or using evangelical clichés. It is then the person's responsibility as to whether or not he receives the message.

One more word about meeting the needs of the poor. It is important that it be done in such a way as to help them lift themselves out of their poverty. Too many economic assistance programs have encouraged people to perpetuate their plight. Where possible, do not give money. Give food, provide shelter, fill the gas tank, pay the rent, give them clothing. At the same time, counsel them concerning God's love and tell them that Christians care about them. Help them find employment or employ them temporarily to work around the church. Take advantage of the opportunity by living your Christian life as they work side by side with you.

In some cases, a person may need training to qualify for a job. If you can secure funds to provide that training, that may be a good way to minister. Perhaps a member of the congregation could provide child care during the process. Use every opportunity to share Christ. Remember, their most basic needs are spiritual ones. Work to solve those needs, and the other solutions will fall into place.

## LOCAL EVANGELISM: NEW BLOOD FOR THE CHURCH

Nothing will revitalize a church more quickly than the inclusion of new Christians into the fellowship. Why do we evangelize? We do so because our Lord commands it and because it is so good for the church. Evangelism is so vital that a church that is not evangelizing may expect to die.

Returning to an evangelistically oriented service as a method of evangelism may, on the surface, seem easy: "All we have to do is use evangelistic songs and have the pastor preach an evangelistic message." Unfortunately, that is not the way it is to be done. A contemporary evangelistic service must take a different form if it is to appeal to the unchurched. The problem is that, if done properly, such a service has the potential for offending many of the established saints.

What should the format be, and when should the service be held? Though most Christians affirm the need for evangelism, many would object to giving up their customary time of worship, the sacrosanct 11:00 A.M. hour on Sunday. As a result, in an established church, an evangelistic service that will reach the unchurched may need to be conducted at other than the usual Sunday morning hour or at a location other than the sanctuary. Here we encounter bad news and good news. The bad news is that studies show that if the unchurched were to attend church they would probably choose the 11:00 A.M. hour. The good news is that you don't have to use the main auditorium for your evangelistic service. In fact, the auditorium may be so churchy in appearance that it would scare the unchurched away.

There are all kinds of alternatives for scheduling and facilities. Find a time when it is convenient for your target audience, not one that suits your church's stereotype. Use a facility in which the unchurched will feel comfortable. That may be a large classroom or a social facility. Make the setting as unchurchy as possible. Allow people to indulge in refreshments all during the program. Remember, this is not a church service per se. It is an evangelistic meeting.

The music should be contemporary and the message unmistakably evangelistic. Instruments could include electronic pianos, synthesizers, guitars, and maybe even drums. Don't major on congregational singing because non-Christians, by and large, do not sing. After all, what do they have to sing about? The majority of the music should be in the form of musical ministry by singers and instrumentalists who are skilled in the more contemporary forms of Christian music. Do not let it get out of hand, however. Instruct the musicians that they are to minister, not perform. Moreover, they are to minister with dignity and restraint. Do not use a vocalist whose words cannot be understood or who has a tendency to scream. Do not allow instrumentalists to drown out the message of the song.

Messages should be geared to the needs of the people but be biblically oriented. After all, it is only the Bible that has decisive solutions to all of life's problems. All messages should be short and to the point. They should be couched in language the audience understands and not in theological jargon. Each message should end by proclaiming Jesus Christ as the ultimate answer and by encouraging people to commit their lives to Him.

Although an invitation should always be extended, it need not necessarily be accompanied by seven verses of "Just As I Am." Indication of need may be expressed by such a simple thing as having a person take off his name tag and give it to the pastor at the door. Follow-up by the pastor or a member of the church's evangelistic team may be made at a social hour following the service or in the person's home. There, another clear presentation of the gospel and an invitation to commitment can be given. Public expression of faith can follow later through baptism and other means of personal testimony.

Careful attention should be given to publicizing the service so that there is a constant flow of unsaved people attending. That may be done through the regular use of attractively prepared bulk mailings. It may also be done through personal invitations given by members of your church who are reluctant to share their faith but who do not mind inviting a friend to this "unusual" service.

I am convinced that the plan of salvation should be presented in some form at all public services of the church, not just special evangelistic services, and that people need to be given the opportunity to respond in some way to that invitation.

A public evangelistic approach is not enough, however. People respond best to the witness of Christians. Therefore, ways must be explored by which to increase the number of contact hours between Christians and "pre-Christians," especially those in the targeted groups.

Who are the best people to employ in the task of evangelism? Those who are new Christians. They are not yet aware that many established Christians view the sharing of one's faith as uncouth. In addition, they have the largest circle of non-Christian relatives and friends. Many of them are not at all reluctant to invite those relatives and friends to an evangelistic service or home Bible study where the gospel is clearly presented. They are still at the point where they are "bubbly" in their faith but cannot begin to answer the hard questions. Employ them in the evangelistic process, but give them plenty of backup.

Does that mean that the entire ministry of evangelism should be done by the newly converted? What a shame if that were the case. Imagine the tragedy of keeping established Christians from the thrill of helping to give birth to a baby Christian. I have suggested that we begin a program of evangelism using new Christians because that is the easiest way to proceed. How do we go about the tougher job of getting established Christians involved? First, we must analyze what they need. Are they biblically grounded so that they can explain and defend the plan of salvation adequately in a personal encounter? If not, such grounding can be done in sermons, Sunday school classes, and special courses set up for that purpose.

How about methodology? Are they aware of the "plans" of salvation available for their use? Are they able to use any of the evangelistic tools that are readily available? Again, they can be taught those things in special classes.

What if they know about these things, have gone through the training, and still are not active witnesses? Then we are faced with an attitudinal rather than a content problem. Do you remember how to work in harmony with the Holy Spirit to change people's attitudes? Now may be a good time for you to review chapter 13.

So far we have discussed using evangelistic services, evangelistic home Bible studies, and individual sharing of one's faith as viable approaches in a program of local church evangelism. Earlier I also discussed the use of Bible clubs as an evangelistic tool for reaching families. These are conventional methods appropriate to contemporary conventional people.

But what about unconventional people? As the church has the ability, it needs to investigate needs and find out what resources are available to minister to those needs. A resulting method for reaching people might be a series of classes in parenting for single parents. Such classes would be structured in such a way that they answered not only the questions posed but presented the gospel in a clear manner. A pressing need expressed to one church was to help people cope with the problems resulting from divorce. Many people attended the resulting classes, and some of those people received Christ as their Savior.

A church in the Midwest is finding its best ministry among recovering drug addicts. Along with the emotional and psychological support these people need, the gospel is clearly presented. Many of them have begun a new life in Christ.

Here in Portland, a youth pastor felt a great burden for kids on skateboards. He found out that there was no safe place for them to skate. Viewing the large parking lot of his church, he enlisted volunteer carpenters to construct ramps. He carefully checked the church's insurance policy and then proceeded. On certain nights, the parking lot became "Skate Church." Kids were free to come and skate, but they were required to listen to a gospel message in return. "Skate Church" won numbers of teenagers who would have never attended a conventional church. Many of those teens now attend his church regularly.

In beginning an evangelistic program, don't start off with a bang that becomes a whimper. Begin with a spark that eventually bursts into flame. Start slowly and surely. When you begin, you may not even want to involve other church members. You may choose to begin an evangelistic Bible study in the home of one of your neighbors. Then, when they come to Christ, you can encourage them to share their testimony in your worship service. Begin to work with them on their extended network of friends, relatives, and fellow workers. As those people also are assimilated into your church, have them share their testimony as well. Instruct the newfound Christians that they will find some aspects of your church service to be strange, but better days are coming.

By this time, other church members will want to become part of the process. Place serious training demands on them. Make them give up their other church jobs and work only in evangelism. Remember, they are the ones who are asking you. You didn't approach them to do this. Make participation in evangelism a highly desirable ministry in your church. Make those who become involved in it sacrifice for the privilege of participating.

By now, you may have enough momentum to begin evangelistic services. Employ your new converts to take part in the work involved in these services, including publicity tasks, ushering, and refreshment preparation. Encourage them to invite their unchurched friends. There are many creative ways in which the unchurched can be reached. Some churches have utilized all kinds of banquets, teas, and other social events geared to target groups. Christian Women's Clubs are past mistresses of using special features that attract women. At each event, they have been careful to share the gospel and give an invitation.

Similar events using athletic or outdoor themes have been used to attract men. One church tells the men in its community, "On Super Bowl Sunday, bring a six-pack of pop at 2:00 P.M. We will supply the large screen TV and all the hamburgers and hot dogs you can eat." This is used to bridge the gap between church members and the unchurched. There is no limit to creativity in using all kinds of viable events to bridge gaps and share Christ.

What about the timid people who steadfastly avoid sharing their faith or even avoid inviting someone to an evangelistic event? Don't make them feel like spiritual lepers. Make them feel part of the evangelistic process by encouraging them to do something that is not threatening. Perhaps they could cook the hamburgers or help prepare mailings. Studies show that when the support of people is enlisted in even the smallest, most nonthreatening way, they are more apt to take the next step and do something that is bolder. When people are made to feel that they are part of the evangelistic team in even the smallest way, they will begin to share the victory. Who knows, eventually so much excitement may build that they may find it impossible to resist getting more actively involved.

## LET'S PAUSE A MOMENT

Instead of suggesting that you begin with a large-scale program, I have encouraged you to start in a modest fashion. Develop one program at a time, and then add new programs as they are needed and can be supported both financially and staff-wise. You don't have to do everything at once. In fact, it is better that you don't. Get each new program fine-tuned and running smoothly before you add anything else. Then, as you have the financial and people resources, launch into something new. Now let's look at areas in which a church can work cooperatively with other churches.

## CHURCH PLANTING: THE FINEST CHURCH GROWTH TOOL

The statistics are impressive. New churches win people to Christ in far greater number than established ones. They also grow faster. Do not take it for granted that because there are already large numbers of churches in a community that God's job is being done. Consider the large number of people who are not being reached by any church. That is the group we are after. To win them we have to plant a church that will minister uniquely to their needs. We can't franchise churches. It doesn't work.

There are many church planting opportunities within your "Judea." Some of those opportunities are among people just like those in your church, but many of them are among ethnic or minority people. Whatever your target group, it is important that your church participate in some way in the rewarding work of church planting.

For such an endeavor it is helpful to belong to a fellowship of churches. So much more can be done when churches band together and pool their resources. Perhaps your church will not be able to help finance a new church. However, there are many other ways you can aid a new work. Consistent, organized corporate prayer is the most important way. Intercessory prayer for the church's leaders is especially important.

In the preparatory stages, maybe some of your people can help put together mailings. Or perhaps you will be called upon to help with a telemarketing program, where people in the target community are polled as to whether or not they are interested in a new church. As the church nears the stage of holding public meetings, some of your people may agree to attend, serve, and give for a period of six months to a year. Do you have any surplus musicians? The new church may find them helpful. A church in Portland that has a large music program regularly "farms out" its musicians to minister in smaller churches.

If the new church is located fairly close to yours, plan to conduct joint events together. Get to know the people who attend there. Participate in pulpit exchanges so that the pastor of the church can keep you informed as to how it is progressing. Designate one of your church members to keep track of what is going on at the new church. Have him report all important developments to your people. As the new church grows large enough to erect a building, perhaps some craftsmen and others from your church can donate their services.

If it is an ethnic church, it would enrich your people to learn of the customs, foods, and unique personality factors of these people. See that invitations are extended back and forth. Broaden your horizons.

More than anything else, constantly keep your people informed of what the Lord is doing in and through these new sister works. Rejoice in the victories. Pray harder when apparent defeats are in the making. Keep your people looking outward instead of inward. It will give their faith a broader base and help keep them from looking only to satisfying their own selfish desires.

## WORLD MINISTRY: THE APPLE OF GOD'S EYE

The best known Scripture verse begins, "For God so loved the world." Whether or not we like it, we are an integral part of a world community. Increasingly there is less emphasis on nations and more interest in regions. For instance, the Pacific rim upon which Portland sits has become so important economically that we have been forced out of small town Western provincial thinking. In the United States and Canada, as our countries become more and more pluralistic, we must keep ourselves aware of the opportunities as well as challenges that this brings.

Other phenomena that intrigue analysts are the Asianization of the world and the fact that the European community is now an accomplished fact. With the collapse of Communist systems, it has the potential of growing still larger. Such developments must impact our thinking in regard to worldwide evangelism.

At a time when there is a great need for Christians with a world view and a world vision, many churches seem content to send a few dollars to a mission program. Through this, they feel, they have met their responsibilities. But they are missing out on some of the greatest excitement in the Christian world.

Giving to "missions" is important. I believe that one reason God has preserved us as a nation is the faithfulness of American Christians who support overseas work. But there is so much more to do. Once again, there is a need for a coordinated program with someone in charge. Here are some ideas such a person may want to help implement.

We can minister to the world by ministering to foreign students currently in North America. They will be the future leaders of their countries. Support missionaries who are evangelizing these students. Ask your people to make their homes available for long- or short-term "exchange" students. Ask for homes to serve meals to these people, and include them in family events such as holiday celebrations.

We also minister to the world by keeping informed as to what is going on. Sometimes secular media sources are helpful, but they are incomplete. We need to keep our people constantly updated by securing news of what is happening among and to Christians. With this information, our people can become prayer partners with those who are overseas.

If we are supporting overseas missionaries, it is reasonable that we hold them accountable to our church. Know what they are doing. Be sure they are expending their energies properly. Harass them until they keep you informed through media other than their periodic, innocuous "prayer letter." Video tapes are an excellent way to keep in touch. Some churches call their missionaries long distance and broadcast the whole conversation over the public address system. Sunday morning calls, for instance, are reasonable in cost.

Lavish affection on your missionaries when they are home on furlough. Keep alert to their housing and transportation needs. Aid them in their adjustment to the North American culture. Look after their kids when they have to leave their parents and come back to North America for schooling.

Periodically send some of your leaders to visit them on the field if you can afford it. This is not to be a mere sightseeing trip, however. It is to be an inspection and ministry trip. Let them know you will be taking a good hard look at their ministry. But be prepared to minister to them as well. If your leader has teaching skills, work with the missionary in a plan to use those skills. If manual skills are his forté, ask the missionary to make definite plans so that your leader may use his skills on the mission field. In this way he will become an integral part of the ministry.

Keep your people informed as to the countries in which your missionaries serve. Travelogues and other media sources usually are available. Show these often in church meetings. Plan international "fairs" where people may see pictures, works of art, and taste food from the countries in which your missionaries serve. Perhaps there are shut-ins or others who will have time to keep up an active correspondence with a missionary. This person can then keep the congregation informed of needs.

Once a year missionary conferences are helpful to draw attention to world ministry. They can be conducted inexpensively if proper planning is done. However, it is not enough to have only one large emphasis on missions each year. The needs of world ministry must be kept before people on a regular basis throughout the year. Only as they develop a worldview will they begin to see the need as God sees it.

Identify young people who show signs of being good missionary prospects. Send them on short-term, summer assignments. But before you do so, investigate the sending agency closely. There are some whose philosophies and methods seem questionable.

Challenge your people to short-term missionary opportunities. Missions agencies now have an abundance of these available for people aged eighteen to eighty. Help provide support for these people as you find it possible.

Undoubtedly you have many more good ideas in each of these six areas. Keep those ideas coming, and keep putting "feet" to your ideas. Even though your church is limited in size, you can be part of an exciting church if you are willing to put in the effort to make it exciting.

This chapter began with an impossible premise, that the past could be erased and that you could start from "scratch" to choose programs. That is seldom possible. Most of us are stuck with a system of programs that may or may not contribute toward reaching the church's basic goals. If that is the case, regularly and systematically review all your programs. You may find that some of them are right "on target."

You will probably want to retain these and revise them to meet your constantly changing needs. Remember, as well, to balance your programs so that the evangelism-edification cycle is enhanced instead of interrupted.

In some cases, existing programs may be basically sound but will need extensive revision to reach goals and meet the needs of your projected target groups. Do this carefully, slowly, and systematically, trying not to injure people in the process.

Sometimes, upon careful examination, you will find programs that need to be discarded for one of several reasons. Either the program itself is unsound, it no longer aids the church in reaching its goals, or there are more programs than the church can handle adequately. Work quietly and carefully to remove these programs. However, be aware that one or more leaders in that program may regard it as a "sacred cow." The abandonment of a program may be desirable, but it is not essential enough to cause a church split. Proceed with extreme caution. Remember, the church is a delicate organism.

## Additional Resources

Black, Cheryl M. "A Proposal for Young Single Adults." *Journal of Christian Education* 1, no. 2 (1981): 43-47.

Hardin, H. Grady. *The Leadership of Worship.* Nashville: Abingdon, 1980.

Neal, Tom W., Jr. "Establishing a Method for Doing Ministry in Relationship to Single Young Adults at Sandy Lane Christian Church, Fort Worth, Texas." D.Min. project, Brite Divinity School, Texas Christian U., 1986.

Sasscert, Grace. "Church Programs for Senior Adults." *Journal of Christian Education* 3, no. 1:65.

Stoner, Thomas K. "Family Life Education in the Local Church." *Journal of Christian Education* 5, no. 2 (1984): 53.

## Questions for Discussion and Helpful Projects

1. In recent years, genuine worship seems to have fallen on hard times in many evangelical churches.

PROJECT: Encourage the worship committee of your church to read and discuss Allen and Borror's book *Worship: Rediscovering the Missing Jewel*. Next, have them analyze three worship services in your church according to the criteria established by Allen and Borror. How do your worship services rate? Make a list of things that need to be improved. Set up a plan to implement those improvements.

2. This chapter has revealed that God does not lock His people into one rigid form of worship. In light of this truth, postulate some creative ideas for upgrading the various parts of worship in your church.

3. Discipleship is often conceived of as the transference of spiritual life from one person to another. Although there is some degree of merit to this definition, the scope of discipleship is much broader than a one-on-one ministry. With that in mind, list some of the dangers of one-on-one discipleship ministry. What steps may you, as a leader, take to see that those dangers do not come about?

4. One of the primary functions of the early church was fellowship. It was one of the dynamics that contributed toward rapid and steady growth.

PROJECT: If you have a fellowship committee in your church, assemble them. If you do not have such a committee, select a group of people whom you know are interested in promoting fellowship. Create a list of ways in which the "out crowd" of your church may be incorporated into a meaningful fellowship structure.

5. Devise a plan whereby a "holy busybody" model of caring ministry may be implemented in your church. In what practical ways can this model be used to assist the poor and needy in your congregation?

6. This chapter has referred to a "made to order" fellowship structure built upon the boards and committees of your church.

PROJECT: Take a survey of your church board to see how well your board and committee structure already functions in encouraging fellowship. Devise ways in which this structure can be made even more effective in promoting fellowship.

7. It has been said that nothing will fan the flames of a dying church more readily than evangelism.

PROJECT: Construct a model evangelistic service designed to appeal to contemporary unbelievers. In what ways does this service differ from your current morning worship service?

8. Why is church planting such an essential ministry for the Body of Christ? List the reasons new churches grow more rapidly than established ones.

# Appendix A:

---

# CODE
## OF
# ETHICS

Throughout this book I have outlined numerous broad ethical principles by which the church leader should operate. Here, however, I would like to become extremely practical. If there is any area in which current church leaders fall short, it is in the area of ethics. Broad violations of ethical principles on the part of well-known Christian leaders have brought untold shame on the church of Jesus Christ. May I suggest that you read carefully chapter 9 in *The Effective Pastor,* from which this list of ethical guidelines is adapted?[1]

## CODE OF CHURCH LEADERSHIP ETHICS

MY PERSON

- I will endeavor to pray daily, to read, study, and meditate upon God's Word, and to maintain extended times of contemplation.

- I will plan time to be with my family, realizing my special relationship to them and their position as important members of the congregation that I serve.

---

1. Adapted from the Code of Ministerial Ethics, Columbia Baptist Conference; for a slightly different wording, see Robert C. Anderson, *The Effective Pastor* (Chicago: Moody, 1985), pp. 122-24.

- I will seek to keep my body physically fit through proper eating habits and planned exercise, renewing myself through weekly times of relaxation and an annual vacation.
- I will try to keep myself emotionally fit, keeping in touch with my feelings and growing in healthy control of them.
- I will strive to grow through comprehensive reading and through regular participation in available training opportunities.

MY CALLING

- I will seek to conduct myself consistently with my calling and my commitment as a Christian leader.
- I will give full devotion to a reasonable amount of tasks to which the congregation assigns me. I will accept additional responsibilities only if they do not interfere with the overall effectiveness of my ministry to my family and to the congregation.
- I will consider a confidential statement made to me as a sacred trust not to be divulged without consent of the person making it.

MY FINANCES

- I will do my best not to be dominated by the love of money or the desire to live in opulent style.
- I will be honest in my stewardship of money, paying bills promptly, asking for no special discounts or other considerations from members of the congregation.
- I will give tithes and offerings as a good steward and example to the church.

MY CHURCH

- I will seek to regard all persons in the congregation with equal love and concern and to minister impartially to their needs.
- I will seek to be friends with all members, yet retain the right to seek close friendships within the congregation.

- I will exercise confidence in other leaders, assisting them in their training and mobilizing their creativity.

- I will work as part of a leadership team, leading the church in a positive direction to achieve the goals we have mutually agreed upon. I will remain open to constructive criticism and to suggestions intended to strengthen our common ministry.

- I will resign immediately from my position of leadership if I no longer hold to the statement of faith and standards of conduct held by my church.

MY FELLOW LEADERS

- I will be absolutely loyal to those other leaders with whom I serve. If I am a staff person or lay leader, I will recognize the pastor as chief undershepherd and honor him as such. If I am a pastor, my loyalty is even more applicable to my relationship with the staff and lay leadership.

- I will not "bad-mouth" or gossip about fellow leaders in my church or leaders in other evangelical churches.

- I will recognize the fact that the local church is wider than my own congregation and affirm that these ethical principles apply in my dealings with other evangelical churches in my community. In no way will I encourage or engage in "sheep stealing" from those congregations.

MY DENOMINATION

- I will acknowledge the fact that churches band together to enhance each other's ministries and to carry on larger ministries that a local church finds impossible to do itself.

- I will be supportive of the denomination to which my church belongs and will work, to the extent I find possible, to further improve relationships and enhance mutual ministries carried on by my church and its sister denominational churches.

- Where possible, I will lend my energies and talents to my denomination to help it perform its mission more effectively. As I feel necessary, I will offer responsible criticism in order that our common service in the kingdom of God might be more effective. I will do so positively and directly to denominational representatives.

- I will not gossip about my denomination and its officials or tear down its reputation either with people in my own congregation or in other congregations, or with outsiders.

- I will not use my influence to alienate this church from its chosen denomination. I will not work either openly or behind the scenes to get my church to join another denomination or become "independent."

- I will resign immediately from my position of leadership and seek membership in another church should I cease to hold practices and principles commonly held by our denominational fellowship.

- I covenant in the sight of God with my fellow leaders in the ministry to keep this code of leadership ethics.

## A WORD OF ENCOURAGEMENT

Finally, do not be discouraged! You are not yet a finished product. God is not through remodeling you yet unless you want Him to be. Maintain the cutting edge by being constantly open to His molding, re-creating power in your life. On the other hand, when you think you have "arrived" and are finished learning, please do both God and His church the favor of resigning as a church leader. If you yourself are not willing to be a constant product of change, you will never be able to help your people to change. Remember, God has never called you to perpetuate the status quo. The meaning of leadership dictates that you lead your people somewhere. To do this, you've got to be going someplace yourself. It is my prayer that you will lead your people on to bigger and better service for Jesus Christ.

Remember that the church is engaged in battle. If it is going to win its war, it must think strategically as well as tactically. Never lose sight of the big picture while struggling to get the everyday work done. Keep the overall mission of the church in sight, and don't get bogged down in trying to reach peripheral goals. Keep these as means to an end instead of ends in themselves.

Yours is a noble calling, and in choosing you as a leader God has indicated His great confidence in you. Live up to your calling. Be obedient and faithful, and God will perform the miracle of taking an imperfect person and doing great things through him. I have seen it happen repeatedly, and I pray that it happens to you.

# Appendix B:

# PARACHURCH ORGANIZATIONS

Parachurch groups perform at least four positive services in behalf of the church. First, they alert the church to areas of deficiency where the church no longer is functioning as it should. An example of this is the great challenge that Campus Crusade for Christ gave to the church in waking it to its responsibilities to evangelize. What a valuable contribution to the church such groups have been!

Second, they develop tools that the church may find helpful in reaching its goals of evangelism and edification. Here, I am thinking of the wonderful discipleship materials developed by Billy Graham, The Navigators, Campus Crusade, and others. The presence of these tools has encouraged the church to work more seriously on its goals.

Third, they are often able to accomplish a mission that a local church by itself would have found impossible. For example, how grateful the church should be for mission boards, which have enabled groups of local churches to work together to send out missionaries. How wonderful that the Gideons have been able to distribute Scripture portions on such a widespread basis. No local church, on its own, would have been able to accomplish such a mission. We need to thank God, as well, for Bible colleges and institutes, Christian liberal arts colleges, seminaries, and other Christian training centers that prepare future leaders for the worldwide mission of the church. Few local churches are able to carry out this technical and specialized work.

Fourth, they provide essential seasoning and training of young people for Christian service. These groups often take impatient but zealous youth, utilize them in a structured setting, and prepare them for later service within the church. Were some of these young people to enter ministry in local churches upon graduation from Bible college or seminary they would be a hazard to themselves and to the local church. Many of them would become so discouraged they would become early casualties to the ministry. Parachurch organizations often carry on a necessary service by the patience they extend to the church's young people and the valuable training they provide for present and future ministry.

Could we get along without parachurch organizations? Certainly, but why should we? Parachurch organizations can be the greatest allies a church can have in helping it to perform its mission. But parachurch organizations must keep in mind that their ultimate mission is on behalf of the church, not themselves. Howard Snyder, who serves with a parachurch agency, writes, "Evangelism, regardless of the agency which sponsors it, is legitimate only as it plants and edifies the church or extends its witness."[1]

Where does the danger lie? Great problems arise when a parachurch group ceases to be truly "para," one called to come alongside the church and assist it, and instead begins to compete with the church or to go off in a direction directly opposite to that of the church.

Only the church is permanent, and leaders of parachurch movements are wise to remember that. Parachurch groups will flourish as they support and enhance the ministry of the church.

How should leaders in a local church view the parachurch movement and its leaders? First, they should remind themselves that these groups are temporary. Then they should be grateful to God for the resources He provides for the church through these groups.

Sincere appreciation for parachurch groups does not mean that the church should give automatic approval or financial support to any organization that asks for it. Nor are they to assume that the programs offered by parachurch organizations are necessarily beneficial and ap-

---

1. Howard A. Snyder, *The Community of the King* (Downers Grove, Ill.: InterVarsity, 1977), p. 164.

plicable to every church. Just as church leaders would carefully investigate anyone they would call as a coworker, so they must carefully evaluate parachurch groups and the individuals who serve in them. Some of the questions they must ask themselves are as follows:

- Am I absolutely certain that this is a legitimate organization? On what facts do I base this judgment?

- Are the goals and objectives of this organization harmonious with the goals and objectives of the Christian church in general and our church in particular?

- Does this organization produce the results it claims? Does it have tangible evidence to support those claims?

- Is this group financially dependable? What percentage of its budget actually is applied to direct ministry? Are its books open to scrutiny and its financial policies above reproach?

- Does this institution provide services that are directly beneficial to the church in general and to our church in particular?

- To whom is this organization accountable? To whom are its leaders accountable?

- Is the organization local-church oriented? Do its leaders faithfully attend a local church? Are they above reproach in their conduct and ethics? Are they accountable to that church and its leaders for their personal and professional conduct and ethics?

- Do the actions and programs of this organization honor the Lord Jesus Christ?

- If I as an individual or we as a church supported this group, would that constitute a responsible use of God's money? Are we getting the best value possible for the amount of money we are investing?

After these questions are answered, it is up to church leaders to decide what kind of relationship the church is to maintain with a particular parachurch organization and its leaders.

How fortunate for church leaders that God has given so many parachurch helpers to provide ideas and tools to aid in the ministry. In return, the church has certain responsibilities to them. We are responsible to pray for them, to interact with them within the context of the assembly, and to look after their families when the breadwinner is out of town ministering. We also have an obligation to see that their financial needs are met. And we have a responsibility to see that they are accountable for their doctrine and conduct to the congregation to which they belong. Support these people. They, too, are worthy servants of the Lord.

# INDEX
## OF
# SCRIPTURE

## New Testament

# INDEX
## OF
# PERSONS

# INDEX
## OF
# SUBJECTS